THE LAST PUNISHER

A **SEAL** Team **THREE**
SNIPER'S TRUE ACCOUNT OF
THE BATTLE OF RAMADI

Kevin Lacz
with Ethan E. Rocke and Lindsey Lacz

THRESHOLD EDITIONS
New York   London   Toronto   Sydney   New Delhi

Threshold Editions
An Imprint of Simon & Schuster, Inc.
1230 Avenue of the Americas
New York, NY 10020

First Threshold Editions hardcover edition July 2016

THRESHOLD EDITIONS and colophon are
trademarks of Simon & Schuster, Inc.

For information about special discounts for bulk purchases,
please contact Simon & Schuster Special Sales at
1-866-506-1949 or business@simonandschuster.com.

The Simon & Schuster Speakers Bureau can bring authors to your live event.
For more information or to book an event, contact the Simon & Schuster Speakers
Bureau at 1-866-248-3049 or visit our website at www.simonspeakers.com.

Interior design by Davina Mock-Maniscalco

Manufactured in the United States of America

10   9   8   7   6   5   4   3   2   1

Library of Congress Cataloging-in-Publication Data is available.

ISBN 978-1-5011-2724-3
ISBN 978-1-5011-2725-0 (ebook)

For G.W. and A.R.

CONTENTS

Foreword by Scott McEwen   ix

Preface   xii

Prologue   1

1. Tadpole   11

2. Newguy   25

3. Charlie 13   36

4. Put Me In, Coach   46

5. A Punisher's First Kill   62

6. Firefight in the Ma'Laab   77

7. Mass Casualties   85

8. Nailed It!   95

9. Don't Get Cocky   103

10. Overwatch at Bernie's   117

11. Chainsaw Massacre   130

12. 23 in 24   140

13. Two-For   155

14. The Mailman Delivers   169

15. Patrol to Contact   181

16. Up the Gut   193

17. Iwo Jima Games   208

18. KYK'ing Ass   216

19. Man Down   226

20. All Stop   236

21. Final Salute   249

22. Payback   261

23. A Final Op   269

24. Leaving   278

    Epilogue   285

    Glossary   291

    Acknowledgments   299

FOREWORD

I FIRST CAME TO know of Kevin "Dauber" Lacz when I was working on writing *American Sniper* in 2009 with Chris Kyle. Chris let me know that Kevin was someone who knew the details of what Chris had done in Iraq and could be trusted. More importantly, Chris told me that he was a close friend. In turn, Kevin became one of the very few men who were interviewed while writing Chris's book. Many, like myself, knew some of Chris's story; few, like Kevin, knew virtually all of it.

A few years later, *American Sniper* was brought to the screen, and Kevin lent his expertise to the filmmakers. Not only was Kevin the only SEAL on the set advising the film's star, Bradley Cooper, and director, Clint Eastwood, he was the only person on the set who had known Chris in any capacity. Without Kevin Lacz, *American Sniper* could never have been as authentic or successful as it ultimately became. Through war, fame, fortune, and death, Kevin has remained true to his friend and brother Chris Kyle.

My initial approach to *The Last Punisher* was that I might read it and learn some new information about Chris. After all, Kevin served two combat deployments with him and certainly has his share of stories about the man we call "The Legend." As I read it, however, I became engrossed in how complex this book is, and how much more to it there is than a collection of war stories, some of which feature Chris Kyle. But this is not simply a book about Chris. This is an important memoir by a man with a capacity for violence.

Devoid of politics, and with unsparing honesty, *The Last Punisher* delves deeply into the psyche of an operator with an unrelenting desire to eliminate his country's enemies. From the very first chapter, when we learn of Kevin's motivation behind joining the military, to the last, we witness the maturity of a SEAL who cut his teeth in one of the Iraq War's bloodiest summers. It is raw, unforgivingly honest, and unique to contemporary war literature. It is historically important not only for its subject matter, but also for taking a new approach to delivering a military memoir in an engaging and unforgettable way.

Knowing Kevin in the capacity that I do now, and knowing he devotes a substantial amount of his time helping others in his chosen medical profession, I believe this book illustrates a particularly important lesson: one can participate fully in combat and still participate fully in society. Kevin gives a new voice to a substantial group of veterans being largely ignored—those who have served, who survived, and who now thrive. His experiences overseas, while gruesome and shocking to some, have not impeded him from reintegrating seamlessly into the civilian world and experiencing success. I applaud him for bringing attention to these men and women who have served with honor, even witnessing and committing acts of violence in combat, and come home to do great things.

This book is about the amazing true grit of SEAL Team THREE Charlie Platoon, in some of the worst days of battle in the history of the U.S. SEAL Teams (and the United States). I was obviously already well-versed in Chris Kyle's story and knew a little of Kevin's. As I read more, I saw that each of these men is incredibly special, and that each has his own unique story of sacrifice and courage. I appreciated Kevin's willingness to share the pages with his brothers and tell their stories as well, because these men are truly the best of what America has to offer. This is not one man's tribute to himself; it is one man's tribute to his TEAM. The epitome of the SEAL attitude of "never quit" runs through Kevin's veins and this book's pages.

Many people change their view of the world once they are thrust into the limelight of Hollywood and acting, but Kevin did not. He remained true to his friends, his family, the TEAMs and the code by which he lives his life. For that I respect him greatly, and am proud to call him my friend.

—Scott McEwen
#1 *New York Times* bestselling coauthor of *American Sniper*
and the nationally bestselling Sniper Elite series of novels
May 9, 2016

PREFACE

THIS MEMOIR CONTAINS my true account of the Battle of Ramadi as I experienced it as a newguy with Task Unit Bruiser-Charlie platoon, SEAL Team THREE. In 2006, western Iraq was embroiled in sectarian violence, morale was low, and a deadly insurgency threatened the coalition mission. As a result, SEAL Team THREE was deployed to fight in the pivotal Battle of Ramadi in an effort to aid in securing Anbar Province's capital city. While much has been discussed and written about our work over that summer, Ramadi was not won by SEALs and special operators alone. There was no single commander who brought the enemy to its knees. Rather, it was the combined effort of the Army, Marines, Navy, and Air Force that turned the tide of the battle against the insurgency. This story is reflective of that cooperation.

Now the work we conducted in Ramadi during the spring, summer, and fall of 2006 is merely a piece of history. The peace we secured block by block, alley by alley, and room by room does not exist today. Those of us who fought there, who bled there, and who lost brothers there can only hope that the many lessons learned in Ramadi may one day serve as guidelines for how conventional units and special operations can work together and win on future battlefields. To that end, I offer this piece of history as a sort of primary source for those who would look into the recent past and wonder what combat looked like at the height of Operation Iraqi Freedom. Peace in Ramadi no longer exists. Our story, however, does.

My decision to join the SEAL Teams was swift and final. The road to earning my trident was long and arduous. During my preparation, I consumed as many firsthand accounts of BUD/S, the SEAL Teams, and combat operations as I could. It was my hope when I took on this endeavor that my story might help inspire the next generation of warriors. I know that somewhere there are special young men reading everything they can about Special Forces, and some of them will wear the trident with pride and continue to serve the Teams, the brotherhood, and our country. In a small way, this story is for them.

One of the basic principles of the SEAL Teams is "Earn Your Trident Every Day." As SEALs, we strive to continually earn our reputation as dependable operators who get the job done. We pride ourselves on our violence of action and our ability to neutralize an aggressive enemy. We are not robotic, nor are we lemmings. Each operator is an individual fighting machine, capable of leading at any level, striving for nothing less than mission success. We are relentless. I tried to convey the dynamic nature of the men I knew in these pages. Together, we formed one lethal task unit, and still as individuals they were brothers, husbands, fathers, and sons.

I have an enormous amount of respect for human life. At a very young age I decided to pursue a career in medicine, and today I serve as a physician assistant. When I joined the Navy in response to terrorism, I knew that eventually I would meet the enemy on the battlefield. As a SEAL, it was my job to engage the enemy and deliver the proper amount of force to disable them. Most people will never understand the simplicity of that concept and violence of action. Most people are not SEALs. I believe that SEALs are born, not made, and that I was fortunate enough to be born with the ability to go downrange and do the job. Many of my fellow warriors who have carried the battle flag understand. For these reasons, no matter how long I live, I will never match the vitality I shared within the brotherhood, among family.

During my career in the Teams, I witnessed feats of heroism and bravery from my Teammates, many of whom are no longer living. This is a written contribution to their legacy, as it is to the entire SEAL Teams. My only hope is that it meets the expectations of the brothers who helped make me the Teamguy I am, and whom I admire and respect.

The decision to write this book was a weighty one, and several other SEALs have asked why I chose to. Some would not. I respect other operators' codes of silence. However, I believe I have a different perspective than a career SEAL with twenty years in the Teams. My eight years in the Navy were relatively brief, compared to many others. I joined in response to 9/11, gave my time and expertise, and then moved on. This is one thing I have done in my life, not the only thing. Many guys I was in the Teams with joined the Teams before the war. I joined the Teams *for* the war. This is my story.

During my time in Ramadi, I kept a journal of my experiences. I hoped primarily to keep a record so I would have something tangible to reflect upon when my memory began to fade in old age. I never anticipated its value when I wrote in it, over poor lighting, as a young Frogman in 2006. It proved to be tremendously useful in writing this memoir. In regard to spoken dialogue, I made my best attempt to capture the spirit of words that passed between men when my memory failed. Unfortunately, nearly ten years later, it's simply not possible for me to remember many of the words that were spoken between us. The actual events that are described, in particular the events described on target, are written as I remember them, and according to the recollection of others who were there and whom I consulted with while writing.

It is important to mention that no classified information was used in the preparation of this memoir. I enlisted some of my closest friends at various stages for clarification and detail. I thank them for their assistance. The manuscript was submitted to and approved by the Pentagon's Security Review process in accordance with the Department of Defense and Naval Special Warfare. In addition, the members of the platoon, as well as other Navy personnel who appear in the memoir, were contacted during its preparation. An overwhelming majority were supportive and willing to be represented. They are described by either first name or nickname. I thank them for their unwavering support. Occasionally, I assigned aliases to protect the identity of certain service members.

My time in the Teams shaped who I am today. I would not change either my positive or my negative experiences. In life, I believe you never move on from a life-changing experience, but you can move forward. The SEAL Teams helped me discover my own potential, especially when I least expected it. When I completed my enlistment, I took my lessons learned and deployed them toward my bachelor of arts at the University of Connecticut in political science and then earned a master's of medical science at Wake Forest University, where I graduated as a physician assistant. I am currently a partner at Lifestyle & Performance Medicine powered by Regenesis, where I help people achieve their potential in a medical setting.

My military experience has allowed me to give back to the people I served with. Inspired by my wife, Lindsey, we launched Hunting for Healing to work with service-disabled veterans and their spouses through outdoor, hunting, and fishing excursions. I believe that stronger individuals make stronger teams. I am not a self-made man. I am merely a product of the company I have been fortunate enough to keep. I do not dwell in Ramadi, the Teams, or my past experiences. I do, however, utilize them to help shape each environment I engage in. For them, I am forever grateful.

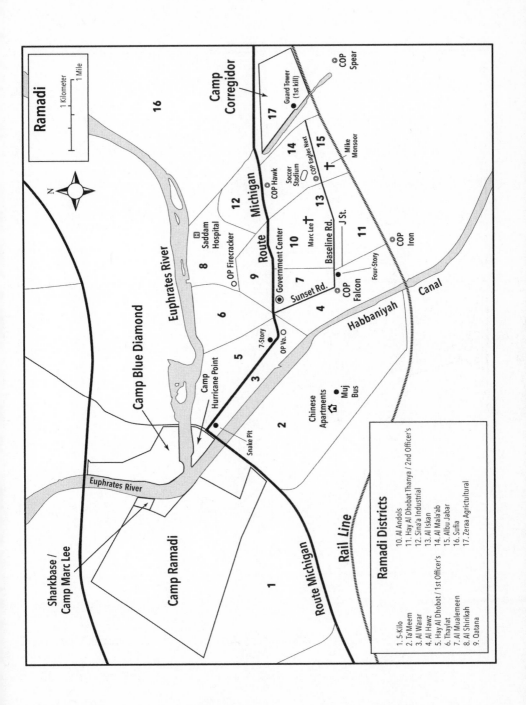

Ramadi

1 Kilometer
1 Mile

N

Sharkbase /
Camp Marc Lee

Euphrates River

Camp Blue Diamond

Euphrates River

Camp Ramadi

Route Michigan

Rail Line

Snake Pit

Camp Hurricane Point

7-Story

OP Va.

Chinese Apartments

Muj Bus

Saddam Hospital

OP Firecracker

Government Center

Sunset Rd.

COP Hawk

Route Michigan

Soccer Stadium

COP Eagles Nest

Mike Monsoor

Marc Lee

COP Falcon

Baseline Rd.

J St.

Four-Story

COP Iron

Habbaniyah Canal

Camp Corregidor

Guard Tower (1st kill)

COP Spear

1
2
3
4
5
6
7
8
9
10
11
12
13
14
15
16
17

Ramadi Districts

1. 5-Kilo
2. Ta'Meem
3. Al Warar
4. Al Hawz
5. Hay Al Dhobot / 1st Officer's
6. Thaylat
7. Al Mualemeen
8. Al Shirikah
9. Qatana
10. Al Andols
11. Hay Al Dhobat Thanya / 2nd Officer's
12. Sina'a Industrial
13. Al Iskan
14. Al Mala'ab
15. Albu Jabar
16. Sufia
17. Zeraa Agricultural

PROLOGUE

G ET YOUR SHIT! All hands to the roof of Shark House!" Marc Lee's breathless bark snapped me out of sleep.

I didn't think as I jolted off my cot, stuck my bare feet in my Oakley boots, and grabbed my web gear, machine gun, helmet, and night-vision goggles (NVGs). I ran hot on Marc's heels, in nothing but a pair of PT shorts and some assault gear, as we raced the hundred yards to the roof like sharks toward blood in the water.

Impending violence permeated the Euphrates's musty breeze.

"Muj swimmers trying to attack Blue Diamond," Marc called over his shoulder as we hit the ground-floor entrance to the house. Camp Blue Diamond was the Marine base across the river to our east. We bounded up the stairs, untied boot laces whipping our bare shins. On the roof, we joined about twenty other Teamguys, most of us in PT shorts and bare chested, the unofficial uniform for middle-of-the-night, just-out-of-your-rack muj hunting. I saw an occasional T-shirt and had to stifle a chuckle when I noticed Guy, one of our officers, and his perfect uniform. A hodgepodge of support guys intermixed among us. When Marc said all hands, he had meant all hands. Everybody wanted to get his war on.

The muj had sent a sorry contingent of maritime fighters to attack the Marine base. Blue Diamond had alerted our tactical operations center (TOC), who in turn had coordinated the perfect L-shaped ambush. We stood poised, waiting for the green light from our base defense operations center on Camp Ramadi. Our mismatched uniforms and patchwork appearance belied our deadly potential. We stood, silently, vipers waiting to strike.

Somebody was going to have a bad night.

Guy was on my left. Marc Lee and Ryan Job fell in alongside him. JP was to my right. We were new to war, but our brotherhood spanned many generations and was forged by a proud warrior tradition. We were ready.

A few spots to my right, a support guy named Neal was armed to the teeth. I stifled another chuckle. His gear was an arsenal of grenades, M4 mags, and trinkets. He had no NVGs. I turned my attention back across the quiet river. My night vision infiltrated the darkness, and I could see movement. I pushed the safety off on my gun and turned on my infrared laser.

Then the command came.

Three, two, one. Execute.

Together, we unleashed hell on the river below and the unsuspecting muj lurking in its waters. It was euphoric. I methodically delivered 150 rounds in precise eight-to-ten-round bursts. The tracers screamed across the water. Some hit and stuck; others deflected and fizzled into the night. The intense energy of American ordnance and thunder of machine guns singing all around left no doubt in my mind: I was born for this.

I looked around me at every other man doing exactly the same thing and realized that this is how it had always been. Since the first man threw a rock, to when a man chucked a spear, to when another man aimed his rifle, it has come down to a man, his weapon, and the brothers who will fight with him. At that moment, everyone who mattered to me was on that rooftop. Nothing existed beyond Ramadi. These were the men who would bring me out alive, as I would them. I had literally nothing but my gun and my brothers. *I hope it will always be like this.*

I didn't notice my scalding-hot shell casing ejecting toward JP's exposed leg to my right. I didn't care. When the abrupt call to cease fire finally came, my ears rang, my hands tingled, and the enemy was dead or dying. I felt alive.

Someone was yelling at Neal for firing six mags at the enemy with no night vision on. We called him Shadow Stalker for the rest of the deployment. A gunner's mate tech asked sheepishly, "Hey, man, am I going to get my Combat Action Ribbon for this?"

"Sure, man," I said, deciding to let him revel in his glory for a little while.

I checked my left flank. Guy, Marc, and Ryan had the familiar look of satisfaction that operating a powerful weapon delivers. JP cussed the burns on his left calf from my brass. I shrugged and took a deep breath. The smell of cordite from hundreds of spent rounds mixed with a breeze from the Euphrates's ancient waters. I put my gun on safe and hit the pressure pad for the laser. I grabbed my gear and began the walk back to my tent, wondering how many similar opportunities I'd have like this over the next seven months. I didn't want it to change me, or us—any of us. I didn't think ahead to the future—where I'd be as a man or a husband or father a decade later. It didn't matter at the time. I just needed to clean my gun. I was in Ramadi, and I'd be back in my rack before the flies found the meat we'd left for them in the reeds.

Later, I lay awake for only a moment before falling into a satisfied sleep, confident in the work I'd done with the others.

I hope it will always be like this.

The bar had a typical college feel to it. The slight touch of hippie made it the type of place that, in my past life, I would have tried to avoid. It was early and the Winston-Salem, North Carolina, night was just getting going. I settled into a much-needed night off from studying and routine grad school life as the opening snap of a cue ball breaking the rack cut into my conversation with my wife, Lindsey. I took a pull from the Coors Light bottle. Some things never change.

My phone vibrated in my pocket. For a moment, I considered ignoring it. I was enjoying a rare night out at a friend's birthday party and I really didn't need a distraction. Then again, I wasn't the average physician assistant student. I had a kid at home with a babysitter, and I had a job outside of school. I checked the phone. The last thing I needed was to miss an important call.

The screen read STEVEN YOUNG—CRAFT CEO.

I thought it strange for the boss to call at 8 p.m. on a weekend. I answered, figuring it had to be important.

"Hey, Steven," I said, my phone held tight to my right ear and my fingers plugging my left to block out the noise of the bar. "What's up?"

I immediately realized something was very wrong from the tone of Steven's voice. The words tumbled out at me and I collected what I could. "Dauber . . . something bad happened earlier . . . *Chris is gone* . . . shot earlier today with Chad . . . *Murder* . . . I'm so sorry . . ."

The phone stayed fixed at my ear, but I didn't hear the rest of what he said. I felt like I'd just been punched in the face. I guess you could call it shock. I shot a look across the bar at Lindsey, whose eyes were glued on me. She knew something was wrong.

I mumbled a thanks to Steven and a request to keep me posted, then hung up the phone.

I walked over to Lindsey. I didn't want to tell her. Since we'd met nearly seven years earlier, we'd grown accustomed to breaking this kind of news to each other. More often it was me who broke it to her, sometimes over the phone when I learned of the death of someone I'd served with, sometimes even via text, other times face-to-face, like this.

I didn't want to tell her.

She was happy, standing there, enjoying a night out. Reluctantly, I grabbed her hand and led her out of the bar. I looked at her face in the streetlight. I thought of the news I'd broken to her over the years, and how she'd taken it on with me, because they were my losses. Each time she had mourned with me, respectfully paying tribute to the men I called brothers. This was going to be different. The longer I'd been out of the Teams, the more my core group of friends had dwindled. Chris had remained constant. I knew this news was going to hurt.

When we were still dating and living in Imperial Beach, California, I took her along on a sniper shoot east of San Diego. All the snipers in the task unit came and a couple of us brought our girlfriends. Chris was solo that day, so we spent the afternoon sighting in the guns and teaching the chicks to shoot. Lindsey had never shot a rifle before, but I could tell she was happy, especially after I watched her hit a head plate target at 500 meters. Chris was the first to praise her with a "Hell yeah!" With praise coming from the Legend, she was especially proud of her shooting.

I thought about the fun we'd all had together over the years. This time it was her loss, too.

As I told her, I watched her crumble. A mixture of disbelief and confusion contorted her face for a few moments before the tears came. She hugged me briefly and silently, obviously in the same state of shock that I was in. As we walked the short block to the car she stopped suddenly, hunched over, and vomited in an alley. Without a word, she straightened back up and got in the car to go home. I felt nothing but unsettled behind the wheel. I had just spoken to Chris the day before about a work project. He texted me hours before his murder. We'd planned to talk the next day. The abruptness left me at a loss for words.

There is an inherent danger to being a Teamguy. Before I took my oath to join the Navy, I realized that I might get hurt doing the job. I understood that I or someone I knew might get killed along the way. There's nothing morbid about it. It's just business. I guess that realization helped condition or prepare me for the bad news, which has come steadily. I was on a beach in Jacksonville, Florida, when I heard the news of Extortion 17 (a helicopter mission in Afghanistan in 2011) and the fate of Jon Tumilson and Darrik "D-Rock" Benson, guys whom I had worked with at Team THREE. I was shocked, but quietly at ease with the fact they died doing a job they wanted. They were fighting alongside brothers. Chris was different.

I called Guy, our old LT, as I drove through the silent streets of Winston-Salem. Voice mail. "LT, this is Dauber, give me a call when you get this."

The texts from other Teamguys began to pour in, but I really didn't want to read them.

U HEAR ABOUT CHRIS? . . . WTF . . .

When I got back to the house, I grabbed the bottle of bourbon and stared at the computer screen. *Murder.* I let the burn of the liquor resonate as I felt the sting of the word on my soul. I couldn't shake the dirtiness of it. Murdered. Chris and Chad. I poured myself another glass and closed my eyes.

I had just visited Dallas a few months earlier for a work trip and sat across from Chris in his Midlothian living room. My belly ached from the jokes we told and the incessant wisecracks that were traded. He was bandaged from his knees down due to an unfortunate sunburn sustained on the Gulf of Mexico. For all the years in the Teams that I spent with Chris, I rarely saw him in shorts. His most recent fishing trip on a flat-bottom boat left him burned and his ego bruised. We sat, joked, drank, and chewed as the Rangers game hummed in the background.

We had been to Iraq together, the place where tough guys go and come out even tougher. We transitioned out of the Teams to the other side comfortably and now worked at his company. For all the experiences shared, we didn't talk about war. I saw the same smile he left us with in Iraq in 2006 when he headed home to be with his kids. We swapped stories about our kids—he couldn't wait for football season to start. I promised to call him when the Patriots won and the Cowboys lost. He told me that I wouldn't have many calls to make. . . . All that would change now.

I opened my eyes as Lindsey cracked open the office door. I had no idea how long I'd been thinking. I looked up at her and then glanced at my phone. She could tell I didn't want to talk. Lindsey is my rock, but there are some things that I just deal with on my own. She knows that. She closed the door as my phone rang again.

I passed along all the information I had to Guy. He was incredulous. Guy served as our officer in 2008 and the three of us had kept in close contact in the years after leaving the Teams. The silence on the phone lingered like a long-range desert patrol in Iraq. "Fuck, I'm sorry, Daubs. Let me know what else you hear. I'm there for ya." I relayed the same and poured another drink.

I sat alone in the room and reminisced about the good times. My transition out of the military changed my affiliation with the Teams. Once I was out, I became a former action guy, a guy who used to do cool things but has moved on. It's not the most glorious self-realization, but it is reality. My departure from the Teams changed my direction. I was on the path to becoming a physician assistant, I had earned a bachelor's in political science, I had a wife and a son and a house and a whole life that separated me from who I was when I was a Teamguy. Yet, somehow, I've always felt drawn back to the Teams. Especially in times like those, at the death of a brother, I realize that a Teamguy is never really out. The brotherhood binds us for longer than a deployment, longer than a platoon, longer than a work-up.

I recalled the phone call Chris made to me to tell me that Ryan "Biggles" Job had passed in 2009. It was my first introduction to loss outside the Teams, and it was raw. I could make sense of dying on the battlefield, but Ryan had overcome his injuries and lived a full life for several years before succumbing to complications from a reconstructive surgery. When Chris called and told me, I felt angry, like we'd been cheated. There was no goodbye. Just a few days before his death, Ryan had called to tell me his wife was pregnant. He was so happy. Then he was gone. I regretted that I hadn't told him more. I hadn't told him how proud I was of him. I didn't say how much of an inspiration he was to others—and the Teamguys—around him. There was no going back. Only memories to relive.

Ryan was the beginning of a cycle. There would be more phone calls and bad news. More anger and memories, and more of the feeling that I am always connected to the brotherhood, no matter how long it's been since I've worn the uniform. Pat Feeks. Nick Checque. Matt Leathers. Tim Martin. The list goes on. Each time the loss brings me back.

And now Chris had left us just as suddenly as Biggles and the others, with nothing but memories to relive.

Each time, the news incites the same rage. The rage is not directed toward any individual, but rage that the world lost a favored son. The memories I had of these individuals strengthen this claim. These were giants among men, and they will no longer walk among us. I feel sorrow for the future that will not know them. I felt the rage boil in me when I thought about Chris.

I downed the last of my bourbon. There is only one place to go when you lose a close friend. A Teammate. A brother. You have to go back. My time in the Teams constantly intersects with the present. It is unavoidable. Each time I suffer a loss, I go back to better times when I knew him living. I go back to the genesis—the beginning of my Frogman days. There is comfort in this journey. It takes me back to the brotherhood, to the blood, the sweat, and the tears endured to earn the beloved burden. It helps me not to lament the passing of a Teammate, but rather to relish in the luxury I was afforded to live and fight next to him.

Many people search their entire lives for meaning or for a single memorable experience. My time in the Teams with the Punishers, with Chris, was my holy grail.

I slid my glass to the side and opened a file on the computer. I stared at the picture of Chris and me at our 2007 awards ceremony. A wave of energy shot through my veins. We had all gone to Danny's Island Bar for the drink-up afterward. My dad had been there, along with Lindsey, Momma Lee, and the hundred or so Frogmen from Team THREE. I laughed out loud as I remembered catching my dad's eye at the bar. We had captured some unsuspecting BUD/S trainees and voluntold them to participate in some "team-building" exercises. I let my mind drift to the following drink-up and after party at Ty Woods's bar, the Far East Rock. The memories were clear. They would always be clear. I smiled as I thought about my progression as a Frog.

I opened a CD case and put on my platoon's video from 2006. I used to watch it religiously after I got out of the Teams, but as the years had gone by the frequency had decreased. Tonight, it felt right to watch it. As the sound came to life and the images appeared, they were as vivid as my memory.

All the way back. I felt drawn to the experiences, the men I fought with, and the memories shared. I felt life lived at its fullest. Although someone had taken Chris's life on that February day, they couldn't take my memories of him. The same is true of Biggles, Marc Lee, D-Rock, JD, and the others who helped shape who I am. I was being drawn to another life. I was back to where I'd started again. Back to the Teams.

ONE

TADPOLE

"It pays to be a winner."
—unofficial motto of the SEAL Teams

W HEN I WAS a child, I was sometimes described as "tenacious," which is really just a euphemism for stubborn. Whatever the case, I've always been one to travel my own path, even when it
meant making decisions that didn't make much sense to others around
me. At times, I refused to give up on things that no one saw much merit
in. Other times, I changed course abruptly when it seemed to make
sense to stay put.

My tenacity littered my central Connecticut childhood with a
strange dichotomy of accomplishments and incompletions: I pitched
on a Little League baseball team that nearly won the New England
title, then quit the next year to focus on soccer, a sport I wasn't
nearly the same standout in. I was a Boy Scout for more than ten years
and then quit before making Eagle Scout because the idea of the project was too tedious to me. Similarly, I quit my high school golf team
when I got bored with the sport, despite excelling at it. Instead, I took
up swimming and competed at the state level by my senior year.

I was in possession of one of the worst things a teenager lacking real motivation can have: God-given talent. It wasn't that I didn't want to be good. I did, and I toed the line. I went to class and stayed on the honors list, but nothing challenged me enough to feel invested. I consistently earned high marks and praise without ever feeling truly tested. At my all-boys Catholic prep school, the stakes were never high enough for me to commit 100 percent of my effort to securing my future.

At eighteen, I saw college mostly as an opportunity to get out on my own. I stumbled through two semesters at James Madison University in Virginia, failing spectacularly with about a 0.7 GPA. By the fall of 2001, I was a nineteen-year-old undergrad with a Mohawk, any number of bruises or shiners acquired in brawls and fistfights, and a general ambivalence toward just about everything that wasn't girls, booze, or rugby.

Although I couldn't make it to class or turn in my assignments, my first attempt at college wasn't a complete loss. Early in my first semester, I stumbled into the Rugby House on Harrison Street, and it quickly became my home away from home. The rugby team took me under their collective wing. They were young men with names like Blumpkin (RIP), Strapper, Spidey, Beardo, Reeper, Snorty, Metal Head Nick, Dirty Dustin, AY, and Weird Jason. On Bastard Wednesdays we finished a keg while listening to metal, playing beer pong, and lifting weights. Chicks dared not enter. We hosted theme parties. We brawled with fraternity boys. We crushed it on the pitch against a large portion of our opponents.

I embraced the lifestyle, some might say a little too much. My parents were not impressed when they showed up at Parents' Weekend and I had a black eye I'd gotten in a match. They didn't love my Mohawk. I found my niche in the team, however, and I did well for myself. If my stint as a young college student taught me anything, it's that I am a pack animal.

I woke up in the Rugby House on September 11, 2001, and logged on to AOL Instant Messenger. The scrolling ticker disclosed the same awful news the rest of the world was learning. For whatever reason, the magnitude of the situation didn't really register at first. It seemed surreal. I brushed my teeth, got dressed, and casually answered my mom's call when my phone rang. As she relayed the details of the two planes hitting the World Trade Center, only two hours from where I grew up, the gravity of it sank in.

I went to the house next door and watched on television the dark clouds of billowing smoke, the people jumping to avoid the searing flames, the pancaking collapse into the massive fog of dust and rubble. I was overcome with the same feeling of anger that gripped the American consciousness.

Later that day, I heard about Bruce Eagleson, a close family friend who had been a mentor to me growing up in Middlefield, Connecticut. Bruce worked for the Westfield Corporation, and he called his son from one of the twin towers that morning. "I've got employees up there," Bruce told him. "I have to go back in and check on them."

They never found his body.

At Bruce's memorial service, I found myself at a crossroads. I was not doing enough with my life. Evil men murdered my friend, and what could I do about it? Playing rugby and beer pong until I puked had suddenly lost its allure. I wanted to kill the men who planned the mass murder of nearly three thousand Americans. It was my generation's Pearl Harbor, and I thought about my family's connection to the Navy in World War II. My grandfather was a machinist's mate on a ship in the South Pacific, and my great-uncle flew a biplane, hunting Japanese in the Pacific, where he was shot down and spent four days floating on the open sea before being rescued by U.S. forces.

At the Navy recruiting station, I was drawn to an old poster for the

SEALs. Five gun-wielding Frogmen in face paint, web gear, and caterpillar mustaches were climbing out of the water. They looked ready to make somebody's day. The poster read simply "SEALs," and I vaguely knew of their reputation. I was interested, and after a little research, it didn't take long to decide I wanted to become one. I was done living a life of mediocrity. It was the first real risk I'd ever taken—the moment I decided to step up and be a man.

When I told my parents, it went over like a turd in a punch bowl. I'm the oldest of three brothers in a proud working-class family from Connecticut. My maternal great-grandparents and my paternal grandparents emigrated from Poland in the early twentieth century. My paternal grandfather was a factory worker and farmer. My mom's dad worked in a factory until he went into business with die molds. My parents have spent their entire lives in central Connecticut in a small, tight-knit community, and they felt I was putting my future on hold by joining the Navy.

I scored high on the Armed Services Vocational Aptitude Battery test, and my recruiter tried to convince me to sign up for the Navy's nuclear operations program. Qualifying test scores like mine are hard to come by, and he talked up the technical training and skills, the cash bonuses and college money. I wanted none of it. My goal was to go into combat and shoot terrorists.

In March 2002, I went off to Navy boot camp at Recruit Training Command Great Lakes, or "Great Mistakes." Boot camp was mostly a giant disappointment in terms of the challenge it provided. The Navy used to have a saying: our ships are made of wood, and our men are made of steel. Based on my boot-camp experience, it seemed more like the modern Navy's ships are made of steel and its sailors are made of sausage. The vast majority of sailors I encountered were not preparing themselves for SEAL training.

After Great Mistakes, I went on to sixteen weeks of training at hospital corpsman school. All I did was work out, study, and think about the challenge ahead. I worked hard, found some time to blow off some steam with my friends, and graduated near the top of my class.

In January 2003, a buddy of mine picked me up from the airport and drove me across the San Diego–Coronado Bridge to report for Basic Underwater Demolition/SEAL (BUD/S) training on Coronado Island. Driving across the bridge in my dress blues, I felt like I'd finally arrived.

Some guys will tell you that SEALs are made. They'll describe BUD/S, tell you about the approximately 80 percent attrition rate, and attempt to illustrate all the ways that Naval Special Warfare takes the toughest men and turns them into SEALs.

I say that's bullshit.

SEALs aren't made. They're born. From the moment a candidate steps onto the beach in Coronado, he either has what it takes or he doesn't. In spite of the Navy's best efforts, there is no real way to identify what that "it factor" is. Men join the ranks from all walks of life, from all regions of the country, of varying heights and sizes. The fastest, strongest, and leanest aren't guaranteed to make it through training. What guarantees success cannot be measured in minutes or pounds. The men who do graduate from BUD/S and SEAL Qualification Training and go on to join the Teams all possess an intangible drive and resilience worth more than thousands of hours of preparation on any track or in any pool.

The Teams don't "make" SEALs, but they do sharpen those abilities a man already possesses. They peel away the layers covering up the killer instinct lying dormant somewhere inside and show him how to be useful. The Teams chip away the excess.

We call it a brotherhood because we forge bonds through our experiences, but also because we are a family of men separate from all others. Our innate warrior spirit unites us. On the most basic, most primal level we are cut from the same cloth.

I was twenty-one when I started BUD/S with Class 245 in early 2003. I completed five weeks of Indoctrination and Pre-Training before starting the first and most challenging phase of BUD/S. Day one started on the BUD/S Grinder, the big asphalt courtyard where students muster in the morning. I looked around at the more than two hundred men who started the six-month course with me. Most of them would be gone by week six. The group was full of guys with beastlike physiques and I-belong-here looks projected with varying degrees of certainty. At six foot three and around 200 pounds, I fit right in. I knew that *my* "unfuckwithable" expression was authentic, and I knew that the vast majority of the others' weren't.

The first quitter DOR'd (drop on request) before PT even started on the first day. In order to quit, you have to ring "the Bell" three times to announce to your classmates that you're not Teamguy material. Quitting becomes extra humiliating when a guy has to cross in front of a formation of 150 of his peers gutting out their three hundredth four-count flutter kick. The Bell goes everywhere the class goes, whether it's to the O-Course, or the beach, or anywhere else. Ringing it promises hot coffee, donuts, and a lifetime of regret.

I quickly found brothers. Meat eaters sense each other. Boat crews are chosen by height, and mine was the six tallest men in 245. As such, we probably should have been the slowest, but Tim Martin pushed us to keep up the pace. Tim was a physical freak of nature from Wisconsin with unreal speed and a persistent positive attitude. No matter how shitty the evolution, he'd flash the same wide, goofy grin and utter some encouragement. His constant reminders that "you got this" got me through more than one of the coldest moments of Hell Week.

When we got fatigued and hypothermic, we turned to Matz. He was a quiet New Englander from New Hampshire with dark hair and a darker sense of humor. During the worst moments, he would unleash some pseudophilosophical babble to distract us. We laughed, when normal people would probably cry. It fed us. BUD/S is the beginning of a bond forged by adversity and strengthened by sacrifice.

The first eight-week phase of BUD/S is an endless physical conditioning exercise and is easily the toughest of the phases. It's push-ups and flutter kicks as infinite as the Coronado Beach sand and as constant as the cold and wet that gets blasted by waves and hoses and seeps into your bones and drenches your spirit in discomfort and misery. It's sleep deprivation and log PT and sadistic instructors determined to weed out those who don't belong. It's beach runs and calves on fire and instructors who keep running you faster to try to make you quit. It's two-mile ocean swims and time limits and unforgiving currents and was-that-a-fucking-shark moments. It's timed obstacle courses and artillery simulators and looking out for your brothers and your brothers looking out for you. It's carrying a 110-pound rubber raft over your head with five other guys until your arms burn and quiver and buckle and then digging deeper and hoisting it up again. It's throwing your boat in the ocean and cherishing the fleeting moment of relief before jumping inside and paddling out past the breakers and back with an impossible time limit looming. It's your instructor saying you didn't make it back in time and that this time around the beach you have to load your boat with sand. It's the constant reminder that "it pays to be a winner." It's the sun setting after a day that started before sunrise and the cold creeping in and the painful awareness that this is just the beginning.

BUD/S wasn't JV soccer or club rugby. The stakes were far higher than they'd ever been for me, and I continuously pushed myself past my limits. For the first time in my life, I wanted something so badly I was willing to give everything I had and more. When we had timed runs, I was a fixture on the "Goon Squad," which is an honor reserved for guys who miss cutoff times. Every time I was "gooned" for running too slowly, I took my punishment and came back for more. I suffered through the extra flutter kicks, surf torture, and the perpetual chafing from wet sand sticking to every inch of you. I kept my head down and pushed on, fed by the knowledge that every man who rang the Bell and quit was weaker than I was.

A few weeks into training, the United States invaded Iraq. The fact that we were at war on two fronts weighed heavily on my mind. "There's a war going on right now, and I'm stuck here teaching you motherfuckers," Instructor Torsen yelled at my boat crew during Hell Week. "You can't even hold up a boat!" It made me dig deeper. Whenever a guy rang the Bell to quit, it reinforced my resolve and motivation. I was always mentally separating myself from the guys who didn't make it. They had been worried about getting through BUD/S. I was worrying about getting to a platoon and into combat.

Hell Week is week four of First Phase, and it's designed to be one prolonged period of stress, in every sense of the word. From the moment breakout starts on Sunday night to when the class is secured on Friday afternoon, students are put through constant physical, mental, and emotional stress, all on an accumulated three hours of sleep through the course of the week.

Breakout is chaos. As darkness falls, instructors light fires in trash cans, shoot overhead, and begin the week of yelling that continues mercilessly while the students scramble to complete tasks in times designed to be unreachable.

My Hell Week was in April. A couple of days in, we were cold, wet, and miserable, and my boat team had pitched our boat up on the beach to block the hail and rain while we ate Meals, Ready to Eat (MREs). One of our instructors, Dale, stood over me and watched as I tried to eat cold jambalaya from a green rectangular pouch that I struggled to open with my hypothermia-blue hands. My entire body jackhammered with violent shivers. Every inch of me was miserably chafed and sore. At that moment, cold jambalaya was my happy place, and Dale knew it. He grabbed a paddle, scooped up a little mountain of sand, and poured it into my jambalaya. Imagine the most ruthless kick to the dick possible. That's what Dale's paddle full of sand felt like. Choking down the sandy jambalaya was brutal, but I can say with certainty that having eaten it made that first bite of pizza on Friday morning better than it would have been if I hadn't.

I learned why Teamguys love the phrase "If you don't mind, it doesn't matter." BUD/S is mostly a mental challenge. It's not just being cold and tired. It's being cold and tired and mentally preparing yourself to do it continuously with no end in sight, while in competition with a bunch of other men, while still more men who have already been through these tasks taunt and berate you. It's intimidating. I watched my roommate ring out before the 50-meter underwater swim, just because he got psyched out. I don't think it was the actual swim, which any of us were physically capable of. It was the entire environment. You have to attack BUD/S, or BUD/S will eat you.

In Second Phase, I suffered a back injury and was rolled back to Class 246 after a brief recovery period. I found a new group of brothers: Tanner, B-Dub, Mikey, Maro, Bito, Gilby, Biggs, KPM, and Clark, aka Billy, among others. For seventeen weeks, we toiled through evolution after evolution on the Obstacle Course, in the pool, and in the sands of Coronado. "The Shady Squad" (as we called ourselves) was motley to say the least. We came from every corner of the United States and ranged from five foot six to my six foot three, from a fresh-faced nineteen-year-old to a ripe old thirty. We illustrated the Teams' most basic truth perfectly: there is no physical trait or indicator for success in BUD/S or becoming a SEAL. Of the more than two hundred men who began with Class 246, forty-four made it through all three phases to graduate. On paper, our differences were vast, but our most vital commonality was the innate resilience and tenacious spirit that a warrior is born with and must cultivate. We learned to recognize it in ourselves and in each other. We learned to call each other brother, and together we made it through.

On graduation day, we mustered early on the beach for our final run with our commanding officer. Our CO was tall and wiry with brown hair and a matching mustache. He was an old-school Frogman and hard as woodpecker lips. He could have easily run most of us into the ground if he'd wanted to. Instead, he led us on a leisurely three-mile run under the rising sun on Coronado Beach, stopping periodically to deliver a thoroughly inspiring oration about the history and legacy of Naval Special Warfare. He told us that we were now part of a proud tradition of elite warriors and a brotherhood that goes back to World War II, from the Navy's original Frogmen to Underwater Demolition Teams to SEALs. I felt every bit of what I'd earned with those forty-three other men.

Later, I stood in dress blues, formed up on the Grinder where I'd started on day one more than six months earlier. My mom, dad, and two younger brothers watched my graduation ceremony with proud astonishment. The only thing I'd ever cared enough to give all of myself to was the Teams. I guess they just hadn't seen that coming. My final day at BUD/S remains one of the most satisfying days of my life.

Graduating from BUD/S is a major accomplishment, but it isn't even close to the end of the road to becoming a SEAL. Checking that graduation box is mostly a mental thing because the worst of the physical torture is over.

From BUD/S I headed to Basic Airborne Jump School at Fort Benning, Georgia, in January 2004. While it's not an elite training course by any stretch of the imagination, Airborne School wasn't exactly enjoyable, either. Some guys love jumping out of airplanes. I am not that guy. Nonetheless, I got my basic-airborne qualification and moved on to SEAL Qualification Training (SQT) in February 2004.

SQT is the four-month course where SEALs start learning the myriad skills and tactics that make them elite special operators. At SQT I learned mission planning and intelligence gathering, communications, reconnaissance, ocean and land navigation, and about a million other things. I did day and nighttime static-line jumps, chased a Zodiac boat out the back of a C-130 airplane and into the ocean, fast-roped from hovering helicopters, and dangled like a dog's balls beneath a helo for Special Insertion/Extraction (SPIE) rigging. I trained with and qualified on the best weapons systems in the world, from the M4 to the Mk 48 to the 84 mm Carl Gustav recoilless rifle. I practiced patrolling, stalking, and military demolition, and learned how to improvise booby traps. And I got a heavy dose of combat conditioning during intense live-fire exercises designed to simulate combat and the fog of war. By the end of SQT, I was officially a SEAL, and I finally felt ready to join a platoon.

Most people assume that graduating from BUD/S must be the biggest accomplishment in a SEAL's life, but it isn't the one that we look forward to most. You don't even get your trident after BUD/S. I relished the end of BUD/S like every other man because it meant no more surf torture, no more getting wet and sandy, no more log PT. But what I looked forward to more than anything was my graduation from SQT, when I would be a certified SEAL with a trident on my chest.

In those days, SQT graduation was a private affair in a hangar with only other Teamguys present. We had a formal ceremony with the awards and certificates doled out, and the CO of BUD/S and Command Master Chief Bro pinned each of us solemnly and welcomed us into the brotherhood we'd fought tooth and nail to join. In a similar fashion to the way he'd spoken to us on our final day of BUD/S, the CO delivered some words of wisdom. He told us we could wear the trident, because we had earned that much. But we weren't Frogmen yet. We weren't Teamguys; not until we'd been tested and done what we'd trained for.

"There are SEALs, and then there are Frogmen," he told us. "Today, you are all SEALs, but Frogmen are warriors. When you go downrange and do what you're made to do, that's when you will truly earn your bird."

Later on at the drink-up, much more primitively, we were stripped bare from the waist up and our newly acquired tridents were stamped into our bare flesh, just over our hearts.

The older Teamguys who pinned us this second time meant something to each of us. My friend Mikey's older brother tagged him. When it was my turn, Ty Woods approached me. Ty was my BUD/S instructor and had helped me get out of some trouble resulting from one of the bar fights I got in while under his care. He was smaller than me, but a true barrel-chested Frogman. He was the type to dole out a punishment with a vengeance and then turn around and slap you on the back a moment later. We stayed in touch for the duration of my career, and his fate on that rooftop in Benghazi, Libya, on September 11, 2012, at the hands of terrorists crushed me.

Before he pinned me, Ty looked me in the eye and I knew he was proud of me. That was what mattered. I wanted to make my brothers proud. We wore our tridents, protruding barbarically from our bleeding flesh, for the rest of the night.

I have a small scar from the pinning over my heart. As I grow older, the hair on my chest thickens, and the scar fades.

But it remains.

———

We were finally SEALs, but training wasn't over. Truthfully, an operator never stops training. Our class had one more block of training to conduct together before scattering to our respective platoons and starting careers in the Teams.

We spent three weeks in Kodiak, Alaska, learning the ins and outs of winter warfare. Everyone had heard a lot about this evolution because of the twenty-four hours we had to spend in pairs surviving after submerging ourselves completely in the frigid waters of the bay. We were told to grab our "Bolt Bags," which contained a few bare necessities, and to jump in the water just long enough to fully submerge and then go out into the wilderness for the next twenty-four hours. As the saying goes, it's the most fun you never want to have again.

On one of the last nights in Kodiak, I was camped with my squad of about ten guys when Matz had the watch. He shook me awake. "Lacz," he hissed, "bear!"

"Bullshit," I answered, still half-asleep.

"No bullshit," he whispered. "Bear!"

I opened my eyes and looked in the direction he was pointing. Sure enough, a large grizzly sow was making her way into our camp. I sat up cautiously and began alerting the others. Bito had already climbed about fifteen feet up a tree and was tossing the bear our freeze-dried Mountain House meals.

"What the fuck," I muttered. I grasped on to a branch and began climbing another tree nearby. I thought we were all safely in the limbs overhead when a flash went off. KPM, a Golden Gloves boxer from Philly, stood about ten feet from the bear with a disposable Kodak camera. He was frantically snapping pictures of her, pausing after each one to wind the film. The clicking sound of his thumb turning the little gear was audible even to me up in my tree. The sow stood up on her hind legs and KPM snapped one last shot before running away. He found a tree of his own and we all waited in silence while the bear rummaged through our camp for a few minutes and then wandered away.

"You're fucking crazy," I told KPM.

"Yo, Kev, but these are going to be awesome pictures," he said.

Because my original military specialty was medical corpsman, I was sent to the Army's 18D Special Operations Combat Medic School at Fort Bragg, North Carolina. In July 2004, I classed up with my 18D peers, training alongside other members of the Special Operations community: Army Green Berets, Navy corpsmen assigned to Marine Recon, or Ranger medics. For six months, we learned tactical combat casualty care.

We also learned a lot of civilian medicine, and I spent a month on rotation in Jacksonville, Florida, at Shands Jacksonville, a level 1 trauma center. As I helped treat car accident victims, gunshot wounds, and drug overdoses, I began to picture myself in combat, practicing what I'd learned. Elbow deep in a body cavity, I could feel my resolve fortifying like armor.

I finished 18D in January 2005, and it was finally time to get to a platoon. It was time to pick our billets and the SEALs who graduated bickered over what was available. I had graduated the highest and could have picked first, but some of the other guys had family ties and reasons to want to go to either coast. I wanted to go to a Team on the West Coast but not enough to deprive somebody of proximity to his family. I let the three guys with preferences pick, and then it came down to my roommate, Sean, and me. There was a spot on each coast, and we both wanted San Diego.

We decided to flip a coin.

I won and got my pick. By a sheer stroke of luck, I was headed to SEAL Team THREE.

TWO

NEWGUY

"Do your job."

—Bill Belichick

I MAY BE THE only SEAL to have ever driven up to the Team on his first day in a minivan. I was twenty-three, fresh out of Special Operations combat medic school, and driving my parents' hand-me-down Chevy Venture. It wasn't exactly cool by Teamguy standards, and it's very possible that I hold this unique distinction because no other newguy has ever been stupid or masochistic enough to essentially paint a target on his forehead by driving Mommy's minivan to meet a bunch of guys who kill people for a living. Eventually, I figured the only thing to do was make it cooler, so some buddies and I spray-painted it flat black with flames on the hood, iron crosses on the hubcaps, and "Polish Pride" across the body. We called it the "Murder Van."

Most of SEAL Team THREE was deployed in Iraq and Asia when I checked in to Charlie Platoon in January 2005. My main objective at that point was to avoid any unwanted attention from the few nondeployed Teamguys whose boredom might bring on any number of sadistic hazing rituals. Of course, as the saying goes, "no battle plan ever survives contact with the enemy." Teamguys never need an excuse to haze newguys, but showing up in that van ended up being the metaphorical equivalent of putting on a pair of pork-chop drawers and jumping into the lion's den.

I had a 0730 muster to make. I faked nonchalance as I followed the flow of personnel to the back of our headquarters building, trying my best to be inconspicuous.

Unfortunately, my height, my blond hair, and being the only one of some seventy-five sailors in dress uniform made camouflaging difficult. As the others mustered by platoon, I slid in among the techs to listen to the brief.

When the command master chief was finished, I was about to attempt a hasty retreat. "Hold it, newguy," somebody called out behind me. I froze.

"C'mere, newguy," somebody joined in. I turned around. Most of the Team had scattered, but about a dozen Teamguys stuck around to size me up. I waited. One of the guys, with Oakley shades and a smile like the Cheshire cat, jerked his head to the right.

"Let's see what you got," he said, motioning to the pull-up bar at the base of the steps. "Give me twenty-five."

"Roger," I said. One of my BUD/S instructors had warned me to show up in shape, because there would be a test. I could do twenty-five pull-ups no problem, but I'd never done them in my dress blues.

I hopped up and grasped the bar, quickly counting out my twenty-five. When I completed the set, I hopped back down and scanned the small crowd. A couple of them gave me short nods before turning to begin their days of work. I stood alone at the pull-up bar.

———

On my second day in the Team, I drove the van to work again and braced myself for another day of team building. When I met my platoon chief, he was wearing a blue UDT/SEAL instructor shirt with the sleeves rolled up, green shorts, and freshly spit-shined jungle boots. A gruff Italian-American from New Hampshire, Tony (of course his name was Tony) wore his jet-black hair greased back like a cliché. His vast experience as a Frogman spanned eight combat deployments, and he had all the tattoos to prove it. A spiderweb tatt splayed out from his right elbow, eventually giving way to at least two other ink jobs on the same arm. On his forearm was a trident and the word *frogman*. He looked me up and down with a disapproving scowl. Then he grunted and kind of jerked his head toward his office as if to say, "Follow me, newguy." I sat down for the first of many one-way conversations with Tony. When he finally spoke, his New England roots announced themselves in his thick, clam-chowda accent.

"Lacz," he said, "you're a newguy; you're meant to be seen not heard. Keep your gear and department squared away, always carry a pencil and paper, and shut the fuck up. Just get your ass to work, and I'll keep you busy. Ya got it?"

"I got it, Chief," I said enthusiastically.

"Good. Now get the fuck out of my office."

Tony was a genuine break-glass-in-case-of-war kind of guy, and I looked up to him from the moment I met him. As I walked out of his office to start my day of team building, I felt good knowing Tony was my platoon chief.

Over the next couple of weeks, my fellow newguys trickled in. There's safety in numbers, and every time I showed up at the Team and another newguy had checked in, I felt a little better about my chances of surviving the day without any major incidents. Plus, I was a little longer out of BUD/S than most of them. Jonny came directly from 18D, but the others came straight out of SQT. That didn't really mean shit in the platoon, but it was a small victory for me mentally.

Eventually, we had a group of four newguys at the bottom of Charlie's totem pole.

Besides me, there were Jonny, Biff, and Biggles. Jonny was a Korean kid from Los Angeles and the platoon's other corpsman. He was also a sniper. He was only about five foot seven, but he was compact and had been a strong high school swimmer, which helped him out in BUD/S. He once told me that his attitude toward BUD/S and most of the newguy shit we had thrown at us was just to keep his head down and complete the task, and never to worry about coming in first. It was actually a pretty effective mindset to have. In BUD/S, I saw a lot of "the best" athletes quit. Guys like Jonny who could just steadily grind it out survived.

Biff was a newguy machine gunner from a couple of BUD/S classes behind me. Like Jonny, he grew up in Southern California and got his nickname from his doppelgänger Biff Tannen. Unlike the character from *Back to the Future,* our Biff was actually likable. He'd been a standout wide receiver at the College of the Canyons, and SEAL training had only built upon his sheer physicality. Biff had a quiet reserve to him but could unleash fury on the turn of a dime.

Ryan Job was also a machine gunner and the funniest guy in our platoon. A doughy white kid from Washington State, Ryan had a baby face that seemed to be perpetually smiling. When he checked into our platoon in San Diego, he wasn't exactly chiseled out of granite. By SEAL standards, he was big and jiggly, so I stuck him with the nickname Biggles. His early days in the platoon were rough. He was consistently last on all our platoon runs and just wasn't in the kind of shape that was expected. Our OIC and platoon chief pulled him aside to deliver an ultimatum: "Tighten the fuck up, or beat feet out of this platoon." Ryan took it as his come-to-Jesus moment. He turned around and worked out harder than anybody else in the platoon and got himself up to speed. He took a lot of crap from everybody during work-up, but the fact that he was always locked on with everything he did, coupled with his knack for self-deprecating humor, made it hard not to love him.

In March, Tony sent me to Military Freefall Course in Otay Lakes, outside San Diego, where I learned that higher altitudes didn't make jumping out of airplanes any more pleasant for me. For three weeks, I learned how to jump with a team of other operators in order to insert into a combat zone. We learned to jump on oxygen, with gear, with a rifle, at night, and at various altitudes.

By early April, SEAL Team THREE had returned from deployment. I showed up for work one morning in PT gear and walked into the platoon space, a common area that housed a couple of computers, a whiteboard, a couch, and anything any of the guys thought might add "character" to the walls. Chris Kyle and Jeremy were on the couch. We'd never met, but I knew who they were because I'd recently been given the newguy task of unloading all the older guys' gear when they returned from deployment. Chris had just returned to the States after his second deployment to Iraq. Chris's first combat tour during the initial invasion in 2003 was, arguably, a warm-up for the extraordinary kill counts that came during his two tours in the Sunni Triangle in 2004 and 2006. After the Battle of Fallujah in November 2004, Chris's reputation as one of the deadliest snipers in the world was just starting to spread through the Teams. "The Legend" wasn't a household name back then, and in the Teams he was still known as Tex. Not exactly the most original nickname ever given to a Texas cowboy raised on rifles and rodeo, but Teamguy nicknames aren't exactly a science. Chris's freckled complexion and ginger hair told me he was a Scotsman, which told me fighting was in his blood. The alpha-male-sizing-up-the-competition look he gave me told me the hazing was not far off, but I played it cool and confident—sustained eye contact, standing tall, ready for anything. He slowly raised an empty soda can and spit dip juice into it apathetically.

"Dauber," he said lazily with his Texas drawl. "We're gonna call you Dauber, newguy."

I had never heard of the affable blond oaf that Bill Fagerbakke played on the nineties sitcom *Coach*, but Chris ignored my confused look as he turned to our platoon's lead petty officer and pointed.

"Tell me newguy doesn't look like Dauber from *Coach*," he said.

They say you never get a second chance to make a first impression. Apparently, Chris's first impression of me was that I was big, blond, and dumb.

"Definitely," Jeremy said, smiling. "Big goofy-looking fucker. He's a Dauber for sure."

As lead petty officer, Jeremy was the second-ranking enlisted leader in our platoon. His job was to marshal the sled dogs—keep us all focused and operating at peak performance. Jeremy was from Ohio and had made rank quickly in the Teams. We were his third platoon, and his attention to detail kept our motley crew on point. I learned quickly that the only thing more impressive than his ability to herd cats was his pop culture acumen.

With Jeremy's blessing, Chris's nickname stuck, and I was Dauber from then on.

Some of the biggest proponents of team building were the guys least removed from their status as newguys. Shedding newguy status requires having completed at least one deployment, and Chucky, Squirrel, Spaz, and Rex had all just checked that box. Our head shed called them the Sister's Kids, as a nod to the movie *Tombstone*. I quickly learned that the Sister's Kids weren't about to let our current class of newguys avoid the miserable indoctrination rituals they'd endured.

Chucky was a pipe hitter from Wisconsin. As a breacher and machine gunner, he had a natural affinity for breaking stuff. Whether it was a heavily fortified door on a hostile target or a punk-ass high on liquid courage at the bar, Chucky could deliver the appropriate amount of force to neutralize a target. He had picked up the nickname "Titties" in BUD/S, but it was used in the way you might call the guy who weighs three hundred pounds "Tiny." Chucky was over six feet tall and built like a brick wall. He was anything but mammary. Squirrel, our secondary point man, was from Northern California and more than capable when it came to getting us in and out of tight spots. Unlike Chucky, Squirrel had earned a nickname based on his physical appearance. He was one of the smallest guys in the platoon, but in combat, he was as lethal as brass knuckles on a soft skull.

Rex was our comms guy and primary radioman. He was a great operator with an incredible gift for multitasking in a firefight. He could maintain comms with our OIC, air assets, ground forces in the area, and our TOC, all while shooting at the enemy. He was a fearless operator with machinelike efficiency.

The last of the Sister's Kids was Spaz. Like Chris, Spaz was a ginger and an effective sniper (like I said, fighting's in their blood). Spaz's approach to hazing newguys was harsher than most of his peers, and we newguys thought it was a little overkill at times. It took me an entire combat deployment and numerous confirmed kills to graduate from newguy status, and for the nearly two years I spent as a newguy, Spaz never cut me any slack. It wasn't until I graduated out of Charlie Platoon and onto my second platoon with my own group of meats to torture that I understood it. The team building kept us sharp. It wasn't personal, and we bonded over it.

Getting a spot in Sniper School was one of those right-place-right-time things. Tony looked up at me from his paperwork one morning in the platoon space and asked, "Dauba', can you fuckin' shoot?"

"Roger that, Chief," I answered.

"Good. Pack your shit. You're going to Army Sniper School."

And with that, it was settled.

Being a SEAL at Fort Benning was a welcome change to being a newguy at the Team. The Army guys hadn't met many Teamguys before, and they treated my buddy Jordo and me like we were rock stars. Jordo was a fellow newguy and 18D medic at Team THREE from another platoon. He was a surfer from California and we used to hang out a lot outside of work, drinking too much and looking for good waves. Our first night there, we decided to go out and get hammered. We took a Ranger named Matt and a couple of other soldiers with us out in Columbus, Georgia, and didn't come home until an hour before our mandatory PT test the next morning. I set my alarm and crashed out, hoping to get about thirty minutes of sleep.

I woke up to the sound of the alarm and immediately regretted the decision to drink myself into oblivion the night before. I threw on my PT gear and tried to wake Jordo, but he was out cold in the bottom rack. I grabbed him by the shoulders and shook. Nothing. I slapped him. Still nothing. Finally, I punched him in the leg. He groaned, but didn't wake up. I shrugged and punched him again. This time, he began to stir. I dug through his bag and found his gear. I threw it at him and ushered him along as quickly as I could.

We stumbled to the track and into formation, fighting the urge to laugh or cry or both. I was shitfaced still and about to submit to the first assessment of Sniper School. If I failed, I'd be out. I swallowed liquor-flavored belches while I finished my sit-ups and then busted out my push-ups as quickly as I could. I glanced sideways at Jordo. He looked the same sickly green color that I felt. We got up to run, and I'm sure I ran as fast as I ever have. I did not want to fail and get sent back to Tony's hard-ass glare. When I crossed the finish line, I slowed to a walk and walked straight into the woods. I leaned over and vomited the entire contents of my stomach, which appeared to be mostly liquor, onto the ground. Then I straightened up, took a breath, and went back to my room to get ready for my first day of Sniper School.

I did a lot of drinking in that seven weeks at Sniper School, but I also learned a lot about shooting. I graduated and was a qualified sniper, ready to deploy with my platoon. Jordo and I had spent the better part of two months practicing long-range target interdiction, and I was ready to put my practice to work.

When I returned from Sniper School, Charlie Platoon was finally all together, ready to train for war as one. Toward the end of the summer of 2005, we began the work-up for our scheduled deployment the following April. While SQT provides the basic skills required for all SEALs, work-up prepares SEALs to operate within a platoon. It's all about actual team building and endless practice and refinement during a series of training blocks designed to sharpen and test the platoon's entire skill set.

For newguys like me, work-up was our first rodeo, and we were expected to carry our own weight and be ready to meet any challenge that was thrown at us. For eight months we traveled the country to various bases and installations, training for everything from close-quarters combat to maritime operations and everything in between.

Work-up taught me valuable lessons about leadership. Each time I stepped into a training scenario, I was a functional member of the platoon. I had to be prepared for any outcome at all times. SEALs are thinking shooters and are always prepared to take control of a situation and lead when others don't. I learned to work in concert with my platoon to realize common goals and to overcome obstacles. No man is an island.

Toward the end of work-up, Charlie Platoon gained another newguy, and our tight-knit "E-Dog" clan grew to five enlisted newguys. On any given evolution, I was packed somewhere among Jonny, Biff, Biggles, or Marc Lee.

Marc had done most of his work-up with another platoon and then rotated over to Charlie around Christmas. Like Biggles, Marc was a machine gunner. At about six one and stout with huge arms, Marc had the Big Tough Frogman physique, but he didn't project the big ego and bravado. He was a devout Christian who had studied theology at the Master's College in Southern California, and his faith seemed to underlie his gentle and reserved disposition. As a talented college soccer player, Marc had barely missed a shot as a pro with the Colorado Rapids after a knee injury cut short his run at Major League Soccer. After his knee recovered, Marc joined the Navy with his eye on the Teams. I could see right away that Marc fit the mold of our platoon, and he and I hit it off.

With his deep tan and black hair, Marc looked Iraqi, or at least we liked to tell him as much. He was a stellar operator who could lay down lead in a firefight with the aggression of a honey badger and then just turn it off and have a normal conversation about family or growing up in Oregon. I bonded with Marc and my fellow meats over the many shitty jobs we were tasked with. We loaded countless truckloads of gear, broke down numerous pallets, and did it all over again because we knew if we shut up and bore it, there was a war waiting for us.

In February 2006, Charlie and Delta Platoons of SEAL Team THREE, aka Task Unit Bruiser, completed the culminating event of our work-up cycle. Cert Ex (Certification Exercise) requires an entire task unit, including support personnel, to prove it's ready to deploy, during an elaborate exercise meant to assess our skills and ability to execute our missions. During Cert Ex, I saw the whole Navy war machine in action and took my place as one of its cogs. I was thoroughly impressed by the sheer power of the American military apparatus, and I felt certain of our ability to wreak havoc on our enemies. We were given an enthusiastic thumbs-up to deploy to Iraq in April, and I thought back to the kid I'd been in the recruiter's office, four years earlier. I felt different. I felt ready.

A couple of weeks before we deployed, retired Lieutenant Colonel Dave Grossman gave me much to reflect on when he addressed SEAL Team THREE at Naval Amphibious Base Coronado. Grossman, an Army Ranger and the psychologist who founded a field of study known as "killology," believes that 2 percent of the population is capable of killing without suffering psychological trauma. They simply flip a switch when necessary in order to commit an action. The 2 percent is heavily drawn to Special Operations, as these warriors forget the direction of their forebrain in combat and operate with the more instinctual, primitive midbrain. These killers are unaffected when killing is justified, and Grossman is careful to distinguish between these warriors and sociopaths in his book *On Killing: The Psychological Cost of Learning to Kill in War and Society*. He merely proposes that 2 percent of the male population is capable of levelheaded participation in combat without psychological ramifications.

When Grossman wrapped up his speech, I looked around me at my brothers in arms, trying to do the math. *Are we all 2 percenters?* I didn't know. Who could predict another man's emotions? I just knew that as operators, we were trained and ready. Grossman's 2 percent explanation made sense to me. I felt ready and willing to kill my enemy. It was simple enough to conceptualize, but applying theory to action was something I wouldn't be able to do until stepping onto the battlefield. In the meantime, I concentrated on why I was there, and what I wanted to do.

Robert Heinlein once wrote, "Fulfillment in life involves loving a good woman and killing a bad man." My early years of Team life had been anything but stable in the relationship category, but my vigilance toward my platoon and mission remained constant. I could have the rest of my life to find a good woman to love, but I might have only seven months to kill that bad man.

THREE

CHARLIE 13

"A true initiation never ends."
—Robert Anton Wilson

THE WHINE OF the ramp door's hydraulics shook me out of a momentary doze. I opened my eyes long enough to watch the slice of sunlight visible from the rear of the C-17 shrink and eventually disappear. I knew it was my last glimpse of San Diego for a while. I hadn't lingered long on the tarmac because I had no reason. I was a twenty-four-year-old single Frogman with no family in California, nobody to kiss. Standing around and watching the other guys kiss their babies was depressing, so I boarded our bird as quickly as I could. I settled into my jump seat and watched the ramp close with one eye open, still shaking off the effects of the previous night's drinking. Around me, the other thirty guys were trying to get comfortable among the pallets of gear. Airmen weaved in and out of the crowded space, locking down pallets, securing the aircraft, checking the manifest. *This is life for the next six months,* I thought. Head counts, gear checks, and hurry up and wait.

The truth was, I didn't really know what to expect. I was Charlie 13, number 13 of 16 men in my platoon. In other words, there were twelve other dudes in front of me with either more rank or more experience. I was a newguy, and I had never deployed before. All I knew was I had a job to do, and I had to do it well. We'd spent months training for combat; I hoped to see some while in Iraq. I knew I didn't want to spend my deployment guarding a forward operating base (FOB) or running personal security for some diplomat. I signed up to shoot terrorists.

The whine of the jet engines grew louder as we prepared for takeoff. It was a long way from Coronado to Iraq. We had flights to Bangor, Maine; Spangdahlem, Germany; and Al Taqaddum, Iraq. I planned on making most of the trip in an Ambien haze, and since I was a medic, I had the ability to make that happen. Newguys generally rank at the bottom of the totem pole in every manner, but it's funny how popular a newguy medic with a bottle full of sleeping pills can be on a long flight.

Once we hit cruising altitude I picked my way through the rucksacks littering the floor on my way to the pisser in the back of the plane. Midstream, I thought I heard my name over the engine noise. I shook it off and kept moving.

"Dauber!"

I heard it loud and clear this time and turned around to see Marc Lee hanging over the side of a pallet he'd claimed as his bed for the flight. Cupping his hands around his mouth he yelled, "Hurry up! I need my night-night pills!"

"Keep your pants on!" I yelled back.

As I made my way back, I fished the bottle out of my pocket and tossed it up to Marc. He shook one of the pills into his palm, slapped it back, replaced the cap, and threw the bottle back to me. Then he rolled over to go to sleep. I found my own space on another pallet, doling out the much-sought-after pills along the way like some humanitarian sleep-aid worker before settling in for the first long leg of our journey. I couldn't stop thinking about Grossman's talk and the Heinlein quote on fulfillment, love, and killing. Sometimes odd things give you comfort: the roar of a C-17's engines before takeoff, the stink of your brothers around you, your favorite quote about killing.

I looked around from my perch. The entire center of the plane was strapped down with aircraft pallets. Their tops were covered in Teamguys sprawled out sleeping, reading, or watching movies. The port and starboard side aisles were littered with Teamguys doing the same. I smiled as I thought of our chariot, a C-17, taking us into the fight. If you're headed to a fight, bring your buddies. If you're going to war, bring your brothers and plenty of awesome weaponry. I imagine it might feel a little overwhelming to someone with any amount of anxiety about heading into combat. Looking around me, there was no place I wanted to be but there among my brothers, riding to war.

The next day we sat inside Spangdahlem Air Base terminal in Germany, weary with Ambien, bored and anxious to get to Iraq. A CNN reporter's voice hummed in the background like the buzz of a fly, annoying and constant. No one paid attention until the word *Ramadi* caught somebody's ear. That word interested us because Ramadi was our destination. We perked up and listened to the report. Casualties were high, fighting intense, and the enemy well supplied. I looked at Nick, our Explosive Ordnance Disposal (EOD) guy, and raised my eyebrows. According to CNN, we were headed into one of the most dangerous cities in the world. On one hand, I was acutely aware of my desire to return to the United States in one piece. On the other hand, I thought about why I had joined the Teams. I wanted to bring the fight to the enemy. I felt my palms sweating a little. Heading into Ramadi, there was a good chance we were going to see a lot of action, and I would have the opportunity to do exactly what I had joined for.

I think a man is the sum of his experiences and that we are constantly changed by what we see and do. Sitting in Spangdahlem, I knew I had already been changed by my SEAL training. I was not the same kid who joined the Navy in 2002. The Teams were chiseling me into something much better than before, bringing out the best in me. Still, I knew combat would require more than holding up a boat for several hours or staying awake for a week. I wondered how Ramadi would change me.

I wondered what else war would chisel away.

When we landed at Al Taqaddum Air Base (TQ), I was surprised to see rain. The next day, all the newguys made the thirty-mile helo ride to Ramadi to do the undesirable tasks of picking up gear, checking stuff in, and generally preparing camp for the task unit's arrival. Bitch work. About a dozen of us loaded up on the Black Hawk bound for Camp Junction City, aka Camp Ramadi. We were battle ready with our web gear, body armor, helmets, night-vision goggles, and plenty of ammo for our M4s.

Every time I get on a helicopter, I remember the full potential of an RPG that finds its airborne target. In 2005, eight SEALs and eight Army Night Stalkers were killed when their bird was shot down in Afghanistan during Operation Red Wings, the mission made famous in Marcus Luttrell's memoir, *Lone Survivor*. One of the pilots was from Washington Depot, Connecticut. I didn't mind riding in helicopters, but I always thought about the possibility of crashing or getting shot down. I understood the necessity of flying by night, and I was glad to be taking the safest course. But I reminded myself again that where we were going, there were insurgents who wanted to kill us. Flying out of TQ, I looked down at the base lit up like a small metropolis. Once out over the desert, there was nothing but blackness. A vast and empty canvas stretched before us. In my estimation, we had six months to fill it up with dead insurgents.

In 2006, the last place in Iraq you wanted to be was in an American convoy on a main supply route. I didn't know a lot about the place I'd flown into two nights before, but I knew that. Sitting in the passenger seat of a huge flatbed truck, I tried not to think too much about the unenviable mission I'd drawn as a newguy SEAL on his first deployment. Newguys always get the crap jobs, and I had drawn the short straw in my leadership's random selection for a convoy op back to TQ to pick up our gear. I would spend the next two days in a miserably hot and dangerous convoy trying to avoid being blown up by an improvised explosive device (IED).

Route Michigan was the main artery of transportation along the western front and a magnet for IEDs. Navigating the serpentine barrier of Camp Ramadi's front gate on our way toward Michigan, our sprawling train of vehicles looked like something out of *Mad Max*. Tactical vehicles the color of Iraq's sepia landscape churned up the desert dust that infiltrated every facet of our existence. We called it moondust. There were armored HMMWVs (Humvees), hulking seven-ton trucks, 10x10 tractors called wreckers that stretched the length of a big rig, and the newest addition to the American military's efforts in western Iraq—the MRAP, or Mine-Resistant Ambush Protected vehicle. The 6x6 MRAPs were called Cougars, but they were anything but catlike. The front end protruded like a hound dog's snout from the armored passenger compartment with its V-shaped underbelly, designed to more efficiently deflect IED blasts. There were boxy and bulbous protrusions all over the outside and conspicuous piping running the length of the passenger compartment on each side. There were civilian contractors driving big rigs—pretty much the same type you'd see on any highway in the States, but with tons of added armor and protection from rocket-propelled grenades. The amount of metal and armor was incredible. I was glad to have it, but its necessity stoked my acute awareness of the IED threat.

At the line of departure, I opened the feed tray cover on my Squad Automatic Weapon (SAW) and pulled some slack from the 200-round drum's belt of ammunition. I laid the first round into place on the feed tray, slammed the cover shut, pulled the charging handle back, and checked the safety one more time. Locked and loaded. On the fortifications marking the base's defensive edge, I saw a sign bearing the brand motto for the American service member at war: COMPLACENCY KILLS. Like "Just Do It" or "This Bud's for You," it was a simple call to action that's supposed to stick in your brain and rattle around in the subconscious, directing your behavior toward a particular end. Buy Nike. Drink Budweiser.

Don't get killed.

The success of any advertising campaign depends greatly upon the individual consumer's willingness to accept its message. With less than a week on the ground in Iraq, I was picking up exactly what that sign was putting down. Four years of training just to get to the war. I came to find the enemy, not to have him find me. The maddening thing about being a Teamguy on a convoy op is that all the training and vigilance in the world might not matter against an IED. IEDs don't care how much of a badass you are. If you're one of the unlucky cats whose vehicle rolls over a pressure-plate detonator, it's going to be a bad day for you. If their triggerman decides your vehicle is in the convoy's sweet spot and presses a button at the moment you roll over the massive bomb he rigged and buried, it's going to be a bad day for you. The thought of having one of those bad days and never getting a chance to fight really pissed me off. As a Frogman in combat, you want your chance to go toe-to-toe with the enemy—to shoot people. SEALs are dynamic. We're thinking shooters. Our selection process is just long enough to weed out those who don't have the warrior mindset. Teamguys all have that mindset. It's in our DNA. Getting blown up by an invisible bomb is no way for a Frogman to go. Complacency kills, but when you're one of thirty vehicles in a convoy, hypervigilance is no match for the detached indifference of chance.

I tried to think about something else.

It was barely eight thirty in the morning, but with full gear, body armor, and helmet, it was miserable-hot inside our seven-ton flatbed. It was only April, and I was not looking forward to the summer. As we started out through the city, I got my first good look at our surroundings. Ramadi was full of two-, three-, and four-story buildings, most of them surrounded by eight-foot walls. Everything was brown. Brown and dirty. That about sums up how I saw Ramadi. There was sparse vegetation and palm trees near the banks of the Euphrates to my left, but not much flora beyond that. There was a drought in Ramadi at the time, but I couldn't imagine a little more water making much of a difference in its general appearance.

We were in the first third of the convoy, and once we got through the outskirts of the city, there was nothing but open desert. It looked like Tatooine, the desert planet Luke Skywalker calls home, and the more I saw of it, the more I did not want to be driving in that convoy. One key difference between Anbar and Tatooine was the endless IED craters. Everywhere I looked along our route, I saw the scars left by massive explosions. There were blow-you-sky-high craters as far as the eye could see. I stopped counting how many we passed when I hit one hundred. I couldn't imagine how the insurgency was even operating out there; there were no houses, no signs of life, just a barren desert.

My driver was Mike Monsoor, another newguy from Delta Platoon. Within the task unit, there was a mixed bag of experience and expertise. I was one of two newguy corpsmen, just checked into the Team the year before. I was also one of Charlie Platoon's six snipers.

The rest of the unit was a variety of machine gunners, communications guys, breachers, upper management, and plenty of guys to fill any other job that might arise. Each platoon had sixteen SEALs and two EOD technicians—the guys who handle the bombs.

Mike was a machine gunner and well liked in the Team. He was a quiet guy from California, about six-one with brown hair and a square jaw. Being in different platoons, we didn't work together much, but I had great respect for Mike. During predeployment training, he and I had beat each other senseless for the viewing pleasure of the seasoned operators in our task unit. SEAL hazing rituals can be pretty sadistic and juvenile in a very elaborate—and often hilarious—way. The older guys liked to fire up the newguys pretty frequently. Getting wasted and having a couple of newguys put on boxing gloves and fight like Roman gladiators was a favorite on long training trips. My battle with Mike was nothing short of epic. I remember repeatedly hitting him as hard as I could, but he wouldn't go down. He just kept coming at me and dishing it back as hard as I was serving it up. Once the gloves were on, my two-inch-reach and twenty-pound-weight advantages didn't matter to Mike. He fought like a lion, and I respected that. When it was all over, we sat down together, sweaty and short of breath. The older guys handed us beers.

"Motherfucker, you hit hard," Mike said.

"Motherfucker, you hit hard," I replied.

Driving toward TQ, we fought the truck's engine noise, talking a little about the IED threats and casualties and whatever else came to mind.

"Dude, what's up with all the chicks on this convoy?" I said.

Most of the soldiers driving the vehicles and running the convoy were women. There was something amusing and attractive at the same time about the often petite women climbing into the massive vehicles and handling them with ease.

"I know, right? I saw a few who I definitely would not kick out of bed for eating crackers," Mike said. I laughed in agreement and settled in for the rest of the ride.

The convoy stopped twice along the way to check out suspected IEDs, which turned out to be nothing. Aside from the constant anxiety over the possibility of being blown up without warning, the two-hour drive to TQ was relatively uneventful. Once there, we had the Team's pallets of gear loaded onto the truck and then chilled out. I sat around, dipping a lot of Copenhagen tobacco, a habit I would only increase over the next several months. TQ had recreation tents where we could access the Internet, so I sent a few emails home. We ate in the chow hall and waited for the next day. Mike and I spent the night talking about nothing in particular.

In the morning, we convoyed back the same way we'd come. We had the task unit's pallets of gear and the guys who'd been watching it. We were a little more relaxed, having made it without incident the day before. I noticed that the Army cats who'd been there for months didn't even bat an eye at the prospect of traveling the route littered with the effects of so many IEDs. I managed to take a cue from them for the ride back.

A feeling of calmness settled over me for most of the three-hour journey back to Ramadi. I remembered a couple of our old mantras: "Calmness is contagious," and "Mind over matter: if you don't mind, it don't matter." The previous day's two stops to check out suspected IEDs had been false alarms, so I tuned out the noise of the convoy and my restlessness and thought about getting past the setup phase and into combat.

About ten miles from Ramadi proper, signs of life increased as more settlements littered the landscape. The calmness evaporated as Ramadi came into view and my hypervigilance switched back on. A dusty haze enveloped the city like a locust swarm. Thick columns of smoke billowed up from somewhere in the middle of the city. The irony of driving toward the aftermath of an IED attack after two days of worrying about one was not lost on me.

War is full of cold ironies. You can spend all your time preparing only to get hit the second you turn your head. You can prepare yourself almost to the point of vulnerability. In the end, you never know when your number is up.

FOUR

PUT ME IN, COACH

**"You got to have smelt a lot of mule manure
before you can sing like a hillbilly."**

—Hank Williams Sr.

A NEWGUY DOESN'T HAVE anything of his own. Not even his weekends. I was at the Team one Saturday morning during work-up squaring away some gear, and was just finishing up. As I secured the last of my stuff and headed downstairs to the quarterdeck, I ran into Tony.

"Dauba," he said, "you're not goin' anywhere. We got some drinkin' to do."

"Roger that, Chief," I answered. An order is an order.

We spent the entire day driving from bar to bar in the Murder Van, getting completely wasted. Eventually, we met up with KPM and Tony's roommate, Jeff Paine. Jeff was about forty and had made a big impression on me as my BUD/S instructor when he chummed the water during my five-and-a-half-nautical-mile swim. He was an old-school Frogman like Tony, and the last of the true pirates.

In the morning, I woke up on Tony's living room floor. KPM was passed out on the couch. Sometime in the night he had taken a piss in their dryer. Jeff ambled down the stairs shakily, a cloud of liquor fumes rolling out in front of him.

"Anybody got any whiskey?" he asked. "I need to get this toothpaste taste out of my mouth."

"Jesus," Tony called from the kitchen. "Don'tcha ever worry about ya liver?"

"That's all right, brother," said Jeff. "That's why God gave me two of them."

I glanced over at KPM, whose slight shaking and stifled laugh betrayed the fact that he had woken up. I strained my neck to look up at my platoon chief in his kitchen, pouring a whiskey for Jeff. *Jesus*, I thought. *I just don't want to let these guys down.*

SHARKBASE, LATE APRIL 2006

I woke up around noon and sat up on the edge of my cot. Four days in Iraq, and nothing interesting yet. Patience is a virtue, I thought, rubbing the sleep from my eyes. I looked around at the gear and personal belongings in various stages of being unpacked that littered the tent. Mike Monsoor and I had brought all our gear to Sharkbase, Task Unit Bruiser's base of operations. Our private little Special Operations compound was concealed behind a big wall. It housed SEALs, Rangers, and Tier 1 assets. We had our own firing range and an old palace we used for our tactical operations center (TOC). Throughout the course of the summer, we'd get tasked to support the Army at Corregidor or the Marines at Government Center, or we'd venture out for a forty-eight-hour sniper overwatch, but we always eventually came home to Sharkbase. I shared a tent with Spaz, Bob, Marc, and Dale, our sister platoon chief.

It was quiet in the tent. I was alone. I scratched my beard stubble, slipped on my flip-flops and sunglasses, and headed for the porta-potties in PT shorts and T-shirt. A belligerent wave of desert heat hit me when I walked outside the air-conditioned comfort of my tent. Sporadic rains had left the desert air thick with moisture, carrying with added efficiency the smell of the American war machine and the Euphrates's mix of shit and decay.

I hit the row of porta-potties and briefly recalled the story I'd heard about the guy who took a direct mortar round after walking out of a crapper on Camp Ramadi. The mortar threat was another unsettling reminder that my war could end in a flash without my ever having had the chance for a fair fight. War is a 360-degree environment.

I finished and made the forty-yard walk to our mission planning space, a plywood building full of all kinds of grenades, rockets, and boxes of ammo—a general cornucopia of small arms ordnance. A life-sized cardboard cutout of Elvis stood watch over our impressive hive of dormant destruction and other mission-essential gear. Young Elvis from the 1950s, not fat Elvis. We'd spent some time training in Memphis during our deployment work-up, and the King of Rock and Roll deployed with Charlie Platoon to Iraq as a reminder of our good times. Elvis never saw combat when he served in the Army in the 1960s, but we figured he could handle the mission of looking cool next to a bunch of explosives. I walked past the King and checked the 3x5 dry-erase board where the head shed would post ops updates. I'd been checking the board every day before hitting the chow hall, and today I saw the green light I'd been waiting for.

"Warning order—1400, Op brief—2100, Roll time—2300."

My heart rate kicked up a notch and sent a jolt of excitement through my body. It reminded me of my first time jumping out of an airplane. I felt like I just got the call up to the big leagues and was about to pitch my first game. I headed to the chow hall with a cheesy grin on my face, barely noticing the fecal smell in the air.

I sat in the middle of the mission planning area, surrounded by the rest of the platoon. We sat on folding chairs or leaned against plywood tables, waiting for Luke and Tony to begin the brief. Elvis stood off to the side, waiting for further instructions.

Guy, one of our task unit officers, sat next to me. Guy checked into Team THREE with me the year before. Although I didn't go through BUD/S with him, we quickly became good friends. He was an Annapolis guy, so he wasn't an E-Dog like me, but he was from Jersey, so we shared a connection as northeasterners. Guy wrestled at the Academy and was built like a diesel engine. He was a Big Tough Frogman who possessed the natural Teamguy ability to turn on the aggression when needed. He was also one of the officers who instilled confidence among the enlisted, which became increasingly important as the deployment wore on. He and I built a great friendship over fine whiskey, good cigars, and the strenuous life of combat.

Chucky, Squirrel, Spaz, and Rex sat alongside Guy. EOD Nick sat to my left. Nick was a former Surface Warfare Combatant-Craft Crewman (SWCC) operator turned bomb nut. Nick's SoCal swagger was juxtaposed with his Polish-Mexican ancestry. He was an avid big-wave surfer and would drop into a dust storm if he could. Nick's operational skill saved lives on more than a few occasions. We were very fortunate to have him attached to our platoon.

Luke was our officer-in-charge (OIC). He kept the warning order quick and simple. It was a straightforward direct-action (DA) mission—our specialty: capture or kill a bomb maker and known insurgent in Tamim, a little village in southwest Ramadi. Tony broke into the details of what needed to get done in the meantime.

We spilled out of the ops tent into the Iraqi heat. There were tasks to be done and little time to do them in. Priorities: Team gear, platoon gear, personal gear. Our next brief was at 2100, six and a half hours away, and I needed to be completely squared away by then. Teamguys take pride in their gear. We live by an old adage: take care of your gear and your gear will take care of you. Simple, but effective. From the earliest days of BUD/S, I remember the people around me constantly prepping and then rechecking their gear. A knife was never too sharp, the gear never quite perfect. The cyclic and repetitive nature of fixing, tweaking, and readjusting gear enhances the effectiveness of the operator. I was no different. Previous proper planning prevents a piss-poor performance.

In addition to running the medical department, I was an ordnance rep, which meant I was responsible for making sure my platoon's vehicles were outfitted with heavy weapons and lasers. I changed into cammies and boots before heading over to where our vehicles were parked. The chariots we rode into battle were the 1152B HMMWVs, armed to the teeth. We named all of them for GI Joe characters and spray-painted their names on the driver-side doors: Snake Eyes, Cobra Commander, Shipwreck, etc. The heavy guns we rolled with were .50-caliber machine guns and the smaller M240B machine gun, which fires 7.62 mm rounds. The big guns laid waste on the battlefield and were always welcomed in a firefight. But in case they weren't enough, we stockpiled LAW (light antitank weapon) rockets and the 84 mm Carl Gustav recoilless rifle as backups in the trucks.

All our weaponry was impressive and deadly, but I was particularly fond of the .50. It is a classic champion of the American combat arsenal and predates World War II. The .50 can easily punch through brick and metal of all kinds. It can tear a small vehicle to shreds within a matter of seconds. Hitting another human being with a burst of .50-cal will turn said human being into a mangled mass of hamburger. There is a vicious rumor in the military that the Geneva Conventions prohibit the use of the .50 on human targets, but that's all it is—a rumor. I read a February 2011 blog entry in Rumor Doctor for *Stars and Stripes* that carefully explained how the .50, though capable of causing horrific wounds, has a military advantage that outweighs the suffering it causes. Therefore, it is not considered an illegal weapon for use against human targets under the Law of Armed Conflict.

I checked the headspace and timing of the .50s, and then conducted function tests on all the guns. I replaced the batteries on the lasers and made sure the hand-grip pressure pads were functioning properly. Later on, before departing, each turret gunner would check all of these again. When I finished, I relayed to Bob, the primary ordnance rep, that I had completed the checks.

Bob was on his third deployment with Charlie. He grew up in California's Central Valley. Fortunately, Bob was spared Valley Fever when he joined the Navy. Bob was a solid 210 pounds on a six-one frame and did the heavy lifting. He was often aloof with the newguys, praised very little, but demanded the highest degree of performance on the job. Uncle Bob made newguys better Frogmen. It's kind of an unspoken rule in a SEAL platoon that after your first platoon you're relieved of the burden of carrying the machine gun (otherwise affectionately known as the "Pig"). On this deployment, Bob still carried the bacon. He led by example and was a core member of our platoon.

I split responsibility for the medical department with Jonny, so I checked the medical equipment in Snake Eyes. The spine board, platoon med bag, and body bags were there, so I went back to my tent to check my personal gear. I had my med bag, plus the same gear everybody else carried. My gear was always ready to go. I've been meticulous since I was a kid. While my brothers used to play with their Matchbox cars and Tonka trucks, I would spend hours organizing and arranging mine into neat rows. I like things orderly. I already had my grenades all taped down and a full set of magazines loaded and ready to go. I made a habit of rotating my mags every few days to make sure I wasn't stressing the springs too much. If you take care of your mags, you get fewer jams.

After prepping the gear, I took some time to write an email home to my parents. I was careful to be vague and ambiguous about where I was and what I was doing. I told them things were fine, and everything was going great. In the back of my mind, I was thinking about going out on my first op. Getting shot or blown up was a very real possibility, but that's not something you share with somebody back home. Those possibilities are part of the job, and how you deal with them defines you as an operator. There's a lot of stuff you don't tell the people you love.

I willed the hours to tick by like a kid on Christmas Eve. I hit the range with my M4 to make sure my dope was dialed in (the settings on my rifle sights) before settling in to prepare the medical brief for the op order. This was one of my biggest responsibilities. The brief covered plans such as what to do if a man went down on the way to the target . . . on target . . . during exfiltration, etc. It's your basic planning for every conceivable mission scenario distilled into a PowerPoint presentation. The medical slides were an important part of the brief. Where someone was going if they got shot and who was going to transport them was nothing to breeze through.

When all the prep work was done, I headed to dinner with the other newguys. We ate lunches in our small, private chow hall on Sharkbase, but for dinner we usually drove to the bigger Army chow hall on Camp Ramadi. Besides, the PX sold Copenhagen, and if you didn't get there on shipment day, the Texas boys would clean the place out in short order.

I piled into a Toyota Hilux with Marc Lee, Ryan Job, Biff, and Jonny. Jonny had just finished his daily call to his girlfriend. He used to take a lot of flak for the amount of time he spent calling, IM'ing, writing letters to, and phoning her. If there was a way to communicate with her, he exhausted it. He probably floated a message in a bottle down the Euphrates one night. If he thought an Iraqi pigeon would have made it with a message all the way to her house in the States, he would have tried it. He once got his ass chewed for sitting behind a generator on the satellite phone during a mortar attack on Sharkbase. The rest of us ran for cover, and he had one of his hour-long conversations, oblivious to the overhead threat because of the noise from the generator.

"So anybody know what's up with this place we're headed into?" I asked from the passenger seat. "What are the atmospherics?"

Jonny was driving dangerously and first to speak up. "Hell if I know, bro. I'm just operating on the assumption it's like the rest of Ramadi: shitty. As long as we don't get blown up on the ride over, I think we'll be good."

"Jonny, you think you're gonna be okay to see the enemy tonight through them tiny slits for eyes?" Marc said from the backseat, recycling one of our go-to jokes. Military humor in general is dark, crass, and often tasteless and offensive by civilian standards, but for us, mildly racist jabs like Marc's were a great way to defuse tension before an op.

"Yeah, I think I'll be okay," Jonny said. "I just hope nobody mistakes you for muj tonight, bro. I don't want to have to bandage you up after Dauber gets too excited and accidentally shoots your ass."

Muj (pronounced "Mooj") was our term for the insurgents we fought. It was short for *mujahideen,* which is a broad term for one engaged in jihad and is what a lot of the insurgents called themselves.

"Ha! No shit, right? Dauber will shoot a motherfucker straight up," Ryan said from behind me. "What do you think, Dauber?"

"I guess we'll see," I said. "But if I do, it won't be Marc. I don't have enough magnification on my scope to see them tiny arms."

"You shoot me in a dream, you better wake up and apologize," Marc said.

The *Reservoir Dogs* reference made me smile, and I fired back. "I wouldn't shoot you, man. You're my favorite Iraqi."

"You two aren't gonna kiss now, are you?" Biff said as we bounced over uneven terrain on our way to Camp Ramadi. The cackling continued as we pulled up to the chow hall.

———————————

By 2300, I was loaded up and ready to go. I wore my tricolor BDUs with my black parachute rigger's belt and Oakley assault boots. In my right breast pocket, I had my blood chit and rosary beads. In my other chest pocket, I kept two hundred dollars cash in case I ever got separated from my platoon and had to barter with the locals for my freedom. After Operation Redwings, escape and evasion were given more attention in training, and carrying cash into combat became standard procedure. Fortunately, in an urban environment, your area of operation is finite and there's an Abrams tank on every street corner.

In my right shoulder pocket, I had a tourniquet. In the left cargo pocket of my trousers, I had a blowout kit: three compressed Kerlix field dressings, a 14-gauge needle, an Asherman chest seal, and a couple of ACE wraps. Each of us carried one in order to hastily treat a gunshot wound until more help could be summoned. I carried a CRKJ folding utility knife, which could come in handy if I needed to dig some brass out of a badly jammed gun or as a last-resort weapon. Under my web gear, I wore a set of low-pro body armor with an American flag folded up with the ceramic plates inside. I carried Old Glory with me at all times, a reminder of the liberty for which we fought.

I carried seven mags, two frags, a smoke grenade, an IR strobe, three sets of flex-cuffs, a battle map inside a Rhodesian officer pouch, pen, and paper. On my wrist I wore a Garmin Foretrex GPS and G-Shock watch. My M4 with EOTech was optimized for close-quarters battle and had a 10-inch barrel with a 6-inch suppressor and Surefire flashlight attached to the rail system. I had it rigged with the old Vietnam-style shortened buttstock and metal handgrip. In a leather Galco holster on my hip, I wore my sidearm: a SIG Sauer P226 pistol with a 15-round magazine. I carried two spare mags on my belt. On my Modular Integrated Communications Helmet (MICH), I mounted my AN/PVS-15 night-vision goggles. Last but not least, I carried my med bag, fully outfitted with hemorrhage control measures, advanced airway surgical tools, needle decompression, bag valve masks, and pulse oximetry. I was wearing fifty pounds of gear, but it didn't feel cumbersome. You get used to wearing combat gear, and it becomes a sort of extension of your body. I felt like I carried no excess, like everything on my person was a completely vital item. I genuinely felt swift, silent, deadly.

I loaded into the back of Big Zev, our hulking beast of a flatbed stake truck, which we named after an old Vietnam-era truck that appeared in *Tour of Duty,* the classic 1980s show about Vietnam. We would binge-watch the show during off hours on Sharkbase, and in one episode, the crew had painted the name Big Zev on the truck's door—a pop culture Easter egg and nod to Zev Braun, the show's executive producer. Big Zev was an ambling beast and sat in the middle of our convoy of four armored Humvees, and as we wound our way through Camp Ramadi, I noted again the half-inch steel walls and sandbags lining the floor. I thought about my beloved balls and wondered to what extent the sandbags could keep them intact in the event of an IED blast.

We were on our way from Sharkbase to pick up our Jundis. *Jundi* ("Jundee") is the Arabic word for soldier, and is what we called the members of the Iraqi Security Forces our team was tasked with training. My platoon was divided into four groups, and each group was given a set of Jundis to work with. My group was assigned the Jundi Special Missions Platoon (SMP). The SMP was theoretically a step up in tactical proficiency compared to the regular-army guys, but a real soup sandwich nonetheless when we first got them. Completely lacking in most military discipline, they were mostly young, skinny Iraqis who played a lot of soccer and smoked a lot of cigarettes. They were in pretty decent shape for Iraqi standards and had been selected for the

SMP as a result. Most were Shias from Baghdad who commuted by bus to Ramadi, where they would put on their uniforms and pick up their guns for training. Their fidelity to the cause of building Iraq into a Western-style democracy was often dubious at best. Some of them believed in Iraq and genuinely wanted to fight to make it better. Some were just there for the paycheck. Some gave off a very strong muj vibe. It was something about the shifty glances—the guys who wouldn't sustain eye contact. They were the ones who got my Spidey senses tingling. You try to embrace the whole "one team, one fight" mentality, but in the back of your mind, you're thinking, *These are some nefarious individuals.* You find yourself wondering, *When's that dog gonna turn on me?* You hold them at a distance because you have to. It's nothing personal; it's just basic survival instinct and combat.

We always waited until the last minute to brief the Jundis on the time and location of our missions because we had to account for the possibility that some of them were muj. None of them knew where we lived because we didn't want any of them tipping off our enemies with coordinates to Sharkbase.

The Jundis' main training facility was an old Iraqi prison on Camp Ramadi's outer edges that once housed Iranian POWs during the Iran-Iraq War. That's where Marc and I spent our first few days in country training them on myriad tactics. We focused a lot in those early training days on how to not accidentally shoot us in the back. We taught them two- and four-man room clearing, how to bound from cover to cover, how to load onto and exit tactical vehicles, how to scale walls and set security on both sides, how to prepare for a breach, and how far away you have to be in order to not get concussed. We applied the crawl, walk, run method. We would talk through the training with an interpreter and then demonstrate the tactics over and over again.

Slow is smooth; smooth is fast. This is your mantra when clearing rooms in urban combat.

When the Jundis cleared rooms in training, it was not uncommon to see guys run into the middle of a room and proceed to wave their AK-47s wildly with no regard whatsoever for the need to identify targets, maintain muzzle awareness, or avoid crossing into a friendly line of fire. Some of them seemed to try to make up for their lack of precision with violence of action. This led to more than one instance of Jundis tripping over their own feet or falling down hard by virtue of general clumsiness. They did not inspire confidence. Officially, we were training the Jundis to take the lead in the fight against the insurgency, but off the record, we were doing the door-kicking ourselves on every mission. The Jundis were always in the back of the assault train. We'd let them handle more menial tasks, like searching buildings after we'd secured them and frisking the women on target.

When we got to the Jundis' barracks, I immediately noticed their lack of urgency. When we're on an op, SEALs have a general sense of urgency in everything we do because we're jacked up on a combat mindset. We have our head in the game. Our pucker factor is elevated, and our energy level reflects it. The Jundis did not share our intensity. Getting them all up and onto the back of Big Zev with all their rifles and extra equipment was like corralling third graders for a field trip to a museum. Their general malaise amplified my own nervous energy and excitement. With all of them packed tightly into Big Zev, we rolled out for the objective.

The roar of the engine and warm humid air made me even more aware of how ready I was to do what I'd been training to do for four years. We reached our staging point a couple hundred meters away from the target. We dismounted and started corralling the Jundis into position at the rear of our patrol formation.

Our terp (interpreter), Moose, was a former Jordanian Special Forces guy who carried a pistol and an M4 on all our missions. He was locked on as an interpreter and could hold his own in a firefight. He was a U.S. citizen, contracted by the State Department. Early in the war, the United States had tried using terps who had acquired Arabic in schools, and saw poor results. Sure, they spoke the same language as the Iraqis, but it didn't mean they understood it. If you stick someone from Alaska and someone from Georgia in the same room they'll communicate, but if the guy from Georgia uses a colloquialism like "that dog won't hunt," chances are the person from Alaska is going to miss something. U.S. officials quickly recognized they needed native-born terps to catch all the nuances that only a native speaker could pick up on. They made the switch and saw much better results. Moose was from Jordan, so he knew the little idiosyncrasies of the region. He had all the knowledge of Iraqi culture that a U.S.-born terp who learned Arabic as an adult lacked. He knew the area. He knew war. He hunted terrorists. Guys like Moose were invaluable and greatly increased the combat effectiveness of American units.

Moose was always giving us the skinny on the Iraqi troops, and he was great at corralling and directing the Jundis and making them move on target. They were like lemmings, and Moose was their pied piper. Without Moose, the Jundis would have probably just walked into each other or sat down and smoked cigarettes.

One of my favorite Jundis was a big Baby Huey–looking dude named Hassan. He wasn't fat, just solid, with a head like a bison. He was a meathead, but he was a meathead who was eager to learn. Hassan may not have been a genius, but he was faithful and squared away. He cared about soldiering, and that's about the most I could hope for from my Jundis. Hassan was always eager to get in on the action, always first to volunteer. He wanted to be there, and I respected him for that. He wasn't anywhere near our level of proficiency, but he seemed to have genuine motivation, and that was a big step up from a lot of his peers.

"Moving," Squirrel muttered via intra-squad comms.

We started patrolling on foot with Squirrel as point man to the target building, and the faint sound of our footsteps barely pierced the sleeping stillness of the neighborhood. To our left was an open field, and to our right the street was crowded with compounds. We didn't have much cover. Luckily, electricity was scarce in Ramadi at night, and we moved stealthily down the road. I paid attention to my surroundings, scanning everywhere and looking for threats. The target building was in a block of two-story houses, the third one in. When we reached it, my assault team set security on the gate to the compound and called up the team of Jundis whose job it was to place a ladder on the compound's wall, get up and over quickly, and unlock the gate.

I had not anticipated that even such a seemingly menial task could be asking so much of my Jundis. We had operated like a true bunch of quiet professionals until the Jundis started getting over that wall. The ladder creaked loudly under the weight of their boots on the rungs; their AK-47s slapped on the compound wall. It was the complete opposite of tactical. It was more like a Benny Hill video or the Keystone Cops. We were the best America can offer, and suddenly we were at risk of getting smoked outside our objective because these fifty-dollar soldiers couldn't get over a wall with a ladder. I rolled my eyes and made a mental note that the list of things to work on with my Jundis had just gotten longer. When they finally got over, I could hear them talking in Arabic on the other side, and after what seemed like two forevers, I heard the latch finally open.

The Jundis opened the door and stepped out of the way as our assault team quickly moved in. There was only about ten feet between the outer wall of the compound and the garage, which we skirted and followed to the front door, where we stacked up. I got the signal and passed it forward. Then we went. Violence of action. Smooth and fast. I cleared into the first room, seeing a series of vague details: a dirty marble floor, a kitchen area, some lights on.

Clear. Next room.

We went.

There was a woman with two or three kids screaming in terror at the Terminator-looking dudes with guns. I yelled at the woman to get down at the same time I wrapped her and the children up and pushed them into a corner so the rest of the train could get through. With three or four SEALs and ten Jundis behind me, I was in the zone, clearing corners and underneath beds.

The next room went quick. I noticed a blur of prayer rolls and mattresses as I cleared my sector, encountering no bad guys. We called clear and stacked for the next room. The signal is given—then go. Onto the next. There was an unarmed man; I threw him down hard and flex-cuffed him. Another unarmed man. We took him down and flex-cuffed him. We were through the entire house. CLEAR! The entire target was secure, and not a single shot was fired. No bomb-maker muj testing my resolve; just two suspected terrorists to take back to base for further questioning. Despite the op's anticlimax, I felt amped and pretty good about my performance. I had just secured my last room and was headed back out to meet the guys when Moose meandered over and met me in the doorway. He handed me something discreetly.

"You dropped this, Jobber," he said quietly, in his accented version of "Dauber." He pressed something hard and metallic into my hand.

I looked at the magazine he handed me and saw the distinct marking of KRL—my initials in my handwriting. I looked at my rifle and the empty magazine well. Before I could look up to say something to Moose, he was gone.

I was incredulous. I had cleared the entire house with nothing but a single round in the chamber of my M4. I had somehow hit the magazine-release button when I entered the house. I was embarrassed, but also grateful I hadn't needed the mag and that it was Moose who found it. If any Teamguys had made that discovery, I'd be known as No Mag forever, and I would have had my dick thoroughly kicked in. I had been all jacked up on cocky-newguy swagger, thinking I'd had the perfect op, and now I couldn't shake the thought of how terribly wrong everything could have gone. As the Jundis started ripping through the place, looking for bomb-making materials, I began mercilessly hazing myself in my mind.

You fucking turd, Dauber. You could have gotten us all killed.

I saw a bunch of propane tanks in the yard and called EOD Nick to check it out. It was nothing. As we started to pack up to leave, Dale approached me.

"Dauber, how do you feel?" he said.

"I feel fucking jacked."

"Don't ever forget that feeling," he said.

Dale seemed to have a knack for creating unforgettable memories in my mind. I thought back to his paddle full of sand in BUD/S. That sadistic blow was nothing compared to what I would have suffered if Dale or anyone else knew about the magazine. I would never again drop my magazine on an op.

We threw the two prisoners up on Big Zev, which was already cramped for room. The Jundis sat on them all the way back to the detention facility. They liked to mess with prisoners. Before we broke out to head home, we got accountability of all our gear and personnel. As we were prepping to leave, Tony said, "Not bad, Dauba', but not fuckin' great."

It was all the criticism I needed to hear. It made me want to work even harder and tighten up my shot group. *You have no idea how not fucking great that was,* I thought. I packed a dip and climbed onto Big Zev for the ride home. I wedged myself in with my Teammates, the men whose combat brotherhood I'd just joined. The baptism might have been ugly, but it had happened. "Not bad, but not fucking great," I repeated to myself and spat Copenhagen juice. No doubt. The next time I'd be better.

FIVE

A PUNISHER'S
FIRST KILL

"May God have mercy on my enemies, because I won't."

—George S. Patton

YOU WOULDN'T BELIEVE the things people ask when they find out you're a SEAL.

"Do they really drown you on purpose and bring you back to life in BUD/S?"

"I heard they issue you each a German shepherd puppy, make you raise it through BUD/S and SQT, and then require you to slit its throat before graduation."

"How many animals did they make you kill with your bare hands to become accustomed to the feeling of taking life?"

The point is not whether any of these questions and statements are fantastically false or contain kernels of truth, or whether the person asking presumes too much by carrying on with such an invasive interrogation. In the Teams, we have a half-sarcastic term for letting these beliefs persist, even the false ones: perpetuate the myth.

It took me a while to understand, but now I see these people don't want to know the truth about me, anyways. They need the myth because they need to believe I was turned into this thing that I am. It's easier to believe this was created through harsh training and torment than to accept that a few of us just are.

The questions are not about me. They're about them.

SHARKBASE, LATE APRIL 2006

I don't know where I get my mean from. I don't know if *mean* is even the right word, but I know I have something in me that's always been there when I needed it, from the rugby pitch to the Ma'Laab. The first time I broke another guy's nose in a match, I said I was sorry, but I didn't mean it. He was in my way, and I was doing my job for my Teammates. I can be violent when I need to. It's just the way I'm wired. I never gave it much thought before joining the Teams, the fact that not all men carry in them this potential for ferocity. I never had a word for it before, or a label. And then I became a Punisher.

It started out small, a Teamguy's simple graphic tagged on the sides of his helmet during our deployment work-up in 2005. I can't even remember who it was. The image of a human skull is traditionally associated with death or mortality, but the Punisher skull reimagines the meaning. The angular, scowling eye sockets and monsterlike teeth express the malice burning in the heart of Frank Castle, the macabre hero of Marvel Comics' *The Punisher*. In the comics, Castle is a SEAL-trained former Marine captain who served in Vietnam. His violent-vigilante persona takes root after his wife and child are killed by the mafia and the police are too corrupt to bring the killers to justice. Something about the Punisher skull immediately resonated with us. It reflected what most SEALs wanted to be downrange: death-dealing arbiters of justice, punishers of an evil enemy. We didn't really talk about this interpretation in Charlie Platoon. It was just one of those things that caught on and spread without effort—a potent meme finding its perfect audience. It was just cool. And we all wanted to look cool.

During work-up, the image quickly spread from one helmet in our platoon to all of them. Eventually, someone made a bigger stencil, and we all tagged the image on our body armor, wearing the Punisher icon on our chests and backs. Guys started tagging the skull on notebooks, assault packs, all over. In Iraq, we added the Punisher tag to our Humvees, blast shields, and just about anywhere we could fit it. It was the perfect icon for a bunch of Big Tough Frogmen, and our platoon was full of those. The phrase "Big Tough Frogmen" became an acronym, which became a noun, a verb, an adjective. We'd say things like "We're just gonna get outside the wire and BTF around" or "Just BTF that gear over here" or "Time to BTF and show these muj what's up." A couple of the guys hated its overuse, which of course led to more overuse. The average SEAL in Charlie, also known as Cadillac Platoon, was at least six feet tall and two hundred pounds—a bunch of steely-eyed killers.

After two weeks on the ground in Ramadi, I was ready to start earning our Punisher moniker. The monotony of unpacking gear, getting situated, and training Jundis was getting old. There is only so long you can keep a hound caged before you have to let him run.

We were tasked to move from Sharkbase to Camp Corregidor, a big Army base in the southeast corner of Ramadi—the area known as the Ma'Laab district. The Army was prepping for a major offensive there, and they requested our support. We were more than happy to oblige by getting in the fight.

The roughly seven-mile drive to Corregidor under the cover of darkness tempered my youthful aggression. Route Michigan, the main artery of transportation along the western front, was an easy target for terrorists and a magnet for IEDs. Michigan meandered lazily through some of the bigger towns and cities in the west. Ramadi was not spared. The terrorists swarmed on Michigan like ants on a syrup strip.

I climbed into Vehicle 1's turret, where I'd have a clear view of the scenery. I preferred the turret to sitting in the truck because of the fresher air and my two hands on a .50-cal to light up any threat that presented itself. I've always been a little claustrophobic, though I never admitted it to the guys back then. I hated being boxed into a Humvee on a blacked-out (no headlights) convoy, especially when the IED threat was high. I preferred to be on the offensive, head on a swivel, above the moondust that obstructs your view and sticks to your gums like the stink of the city.

The night was inky black and silent. I strained through the grainy green image of my night-vision goggles as the vehicles came to life, one by one. The low rumble of engines filled the air around me, and I hit the pressure pad on the .50's infrared laser. The night began to light up with beams of green from our guns.

Downtown Ramadi had several recognizable landmarks. We rolled heavily past the seven-story where Chris Kyle would later kill seven muj in a day. It was one of the taller buildings in Ramadi, and even then seemed to stand out, as if beckoning us to come and play. The southeast corner of the roof sagged from where it had been hit with an American JDAM (Joint Direct Air Munition), looking severely strained under the burden of war. I inspected its blackened windows, looking for insurgents. In the back of my mind, I was also looking for a good place to snipe from. Seven-story provided vantage points, security, and a nice egress route to Observation Post Virginia, a Marine outpost just south of the building. *Another time,* I thought, and continued scanning my surroundings.

I strained my neck to get a better view at the tangled mess of IED craters and suspect wires at the intersection ahead. "Holy shit," I muttered under my breath. We approached the intersection of Route Michigan and Sunset with caution, as it was a major impact zone.

"Shift left," came the order over the radio from Squirrel, our convoy navigator, and my vehicle began tracking around the mess. The others followed our lead as we continued down Michigan.

I thought again how much I liked Vehicle 1's turret. I had more than 180 degrees of free-fire zone and could really lay down some lead. Besides rear security, the other positions didn't offer the same expansive field of fire. Another benefit of riding lead is that an insurgent usually couldn't hit the first vehicle with a command-detonated IED. A pressure plate was a different story, but you take the good with the bad. Once again, I thought of my nuts.

I would have welcomed a chance to relax my senses and breathe easy, but as the convoy slowed in the soul of the city, it wasn't the time. The Government Center was home to Ramadi's municipal buildings and where the Marines operated from. It was taking some of the heaviest pounding by insurgents holed up and operating out of the surrounding city blocks. They hid with ease in the apartments and homes piled on top of each other and wedged onto the dirty streets like a Tetris game.

Government Center gave me my first real idea of what I was up against. Around it, the scars of battle were evident. Rubble littered the streets, the result of IEDs, small arms fire, RPGs, and the general havoc of war. IR netting attempted to hide the observation points along the roof. I scanned the rooftops of surrounding buildings, searching for our enemy. The scene around us proved they apparently knew where to aim, and it made me uneasy to be in that position. There's a hum that runs through an element when everybody feels the same sense of unease. Call it warrior instinct. You don't have to say it; everybody's automatically locked on and knows things can go bad real quick. From the amount of wreckage piled up around us, even the smell of carnage, I could tell the Marines had dealt some serious death from that roof. It wasn't a position I was eager to hang around.

The rest of the convoy didn't get much better in terms of the warm-and-fuzzies. Muj controlled the battle space between Government Center and Corregidor, and driving through that area in the darkness kicked my hypervigilance into overdrive. That uneasy hum stayed with us as we rolled smack through the middle of enemy territory. I gave tight, nearly imperceptible nods to the Abrams tanks and Bradley Fighting Vehicles providing security on the corners. *Damn right*, I thought. *We're gonna weed these assholes out if we have to do it block by block.* Little did I know, that's exactly what we'd be doing in the coming months.

Up ahead in the distance, I could make out the shapes, glowing green on my NVGs, of the Marines patrolling for IEDs. I felt bad for the grunts out there, trekking through the dirty city streets, sweeping for bombs at night. On one side of the street was a river of human waste. Shit creeks were Ramadi's version of a modern sewage system. Ramadi always smelled bad, but with the lack of airflow and the steam-room humidity, the smell was overwhelming.

Since arriving in country, we'd heard the IED detonations on Michigan every night. When you hear that sound in the distance, you know there's a good chance some Marines or Army cats just died. I'd usually bow my head for a moment in a sort of silent prayer. With the sound of far-off detonations in my mind, I thought about the grunts' courage and was thankful for it. Patrolling for IEDs wasn't a job I would have wanted. I preferred the hunt. Patrolling for bombs was waiting to step in the snare. I am not prey.

We left the Marines behind, but the smell of the shit creeks came with us. They reflected ink black in the green hue of my NODs. It was like the city had been gut-shot and was spilling its bowels out onto its streets. From what I knew of gut wounds from my combat medic course, it's possible to die a slow and miserable death of sepsis after a wound to the abdomen, a death that creeps up slowly from your own feces infecting the rest of your body. It might take days to die, as you suffer the whole time from fever, pain, thirst, and coma. I looked around at the city streets of Ramadi, all shot up and infecting themselves with their own shit, and wondered how thirsty they'd get before they'd eventually die.

Finally, we arrived at Corregidor, which was blacked out like every other installation according to an overall rule, because of the mortar threat. The gate opened as I wiped the sweat and moondust from my brow, feeling relieved the drive was uneventful. Shooting bad guys was at the front of everyone's mind. We could feel the storm coming, but we wanted it to be on our terms, on ops that we planned, moving silent and deadly and so fast that we were literally on top of the enemy before they knew what hit them. Nobody really wants a firefight in a convoy.

What we'd heard from SEAL Team TWO was that they'd only just gotten started in Ramadi by the time they had to turn over to us. They'd been handed a new model to work with—the now well-known counterinsurgency tactic of tribal engagement. They were supposed to build bonds with village elders in hopes the elders would cooperate with coalition forces. But it was going to take more than just a month or two to inspire enough confidence in the local sheiks to convince them to start identifying the terrorists hiding in their communities. To us, a Syrian posing as an Iraqi looked like an Iraqi. An Iraqi religious leader, however, knew immediately when eight or ten guys who had never been in his neighborhood before took up residence in an abandoned house. What we really needed was for the leaders of the Iraqi communities to recognize that the insurgency was just as bad for Iraq as it was for the coalition forces and to help us out. When Task Unit Bruiser got on the ground in Anbar Province, there was still more civil war than Sunni Awakening going on and the troop surge of 2007 hadn't quite begun. In other words, the Punishers were primed to do some killing. I was closer to my original goal.

SEALs don't normally own battle space, so wherever we went our head shed had to coordinate with whoever was in charge before we could actually operate. Corregidor was an Army installation, so in this case that meant planning with the Army brass how to best employ us. Good commanders immediately saw the value of utilizing our expertise to mitigate the threats their soldiers routinely engaged. However, it can be a delicate interaction, not unlike a negotiation. It's the Army's space and they've been gutting it out against the insurgency for years. They don't want to hand over their autonomy. SEALs come in eager to do a job they know they're good at. They don't want to take orders from conventional ground forces. The head shed has to make sure early on that the working relationship is a good one.

For anyone not involved in that tap dance, that translated to more hurry up and wait. We were told to stay out of trouble until we received marching orders, so we mostly spent our time on the range, cleaning our weapons, practicing our patrols, training the Jundis, and rehearsing our missions.

The best-case scenario was that the Army would pretty much let us do whatever we wanted. In an effort to appease those who chose to be all they could be, our task unit commander sent down a directive that we would all maintain Army standards of grooming. For a SEAL, this is kind of a kick in the pants. We're proud of our reputation for being cocky and arrogant, and we normally flaunt our relaxed military grooming standards. It's not uncommon to see a Teamguy in Coronado with sideburns nearing Elvis proportions or hair a couple of inches too long. It's just his way of saying he's not regular Navy, and the rules don't apply to him. Deployment is often an opportunity to forget regular haircuts and shaves. This time, it appeared, that would not be possible. Short hair and regular shaves would be mandatory. I groaned inwardly.

"Cheer up, Dauber," said Marc Lee. "Nobody'll notice if you don't shave that baby face. Can you even grow facial hair?" Marc's thick black beard normally showed a five o'clock shadow sometime around noon.

"What does this have to do with work?" I asked. "And when are we going to start doing some?"

Guy walked up. "We keep them happy, thinking we're falling in line, they keep us operating. Just shave your fucking beard and cut your hair." He smiled before walking off. "Know what's within regs, boys?" We shrugged. "A nice eighties, caterpillar war-stache."

We shaved our beards and cut our hair, but several of us started growing our mustaches. They were hot and gross and Copenhagen stuck to them. They filled up with moondust like everything else, but there wasn't a damn thing anybody could say to us about them. A year and some change later, I returned from a training trip in Niland, California, after a couple of weeks in the field with a mustache, and my girlfriend, now my wife, dubbed it "the molestache." Some guys could grow Tom Selleck works of art. I grew a patchy molestache.

There was plenty to be learned from the Army if you knew where to look. A typical Army deployment was twelve months, so a seasoned soldier could be a wealth of information. Tony and the other senior Teamguys were excellent mentors when it came to Team tactics and operations in Iraq in general, but Ramadi was new to all of us. I was looking for somebody to give me the skinny on Ramadi's ins and outs, and I found my source when I met an Army sniper named Adam. Adam was a sergeant in the 502nd. He was in his early thirties, short and balding with a medium build. He was a good soldier and a smart guy, and I liked him because he was eager to share information and advice. Eight months in Ramadi had put Adam's finger on the pulse of the battle tempo. He knew Ramadi. He knew the Ma'Laab. And he knew the enemy.

"There's a guard tower that's constantly getting rocketed and hit with small arms fire," Adam said with his generic southern accent. "It provides a good vantage point overlooking the canal and a good angle down most of the alleys on the eastern side of the city. Prime real estate for sniping."

The next afternoon, I awoke and sat up slowly on the edge of my rack. As I rubbed my eyes and ruffled my matted-down hair, I wondered what was in store for the day. *I'm gonna lose it if I have to train more Jundis today,* I thought. Adam's words from the morning before still echoed in my mind: prime real estate for sniping. In high school, I studied Latin and the phrase *Audentes Fortuna iuvat* (Fortune favors the bold) drifted into my thoughts. *Virgil,* I remembered, before sleepily winding down a tangent of other Latin phrases I had retained: *si vis pacem, para bellum* (if you wish for peace, prepare for war), *aut viam inveniam aut faciam* (I will either find a way or I will make one), *semper ubi sub ubi* (always where under where). I quit the underwear thing a long time ago. Frogmen don't wear briefs.

I ate hurriedly and came back to my room to put my tricolors on. Around 1400, I made my way to the ops tent and looked up at the whiteboard. Nothing planned for the day. With Virgil's encouragement in mind, I peeled the Dauber magnet off the board and placed it with confidence at the guard tower position. I stopped momentarily and contemplated my move.

I was ready to go hunting.

Over breakfast, I had briefed my chief, lead petty officer, and officer in charge on my plan. "Get some, Dauber," they said. And I planned to do just that.

I barely noticed the weight of my Mk 11 as I began the walk to the guard tower. My Oakley assault boots kicked up little clouds of moon-dust as I trudged through the tracks left by various vehicles. As I moved through cover, I kept a regular pace. At the last piece of cover I started moving tactically. Muj didn't have a direct bead on the facility, but I took no chances as I zigzagged, low to the ground and as quickly as I could.

The tower itself was a stone structure. The pockmarks left by small arms fire alerted me not to linger outside, so I pushed the door open and trekked straight up the spiral staircase. Upstairs on the top floor, I found a couple of soldiers on watch.

"What's up, guys?" I said casually. "Mind if I hang out here for a while? I heard this is a good place to smoke some muj." I set my rifle on the table and pulled out my laser range finder. Looking out on the Ma'Laab, I began checking my reference points across the canal. End of the alley—500 yards, red car—300, etc.

"Sure, man," said one of the soldiers. He introduced himself and told me his buddy's name.

"I'm Dauber," I said. I settled my nerves as I rested my gun on the platform and began to glass the alleyways. I felt eyes on me and looked up at the soldiers. One of them was looking at my sniper rifle.

"So you're a SEAL, huh?" he asked.

"Yup," I answered, my eye back on my scope. On the other end, a dirty alleyway was crowded with garbage, clotheslines, and the occasional car.

"And a sniper?" he continued. I cleared my throat.

"Yup," I said again. These kids were pretty green. They didn't know I was probably just as new. I noticed how much bulkier they looked than I did in my low-profile body armor under my Rhodesian vest.

"Damn, dude," said the other one. "Is that a Nightforce? That's a sweet scope. And a Mk 11? You guys get all the good shit."

I turned my head to him for a moment and smirked good-naturedly. "Yeah, man, it's pretty nice," I said. I didn't tell him that my weapon was actually a bit of a sore spot for me. I had attended Army Sniper School instead of Naval Special Warfare (NSW) Sniper School. It just happened to be where a spot was available when they needed to send me. Because of that, however, the Teams didn't see me fit for a full sniper suite and only outfitted me with an Mk 11. It's a great gun, but it was a constant reminder that I had something to prove when we were heading out on an overwatch op and I saw the other snipers choose their weapons while I picked up the only one available to me. I had to earn my .30-cal sniper rifle with blood. Honestly, it made me appreciate it that much more when I returned to Iraq in 2008 for my second deployment with the full sniper suite.

I probably should have been thankful just to have a rifle to myself. We spent a lot of time in an area just north of Ramadi, working with a group of Army National Guard soldiers in farm country. The Army cats were from Kentucky, and their Appalachian accents were so thick, you practically needed a translator to understand anything they said. They were a bunch of good old boys who were eager to take the fight to the enemy. We ran sniper ops with them, overwatching a medical clinic that had fallen into muj hands. Coalition forces had been taking a lot of fire from the clinic, and our orders were to kill anyone who presented as a combatant.

Every SEAL sniper had a sniper rifle, but the Kentucky cats had one gun, which they would rotate every time somebody got a kill. When their gun rotated into the hands of their first sergeant, he was hesitant to shoot anyone and ended up keeping the gun for an excruciatingly long period. This greatly frustrated the young guns, who were eager to engage the enemy. I felt their pain.

"So what's going on this morning?" I asked. "Any action out there?"

"Nothing so far," said the first soldier. He gave me a SITREP of the area, which turned into idle banter that I tuned out. I knew a target wouldn't present itself willingly. I would have to be vigilant. The minutes began to slip by quickly. My heart beat steady through my blouse. I packed a dip of Copenhagen to settle the nerves.

About an hour into the watch, the alleyways started buzzing with activity. The afternoon call to prayer seemed to set the locals free. I saw women with kids, goatherds corralling one or two of their animals here or there, and the occasional vehicle moving down the canal road. I gathered intel as I waited.

I stood and watched, my rifle about chest level set up on a high table in front of me. With my boots firmly planted a couple of feet apart and my waist slightly bent, I kept my eye on my scope and waited.

Two hours into the hunt, my target appeared as the sun began to move behind the buildings. As I peered out from the crack in the bulletproof glass, he moved from the back of the alley and paused in a doorway, staring in our direction. I felt the hair stand up on the back of my neck. He was wearing a blue shirt, black Adidas pants, and leather sandals. His clothes were covered in a thin coat of dust. I watched him back behind a wall momentarily as I checked my lased reference points, fixed objects that I knew the distance of. I had my dope dialed in at three hundred yards, which left plenty of room to hold on a target that was near or far from that position. My target disappeared behind a wall three hundred yards out.

Suddenly, he scurried across the alleyway from my left to right. He had nothing in his hands. My 22x scope left no room for error. Although his behavior had insurgent written all over it, the rules of engagement (ROE) were clear: without the clear presentation of a weapon, IED, or other threat to coalition forces, I couldn't shoot him. Looking shady wasn't enough. He hugged tight in a doorway, gazing in our direction, and I watched his face as the sun caught the sweat. It shined bright and dripped toward his angry beard. Again, he sucked into a doorway and out of my sight. I readjusted my cheek weld and spat a fresh shot of Copenhagen onto the table. The Army guys began to notice me tracking the guy. Their chatter trailed off into silence in the tower. My own breath and the hammer of my heart rushing blood to my brain were the only sounds to breach the stillness.

He peeked out from the doorway, and I adjusted the clarity of the focus on my scope, fighting the light distortion from the afternoon heat. Then I saw it; cradled in his arms was an AK-47. Unmistakable. This guy was now muj; a legitimate target.

I fought the elevated pulse in my temple. My breathing grew

heavier as I flicked off the safety on my rifle. Unconsciously, I worked through my points of performance and prepared. Suddenly, the insurgent bolted across the alley from right to left. I placed the second Mil-Dot on him at shoulder level, tracking him as he jogged, and smoothly squeezed the slack out of the trigger as I exhaled to my respiratory pause. The 7.62 round sprang from the rifle, and I barely noticed the recoil on my shoulder as I watched the reticle track the target. He fell face-first in a heap, his AK hitting the dirt and his feet kicking up behind him. The shot had torn through his upper torso and both his lungs. The gun cycled another round. The reticle continued to track the line, but no target followed.

My first kill.

"Fuck yeah!" the Army cats cheered.

I cracked a smile, staying on the gun and scanning for more targets. No time for celebration. I stayed fixed on the expired insurgent, waiting for further movement. There was none. He lay dead in the street as we braced in the tower for the retribution that never came.

The soldiers' cackles and quiet cheers faded away as I focused on my breathing. The biggest point of failure usually comes after an epic high. I wasn't about to drop a mag again. I was growing as an operator, but you can never get too big for the basics. They keep you in the fight for another day. I welcomed the warm air into my lungs as my breathing remained at a constant twelve breaths a minute. I suffered a temporary lapse of focus as I remembered the words of a Marine captain interviewed on CNN after the initial invasion of Iraq. The innocent reporter asked him what he felt after he shot a terrorist. The captain's answer was simple: "Recoil." A thin smile tugged at my lips. My Mk 11 was suppressed. I'd barely even felt that much.

Later, the insurgent's friends would come collect him, waving white handkerchiefs and napkins. They'd scurry out of a doorway and pull his limp body out of the street, leaving nothing but a bloodstain and his AK-47.

That night I lay in my rack and thought about how easy it had been. The only thing I spent much time contemplating was that I wasn't surprised by my lack of reaction. It was like taking a peek in a mirror to just make sure you still look the way you think you do. In this case, I did. I hadn't expected to mind taking a life, and I didn't. I was neither happy about it, nor sad, nor confused, nor angry. I was satisfied.

My entire life, I'd been taught that evil exists in the world. When training to become a SEAL, my instructors had reassured me that wearing a trident would provide me an opportunity to meet it. That afternoon, I'd looked at an evil man through my scope and known exactly what to do. I felt sure.

In the past, I used to chuckle when I heard a rumor that someone quit BUD/S because they "couldn't handle the pressure of possibly taking a life." I didn't understand. If you volunteer yourself to do the business of doing bad things to bad people, you have to be prepared for the eventuality of being required to do it. Teamguys get paid to take the fight to the enemy. How I had handled my first enemy KIA was a reassurance that I had made the right decision to join the Teams.

I settled into a contented asleep, proud of a job well done. Many guys go through entire careers and never kill anybody. I'd been on the ground for two weeks as a newguy and had a clean kill.

I wanted another.

SIX

FIREFIGHT IN
THE MA'LAAB

"War is hell, but that's not the half of it, because war is
also mystery and terror and adventure and courage and
discovery and holiness and pity and despair and longing
and love. War is nasty; war is fun. War is thrilling; war is
drudgery. War makes you a man; war makes you dead."

—Tim O'Brien, "How to Tell a True War Story"

S AN CLEMENTE ISLAND is home to the last three weeks of
BUD/S training. In these final weeks of Third Phase, students
conduct numerous exercises combining the skills they've honed in the
previous months, from patrolling to shooting to small unit tactics.

Our instructors put us through a timed stress course, the object of
which was to move quickly from cover to cover and shoot steel targets.
I held my M4 as if it were an extension of myself and moved smoothly
through the first few targets, gaining confidence from the metallic
ping! each time I hit one. When I came to a window, I took a knee and
prepared to shoot at the next target.

For some reason, I got frazzled. I'm a competitive guy, and once I let myself think about my time and tried to beat the other guys, I was screwed. I overthought it and I couldn't hit that steel to save my life. It took me completely resetting, changing the mag, taking a breath, and clearing my head to be able to hit that target and move on.

I never once choked like that in combat, and I think it's because I wasn't trying to beat the guys next to me; I was fighting for them. In Ramadi, our reasons for fighting had nothing to do with politics and everything to do with the responsibility you feel when another man trusts you with his life. And that made us the most dangerous men in the world.

CAMP CORREGIDOR, LATE APRIL 2006

On April 17, Al Qaeda forces led by Abu Musab al-Zarqawi launched a series of attacks against American outposts all over the city, marking the official start of the second Battle of Ramadi. A suicide bomber drove a yellow dump truck up to the gate of Observation Post Virginia and detonated his thousand-pound payload. OP Virginia was on the south side of Route Michigan about a quarter mile from the eastern shore of the Euphrates. The massive explosion was the primer for a force of insurgents who attacked the outpost with small arms and rocket-propelled grenades. Marines from Lima Company, 3rd Battalion, 8th Marine Regiment, fought them off, killing dozens, with only a few Marines wounded. A week later, we found a muj propaganda video of the attack during a DA and watched it when we got back to Sharkbase. It included footage of Zarqawi himself planning the operation. Zarqawi was the brutal leader of Al Qaeda in Iraq and is said to be the executioner in the infamous AQI propaganda video showing the decapitation of American contractor Nick Berg in 2004. Zarqawi was the embodiment of the evil we were fighting in Iraq, and all of us would have given just about anything to put an end to him.

OP Virginia was just the beginning. The muj launched attacks on the Government Center, Snake Pit, and Camp Ramadi. It was a major enemy offensive, and the American brass was ready to strike back. The 1st Battalion of the 502nd Infantry Regiment was tasked to push through the Ma'Laab and clear the entire district of insurgent forces. It was a large-scale op for which the brass had estimated a casualty rate around 50 to 70 percent for coalition forces. Our mission was to act as force multipliers. We would occupy strategic positions and provide eyes on the battle space as forward observers and snipers. We had joint terminal attack controllers (JTACs) to coordinate direct air support and plenty of snipers to provide overwatch security. The overall objective was simple: root out and destroy the enemy. What this boiled down to for me as an E-5 shooter: target-rich environment.

In late April, we piled into some Army Cougars in the early morning hours and headed into the gauntlet. Our force was about four SEALs, six Jundis, and Adam, the Army sniper. I felt more cumbersome than usual because we'd prepared to be out in Indian country for an extended period. In addition to my regular load, I was carrying an Mk 46 Squad Automatic Weapon (a light, belt-fed machine gun) with one thousand rounds of ammunition, ten liters of water, and several MREs. I knew we were going into a dangerous area, so I was pretty buttoned up armor-wise. I once saw Tony leave for a two-day overwatch with nothing but two cans of Copenhagen and a liter of water. I admire Tony's BTF credentials, but I'm a big guy. I have to eat.

We headed toward a soccer stadium a couple of miles west of Corregidor. It was a major landmark in the Ma'Laab and smack in the middle of muj land. The Army bomb techs we rolled with made several fake pauses along the way to our objective. This was an attempt to confuse any insurgents who might be watching and keep them off our trail. When we reached our real insertion point, we exited the vehicles and quickly found cover, inhabiting the shadows in the dimly lit streets. Everyone took a knee and waited for a signal.

Bryce from Delta Platoon was the patrol leader and our sniper for the mission. He was five foot seven with sandy blond hair and a hint of a midwestern accent. His unimposing stature belied his proficiency as an operator. Ramadi was his third deployment. He'd fought in the Battle of Fallujah with Chris Kyle, and nothing ever seemed to faze him. Bryce was the epitome of a quiet professional.

Bryce gave the signal for a tactical pause. As the dull roar of the vehicles' engines faded into the distance, we all stayed as still and quiet as possible, scanning our surroundings. Heads on swivels, we waited. The area looked to me about like every other street in Ramadi. The effects of prolonged combat had scarred the urban landscape in every direction. There was broken glass and refuse all around us. Packed down like a camel, kneeling in silence for almost ten minutes, I thanked God for my knee pads. Finally, Bryce gave the signal to move.

We patrolled to a house whose rooftop could serve as a good overwatch position for the battle space and employed our soft-knock tactic to enter and clear the building. A soft knock is literally where we knock on the door of a residence and ask the inhabitants to let us in. We liked to ask to make the family feel like they had a little autonomy, but in reality they didn't really have the option to refuse. In this case, when the man of the house opened the door, our terp explained the situation, and the man welcomed us inside. The man had a wife and two kids. We entered and turned off all the lights, clearing the building on night vision. We left some Jundis to pull security inside and then headed to the roof to set up our sniper position.

Bryce made the call to use the sledgehammer we'd brought to punch a sniping hole in the three-foot wall around the roof's perimeter. The idea was that the hammer would be quieter and draw less attention to our position than the small explosive charges we often used. It didn't quite work out that way. When Bryce started knocking the hole, every strike sounded like someone hitting a gong. The reverberation echoed through the neighborhood in the early morning hours.

Instead of a single loud blast, we provided a brief rhythm of gong strikes that broadcast our position to any nearby muj who might have been looking for some Americans to kill.

The reality is, the muj always knew where we were anyway. We could be quiet and evasive, but we couldn't be invisible. The city had eyes in places we couldn't imagine. We could have tunneled into that house, and the muj would have known about it. Regardless, I didn't like the sledgehammer making the extra noise. It was like advertising to any off-duty muj that if they didn't have plans for the day, the game was on. Still, Bryce had his reasons for using the sledgehammer and it wasn't my job to question his judgment.

Once the hole was made, the position provided a clear line of sight for about three hundred yards and into an alleyway on the north side of the target area where the grunts would be operating. Time to watch and wait. I put in a chaw and scanned my sector with the SAW.

"You good, Dauber?" asked Evan. He was a cowboy from Wyoming and Delta Platoon's JTAC. He knelt to my left. An Irishman with a great sense of humor on his second deployment to Iraq, Evan exhibited the same Zen-like calm under fire that I saw in a lot of seasoned SEALs. He had a habit of calling in air strikes that delivered an awesome payload of American ordnance, and afterward, he'd nonchalantly declare, "Good hit." He was a lot of fun to be around.

"You look like somebody farted in your canteen," he said.

"I'm good, man," I answered in a low voice. "Just BTFing all this extra shit around." He chuckled and continued scanning his sector. Before the op, Adam had made sure to point out the enemy's habit of lobbing grenades onto the rooftops where Americans operated. I tried to account for this threat by keeping my head on a swivel, scanning my periphery, and looking down the road.

As usual, the city came alive after the morning call to prayer. Dogs meandered through the streets scavenging for food. People came out of their houses, moving up and down the street, and we noticed that a lot of them were looking in our direction. "Fucking sledgehammer," I growled to myself.

A black four-door sedan pulled to a stop about two hundred yards out. Three men slowly exited on the side of the vehicle opposite my position. They stood there for a minute and stared up in our direction. My instincts were going crazy. I watched them through the SAW's ACOG scope, and they looked suspicious as hell. I had the gun trained on them, ready to open fire if any one of them showed hostile intent. They stood there for fifteen minutes, and for fifteen minutes every muscle in my body—every fiber of my being—was on high alert. It felt like hours.

"What do you think, Bryce?" I said.

"Just hang tight, Dauber."

By 8 a.m. the sun was high in the sky. We'd been on the rooftop for several hours, wading through periods of intermittent high tension and relative low alert. I was reaching into my pocket for my can of Copenhagen when I heard the snap of small arms fire whizzing over our heads, followed by the call of "Contact!" over the radio. I ducked down lower against the wall and looked to my left at Evan, who gave me an exaggerated wide-eyed look and an impish grin. Over the sound of the gunfire all around us, we heard what sounded like World War III coming from the other side of the soccer stadium. Another group of SEALs was on a rooftop there, and we assumed it was a coordinated attack.

I was thinking about those grenades when the leadership made the call to get downstairs. I gathered up the gear that I'd shed during the night and low-crawled to the doorway, mindful of my SAW and my ruck as I scraped across the rough roof. On the second floor, Bryce did a head count and we cautiously took up window positions, scanning for targets. Everybody was on the same adrenaline high and ready to send a wall of lead at the enemy.

"Anybody see anything?" Bryce asked.

"Nah, I can't see shit," I said.

"Nothing here," Evan said.

The only thing more frustrating than being in a firefight with nothing to shoot at is being in your first firefight with nothing to shoot at. We had just taken fire from an enemy we couldn't see, and now we were unable to do anything about it. It was painful.

"Hostiles moving behind the wall of the soccer stadium," Bryce said. "Out of range," he added with disgust.

"Roger that," Evan said. "I've got eyes on them. You want me to call in a Hellfire missile?"

"Fuck yes," Bryce said.

Evan called in the Hellfire, but we were still stuck. Our position was compromised, and we had no choice but to call for extract. A quick reaction force (QRF) of Humvees and Bradley Fighting Vehicles arrived within thirty minutes, and we prepared to bound the few hundred meters to the vehicles Frogman-style, basically leapfrogging from covered position to covered position, the men in the rear providing constant cover. It was hot as hell, and the fact that I'd loaded down with so much extra gear just to turn around and go back to base was pissing me off even more. *Please let a motherfucker shoot at me,* I thought. *Show me a hostile threat and I'll put him down.*

We started our peel, and the first two hundred meters were uneventful. With about one hundred meters to go, we hit an intersection. I saw a flash out of the corner of my left eye.

"Contact left!" I yelled, as the gunfire came at us from somewhere down the road on our left flank. I took a knee as I returned fire, and those around me did the same. The act of aggression was cathartic as I laid down a wall of lead, shooting at the profile with the AK-47. The violent rhythm of the gun provided a sudden release of tension that was almost euphoric. I felt calm, like I was finally in control. By the time we reached the vehicles, I'd spent at least four hundred rounds. Everyone piled into the back of the Bradley waiting for us, and Bryce got a head count. We were jam-packed like a can of sardines, sweaty and short of breath. The Bradley's ramp began to close, and we watched the daylight disappear behind the thick armor barrier as the track roared to life and headed back toward Corregidor.

I wasn't sure if we got the muj in the alley, but I wanted to believe we had. I thought about it for a moment—how I didn't care who killed him, as long as he was dead.

And then I didn't think about him anymore.

SEVEN

MASS CASUALTIES

"War is a game that is played with a smile. If you can't smile, grin. If you can't grin, keep out of the way till you can."
—Winston Churchill

M Y WIFE, LINDSEY, told me a story about three Vietnam veterans who came to speak to her History of Air Power class when she was studying history at the University of North Carolina at Chapel Hill. For forty-five minutes, they relayed everything they could remember about being grunts in 'Nam to a lecture hall of two hundred attentive nineteen- and twenty-year-olds. "I saw some terrible things," one of the older men recalled. "But when the sun came up and I'd see those little Vietnamese women walking through the rice paddies, their sedge hats the only things visible, just gliding through the rice . . . it was the most beautiful thing I've ever seen. It was fucking beautiful, man."

I didn't have any beautiful moments like that in Ramadi.

I told Lindsey as much and she nodded and smiled sadly. Then she said, "Good."

"What do you mean?" I asked.

"The way he said it," she answered, her voice breaking. "It was the saddest thing I ever heard."

CAMP RAMADI, EARLY MAY 2006

I was eating in the chow hall on Camp Ramadi when an Army medic rushed in, yelling urgently, "We need litter bearers! We've got vehicles coming in. Triple-stack IED. Lots of casualties." I looked at Jonny, Guy, and the other SEALs at the table. Without a word, we dropped our forks and rushed outside. The insurgents had rigged several 155 mm artillery shells together and detonated them when a small convoy of Marines entered the blast zone. It was a massive explosion. Guy approached the medic in charge and told him Jonny and I were Special Operations medics. The medic was glad to have us there.

I had heard the IED detonations in the distance many times before, and I always thought about the death and destruction they wrought. Seeing the carnage firsthand was a completely different level of grim reality. You can push it further back in your mind until you cross the barrier between hearing or reading about the casualties and actually seeing them up close. The image of those American Marines maimed or dying at the hands of cowards filled me with rage. I wanted to do something about it. I wanted to strike back.

I would get my chance soon enough.

Charlie Med was just a quick run from the chow hall, and we booked it as fast as we could. Initially, we went to the vehicle staging area where the casualties would be delivered, but after we were identified as combat medics, we were ushered inside.

"We're probably going to have more casualties than initially expected," said an Army medic. He walked briskly through the hectic scene inside, indicating we should follow him. "We're gonna need you each to run your own bed. I can give you each three or four medics to help you out. Can you handle your own patients?"

"Roger that," we replied.

He nodded quickly and left us at a pair of empty beds. I looked around at the scene beyond my bed, which looked like a modern-day M*A*S*H episode. Around me, various medical personnel scurried in preparation for the incoming casualties. Crash carts, EKG monitors, IV fluids, and solar blankets were being gathered and distributed. The medics assigned to me came and stood by, waiting for the action they were unfortunately accustomed to. They were young, but they knew what they were doing.

I felt anxiety as the casualties started coming in. The blast had burned off some of their cammies. There was so much blood. *I don't know if I'm ready for this,* I thought, nervously eyeing the other medics. We had trained for mass-casualty scenarios at the 18D combat medic course, but it's different in real life. I was about to attempt to stabilize a person, a uniformed American, not a goat. I hadn't felt this level of tension on any of the ops I'd gone on. Treating someone who's been blown up and is fighting for his life is a heavy load to carry. You know that person's survival depends almost completely on you. They need you to make exactly the right decisions, and you have to wrestle with a flurry of thoughts and emotions while trying to stay calm and focused enough to save them. It's difficult to convey the amount of pressure that comes with that feeling. "ABC," I kept repeating to myself. Airway, Breathing, Circulation.

There was an atmosphere of organized chaos as beds filled around us. When I heard the announcement that all casualties were accounted for, I realized I would not have to run my own bed. I should have been relieved, but I felt frustrated by my own helplessness. I didn't want to sit idly by. I looked over at the bed closest to me. The doc stood at its head assessing a young Marine laid out on his back. A couple of privates worked quickly on either side of him, cutting off cammies, checking vitals, taking orders. I stepped up assertively to the doc's side. "Sir, I'm an 18D medic," I said quietly. "Can I be of any assistance?"

He glanced at me quickly before returning his attention to the penlight he was using to check the Marine's pupils. "Start an IV in his right leg," he answered.

My anxiety melted away as my hands found their purpose. I worked efficiently on the Marine, who appeared to have suffered a blast injury to the head. He wasn't conscious. The intracranial pressure that results from such an injury meant this Marine needed to be flown out of Ramadi immediately. Even if he got to Germany, where all serious casualties were flown for treatment, I didn't like his chances. I could tell the doc didn't, either.

I felt a sudden surge of rage as we packaged up the young Marine and ran him out to the awaiting helo. He was blond, ashen, and groaning. I noticed his recently cut hair shaved in a fresh high-and-tight. He looked no older than eighteen or nineteen—about my youngest brother's age. I felt the urge to curse aloud as I looked at his pupils, one constricted and the other ominously dilated. Basal skull fracture. Not good. The rotor wash of the UH-60 helo blew dust into the tent as we lifted the young man up and ran to the helo pad. A quiet calm washed over me as we passed him to the flight surgeon and crew. There was nothing more we could do for him. He was in their hands. I ducked and ran back outside the radius of the rotors. As the 60 lifted and flew off, I stood there in silence. I thought about the Marine. I wasn't likely to ever learn his fate. As Americans, we fight together—one team, one fight. I turned around and looked out over the city, my jaw clenched. I felt like a hammer, ready to smash every muj in Ramadi.

An hour later, Jonny, Guy, and I left Charlie Med in a somber silence. I stomped heavily through the moondust back toward the chow hall, eager to return to the order of my little tent. My SAW, my M4, my

Mk 11—those things made sense to me. But a dying Marine, not even as old as I was—I couldn't rationalize what the muj were doing with those bombs in Ramadi's streets. I wanted a stand-up fight with the enemy so bad I could taste it.

A week or two after I worked triage for the IED attack, we got another mission to roll up a bomb maker in southwest Ramadi. A few weeks in country and I was settling into a battle rhythm. We had about fifteen ops behind us and plenty more ahead. My combat mindset was evolving. War, like anything else, is a routine, a matter of muscle memory. Get an op, prepare, execute. Anxiety became less of a factor. Hatred for the enemy and his cowardly tactics grew.

We were all amped to go after another bomb maker and hopefully have an impact on deterring the IED threat. The area we were headed into had a high concentration of insurgent activity, and nobody had ever pushed through and cleared it. Our target was a compound with a cluster of homes, which we were to clear one by one. It was another early morning op. We almost always operated under the cover of darkness. With our night-vision capabilities, we owned the night. Unless they were planting bombs, the muj mostly operated in daylight, when they could blend in with the local Iraqis.

We launched later than usual, leaving around three in the morning, which meant we'd be operating in daylight within a few hours. For direct-action missions, we usually launched no later than 2 a.m. so we could be back before sunup. With our full SEAL platoon and about twelve Jundis, we had about thirty guys. Movement to the objective took approximately forty-five minutes. As usual, we established security around the compound with our vehicles and foot-patrolled up to the main objective. The streets were narrow, with low-hanging wires everywhere. It was only May, but the temperature at night was already in the nineties. As was often the problem, the humidity fogged up my protective lenses and began to screw with the view through my night-vision goggles. I decided to stow the Oakleys in a cargo pocket.

Chris Kyle led the patrol. Chris had straggled into Iraq a couple weeks late after the main element and had missed our push over to Corregidor. It was good to have him back in the lead. We reached our first target, set in security on the door to the building, and called up the breach team. Bob came up, set a strip charge on the door, and then signaled for us to get to the minimum safe distance. When Bob blew the breach, the deafening blast cued us to assault. The noise and confusion caused by the explosion provide a tactical advantage. Anyone who might be inside is temporarily stunned while we move in with extreme violence of action. Dust and debris filled the air around us as we lurched forward and funneled through the door in standard fashion. We cleared through the entire building with zero resistance. We left some Jundis to detain the women and children on-site and to conduct the sensitive site exploitation (SSE) phase—basically a thorough search to collect as much intel as possible—and moved to the next house. The second house was more of the same. We called in the Jundis to search and moved on.

In the third house, there was a surprise waiting for us.

It was a walled-in structure and a lot tighter space to operate than the previous buildings. We'd been operating for several hours with the same level of intensity we always applied, and I could feel myself wearing down a little as the sun started creeping up toward the horizon. We stacked, breached, and went. The building had two stories, and we cleared all the way through, finding nothing. The last place to clear was the roof. We figured the muj had heard us hitting the other houses and were holed up on the roof waiting for us. I expected to rush into a swarm of insurgents, eager to be martyred in a violent last stand on the rooftop.

Here we go, I thought, my jaw clenched. *Whoever's up there knows we're coming and is ready for us.* My heart was racing, adrenaline surging. I got the signal from Jeremy and passed it to Bob. I was ready for hell on the other side of the door. We spilled onto the roof berserker-style, ready to cut down anything in our path.

Goats. The entire rooftop was swimming with goats.

A meandering horde of gray and white livestock was bleating lazily in a way that almost felt like taunting, as if the insurgents were pranking us.

"What the fuck?" Jeremy said.

"Are you fucking kidding me?" I said.

"Well, there's something you don't see every day," Bob said.

We all just looked at each other and laughed. Only in Ramadi.

We were all pretty spent and ready to get out of there. Being in bad-guy territory in the daylight was never smart. Luke called in the Jundis to search, and we all started gathering whatever intel we could find. We found computer parts, cell phones, a bunch of CDs, and Iraqi dinars (money). The place was rife with all the signs of being a muj house, except for the muj. We stuffed several trash bags full of the valuable items and headed out to the vehicles.

I tossed a trash bag onto the back of Big Zev and was about to hoist myself up when I heard the roar of a diesel engine and the screech of tires in the distance. My hold on Big Zev slackened as I went for my weapon and turned toward the noise. A city bus came screaming around a corner. Our radios came alive with the call: "MUJ BUS! MUJ BUS! FOUR O'CLOCK!" It was barreling toward us like an angry bull. *You've got to be kidding me,* I thought. *These dudes are about to get chewed the fuck up.* There we were, some of the most highly trained and best-equipped warriors in the world, and we were being chased down by a bunch of muj who'd just hijacked a scene from *Speed.* I shook off the sheer absurdity of what was happening and calmly raised my M4 to my shoulder.

The bus screeched to a halt about two hundred yards out, and several muj piled out and ran toward us with AK-47s and RPGs. They may not have been tactical, but they were prepared.

"Heads down! Heads down!" Guy yelled from behind Big Zev's .50 above us in the turret. Often stuck in the TOC, Guy loved an opportunity to get his war on, and he didn't hesitate when the opportunity presented itself. We all got low as he trained the gun on the bus and opened up with a vengeance, unleashing a deafening stream of hot metal just a few feet over our heads. When you're behind the .50, the explosive chug-chug-chug rhythm is loud, but the decibel level is tolerable. Being just a few feet below and in front of it is a completely different story. The concussive blasts of each thumb-sized round leaving the barrel at a muzzle velocity of 2,900 feet per second make your head rattle like someone slamming two frying pans together with your skull in between. To say it's an uncomfortable feeling is a gross understatement.

We all stayed low, creeping away from Guy's line of fire and over Big Zev's sidewalls to join in the turkey shoot. "Muj bus!" had been the only order and we didn't need another one. It was read and react. Instinctively, we fanned out on line and engaged. The whole thing was too absurd to process while it was happening. It reminded me of the scene in *Star Wars* when Han Solo takes off running in a kamikaze charge after a few Stormtroopers on the Death Star, only to turn a corner into a horde of enemy waiting to blast him. The main difference between that and our scenario was that Stormtroopers couldn't hit water if they fell off a boat.

SEALs, on the other hand, are not Stormtroopers, and even my Jundis could hit a muj bus.

The .50 gunner from the Humvee opposite Big Zev on the other side of the street unleashed holy hell on the muj bus, and I saw pops of sparks and little flames erupting all over it as both our .50 gunners ripped it to shreds with a steady stream of red-hot metal. The guys who made it off the bus didn't get far. I imagined what it must have been like for the muj, screeching around the corner, all amped up, chanting God is great, ready to surprise and kill some Americans, only to find themselves staring down a platoon of heavily armed SEALs ready to settle the score through an awesome display of superior American firepower.

We were finally getting an outlet for all our built-up aggression. For once, we had a stand-up fight. An incredibly lopsided fight, but a fight nonetheless. Every one of us poured hate into that bus and the handful of insurgents who managed to get outside just in time to catch a hail of bullets and crumple in a bloody heap. I fired at the bus, at the insurgents, and at anything hostile coming from that doomed vehicle of death. I'd heard the old cliché so many times: like shooting fish in a barrel. Now I'd seen it firsthand. The barrage lasted about two minutes, and when it was done, there was broken glass and carnage all around and inside the smoking bus, now peppered liberally with hundreds of holes, giving it a spongelike appearance. The call to cease fire came over the radio, and all of us just sat there for a moment, waiting for anything to move. Nothing did. We looked around at each other, and everyone began to laugh.

"Dude, did that just fucking happen?" I said, to no one in particular.

"That was some Highway of Death shit right there," the Legend said.

"I don't know what to call it, but it was fucking awesome," Guy said.

Bob, who'd been closest to the .50-cal, yelled, "What the fuck'd you say? I can't hear shit!"

Everybody laughed, and Luke called over the radio, giving the order to move out. The truck rumbled to life as we all sat back on Big Zev's sandbags, smiling with a mixture of satisfaction and incredulity. Riding back to Sharkbase in silence, I remembered stories about the initial invasion of Iraq in 2003, and how the Iraqi soldiers and Fedayeen fighters would sometimes roll up to the fight in school buses. Muj buses were apparently a thing in Iraq . . . a very ill-advised thing. The whole absurd tactic made me think of my favorite passage from George C. Scott's classic opening monologue in *Patton*. The film was a regular fixture for our platoon in Iraq. We watched it religiously during our downtime and frequently quoted Patton's opening speech to his troops:

> Now, we have the finest food and equipment, the best spirit, and the best men in the world. You know, by God, I actually pity those poor bastards we're going up against. By God, I do. We're not just going to shoot the bastards. We're going to cut out their living guts and use them to grease the treads of our tanks. We're going to murder those lousy Hun bastards by the bushel.

Muj bus. Our first bushel. I couldn't help but grin. I preferred it when the mass casualties were on the enemy's side.

EIGHT

NAILED IT!

"Aim towards enemy."

—instruction printed on U.S. rocket launcher

S EVERAL YEARS AGO, I was out in the surf near the Imperial Beach Pier with KPM early one Saturday morning. I was riding my longboard and trying to wash away my hangover. When the surf was good, it was chest to head high and I spent many of the weekend mornings I wasn't away on a training trip in the same spot.

As I went down the line on a clean head-high wave, the set closed out and I jumped off my board. When I popped up to the surface to grab it, I felt a sharp stinging pain in my right cheek and grabbed at my face. Something was tugging at me. I'd been hooked by one of the fishermen on the pier and was getting tangled in the line. I could feel the weights and bait swirling in the water around me.

My board was being pulled toward the shore and yanked me underwater by the ankle. I didn't know what else to do, so I grabbed as much line as I could and wrapped it around my hands to protect my face. With both of my hands literally tied, my board pulled me under each time it got tossed by the churn of the surf zone. It took me several large gulps of air and submersions, and several attempts before I finally bit through the line and cut myself loose.

I made my way back to shore with a fishhook in my face and my board still lashed to my ankle. Onshore, I untied the shrimp and weights from the line, then packed up to head home so I could cut the barb off the hook and push it the rest of the way through and out of my face.

At the time, I never thought much about how lucky I'd been to get out of that situation so quickly and without a real injury. I never considered that it could have hooked my eye. Some things just happen the way they happen. They make good stories to tell over beers later, but dwelling on them too much is an effort that yields no profit.

NORTHERN RAMADI (MC1), MAY 2006

Our target was a couple of compounds in a rural area north of Ramadi. We took a big convoy up Route Mobile to a farming area north of the Euphrates. The land was flat and well irrigated with green fields, hedgerows, and date palms. The vehicles dropped us off a few klicks out, and we patrolled on foot to our objective, following the mud-soaked drainage ditches, which provided some cover and concealment as we went. As usual, it was hot and humid, and the mosquitos were savage. Walking with night-vision goggles over slippery or uneven terrain can be a challenge, and Bob, who was usually a stickler for noise discipline, kept slipping and falling on his ass, making a racket as he went. I snickered loudly, which was my way of letting him know each misstep he made was noticed, and he was going to hear about it later. "Get your shit together, Bob," I'd tell him. Newguys have to exploit whatever opportunities we get to give back some of the shit the older guys give.

After about forty minutes, we arrived on target. At our waypoint,

I took my place in the front of the formation for the patrol to the compound. Our security element covered all avenues of approach as four of us ran up and stacked against the compound's eight-foot wall.

Time to go, I thought, preparing to lead the way over the wall. I remembered the Jundis on my first op and the loud banging of their AK-47s against the ladder as they scaled the wall. There would be none of that tonight. The wall was about twelve inches wide, and I hoisted myself onto it with ease. I straddled and hugged the top of it momentarily, keeping a low profile and then swinging my other leg over and dropping down. With all my gear, I must have weighed at least 275 pounds. My left foot hit the ground first.

At least, my left foot was supposed to hit the ground.

Instead, it came down hard on a long nail, which punched through the sole of my Oakley boot, punctured the bottom of my foot, and proceeded right on through my whole foot until it was poking through the top as if to say, "Hey, Dauber, fuck you!"

For a moment, I just stood there, wondering what the hell had just happened and why there was such an excruciating pain in my foot. I looked down and saw the night-vision-green image of the tip of the nail sticking out of the top of my boot. Somehow, I managed to muffle the instinct to scream obscenities at the top of my lungs. Behind me, the rest of the guys were about to come over the wall. I exhaled hard and let out a muffled grunt. I trained my infrared laser on the front door to the first house and then slowly pulled my foot off the nail while the other SEALs made their way over. It took only a second to slide the metal out of the flesh, past the bones and thousands of nerve endings, but it felt like the longest second of my life. It was hard to focus on anything other than the horrible pain, but I did not have the luxury of feeling sorry for myself. I was on target and it was time to move.

BTF it the fuck up, Dauber. You're a Frogman.

Our raid force was eight SEALs and four Jundis, and the others came over one by one, each picking up a field of fire until everyone was over. We knelt in the wall's shadow, ready to traverse the fifty yards to the house's front door. At the same time, the other half of our platoon and four more Jundis were infiltrating the next compound over, about 150 yards away. The plan was to breach and clear two compounds simultaneously. We moved up and set security, covering all threat points while the breach team moved up. I trained my gun on the door, peeling past the hinge side to cover the side that opens. Chris peeled with me, falling in behind me to cover my back. We called up Squirrel, our breacher, and he moved up to put the strip charge on the door. With the charge in place, Chris and I rolled back to the minimum safe distance, a little past a window on the front of the house. We took knees and waited, scanning our surroundings. He glanced at me and gestured with a hand as if to ask, "What's up?" I was wiping blood off my mouth. I realized I must have bitten my lip when I pulled my foot off that nail. It wasn't a little blood, and the shine of it on night vision had caught his attention. I waved him off, back to scanning the scene. *Tell you all about it later,* I thought.

At this point in the op, communication and timing are everything. The plan was to blow the doors to both houses at the exact same time. The element of surprise is crucial on an op like this. Luke called it over the radio: "Breach team one set." Within a few moments, we got the report from team 2: "Breach team two set." Luke counted it down over the radio: "Three, two, one, execute."

When something like this goes down the way it's supposed to, it's nothing short of spectacular. Two assault teams, two locations, two explosions, two simultaneous works of art.

When it goes wrong, it can be a shit show.

Chris and I heard the "Three, two, one, execute" call over the radio and braced for the breach. Behind me, Squirrel pressed the firing button on the charge, and nothing happened. At the other compound, team 2's charge blew as expected. Loudly. Conspicuously. We waited there, giving each other looks of *what the . . . ?* as precious seconds ticked by. It quickly became apparent that Squirrel's firing device had been jarred loose, probably on the hop over the wall. Murphy's law applies to Teamguys, too. He started fumbling with it furiously.

"Come on, Squirrel," Luke hummed over the radio. "Hurry up, Squirrel. Muj is waiting for us, Squirrel."

When I was back in SEAL Qualification Training (SQT) in Niland doing a training block, I'd struck up a conversation with a salty old chief in Golf Platoon at the weapons cleaning station one day. He looked like the badass from the movie *The Boondock Saints* with his ragged white hair and evil eyebrows. He had a tattoo of Jesus on his right forearm and "666" on his left. *Conflict makes you stronger,* I thought. As I extracted the bolt to my M4, he quietly asked me, "What is the best type of ambush?"

I thought for a second. "The one that you win?"

He smiled. "Exactly," he said. "You want to sneak up on those motherfuckers like a sleeping baby. You have the arsenal to smash them into oblivion. Never give them a fucking chance and drop the fucking hammer."

The muj have their chance here, I thought, worrying about the failed breach. I could hear Squirrel, digging through his breacher pouch. *Come on, Squirrel,* I thought. *Find the nut.* I could sense him going through his points of performance. He was an experienced breacher and good at his job, but about twenty seconds passed before Squirrel went to a secondary firing device. We were in the most vulnerable part of an assault for much longer than we'd anticipated, and assault team 2 had already executed the breach, giving the enemy time to prepare. There's a term in the military for the position we were in: hanging out like dog's balls. After what seemed like an eternity, Squirrel pressed the detonator and finally blew the door.

It's hard to describe the sound of a strip charge to someone who's never been close to one when it detonates. The sound is one thing, but it brings with it a concussion and back-blast that overwhelm your senses. Even at minimum safe distance, the explosion will rattle your teeth. I knew guys who wore ear protection in combat, but I didn't like the idea of numbing any of my senses when we might encounter the enemy.

When the charge went off, I sprang from my position toward the door like a racehorse through the gates. I barely noticed the shower of glass that rained on me from the blown-out window above. I was first into the building. With a couple steps, I closed the distance between me and the jagged opening where the door had been moments before. My flashlight shone through the dust and hazy smoke as I cleared my sector of the room.

"Clear!" I yelled. Bob followed immediately with "All clear," and I moved toward the nearest threat—a closed door at the far corner of the room. Behind me, I heard the Jundis streaming into the room at the end of the initial assault team.

Clearing a target is organized chaos. I've never been in a house fire, but I imagine it might be a lot like hitting a house after an explosive entry. You're struggling not to cough or choke on the dust and smoke. You're sweating and high on adrenaline, moving as quickly as you can while maintaining efficiency. You're fighting the darkness and any obstacles in the room—bedding, furniture, rugs.

And muj.

The beginning of the op had gone south with the failed breach, but I felt like we were making up for it in the initial room. We moved with urgency, and I was ready to open the door and press the next room. I was about to reach out for the handle when a burst of gunfire exploded just to my right. Bob held me back by my gear. Someone had shot up the doorway I was about to open, about three or four shots. About six feet away, standing right in front of the door, one of our Jundis stood frozen. He'd attempted to roll the doorway when the gunfire erupted.

"CONTACT HALLWAY!" Bob yelled as we stood stalled for a second, thinking the bad guys were holed up on the other side of the door shooting at us. Suddenly, before I could pull out a grenade, the door opened and I saw into the room. An old man stood in the doorway with his hands up in surrender. Without even thinking, I hit the guy with a left hook and laid him out, deferring to my training: get in fast and kill whoever else is in there shooting at us. There's a reason doorways are known in urban combat as "the fatal funnel." It's not the place you want to linger. We pushed into the room to clear. There was a woman on the floor with her hands up. I checked her for explosives, found none, and held on for a Jundi to come over and detain her. The room was clear. There was no resistance. No bad guys. Who the fuck shot at us? Within seconds, the call came that the rest of the compound was clear, as well.

I walked back toward the old man I laid out. He was wearing a man-dress, balding with a big nose and hairy ears. His nose was crooked and bleeding. Seeing this, I felt bad, but I also knew hitting him was the right call. I had just been shot at from inside the room where the man was, or so I thought. I looked up and saw the same Jundi who had been there before we went in—a skinny guy with a mustache. He was still frozen. It took a minute to put it together. The Jundi had stitched up the door right next to me with an accidental discharge, an AD. This kid had nearly killed Bob and me with his itchy trigger finger. His lieutenant walked up, cleared and safed his weapon, and proceeded to chew his ass in Arabic. I walked over to Moose and asked him what the lieutenant was saying.

"The kid's done. The LT just told him he's out of Special Missions Platoon."

The guy looked dejected. I didn't really care. I was pissed and uncomfortable with the fact that his ineptitude had almost killed me. I'd known Teamguys to be kicked out of units for having ADs. As far as I was concerned, they had deserved to lose their jobs and this Jundi did too. I stalked outside to get some air. The target was secured, and the Jundis began to search the place for any sensitive items. I went to find my boys. Marc and Ryan had been on external security.

"What the fuck happened, man?" Marc asked.

"Jundi had an AD, man," I said. "He stitched up the doorway right next to my face. Almost the end of Dauber and Uncle Bob. That'll pucker you up."

"Dude," Ryan said, "you almost got killed by a Jundi. That would have really sucked."

"Yeah. I'd say," I replied.

That incident went down in our mental notebook of lessons learned. In addition to worrying that some of the Jundis might be muj, now we were a lot more worried about the possibility of being accidentally shot by them. SEALs pride themselves on being professionals, and weapons safety is vital. A minor mistake could turn into a catastrophe. There's just no room in the Teams for anything less than the utmost respect for protocol when it comes to safety. The idea that I was going to be forced to go on target with guys who didn't share the same commitment was unnerving. Since our orders prohibited us from running unilateral ops, we were required to bring Jundis on every patrol, DA, or sniper overwatch. We always had to bring at least a few with us. Before the Jundi's AD, I always thought we were good as long as they stayed behind us. Now even that seemed questionable. From that point forward, we became a lot more selective about which Jundis we brought with us, and tried to be constantly aware of their position.

"The lemmings are going in front of me from now on," I told Marc and Ryan. I climbed into Big Zev, noticing the pain in my left foot for the first time since the assault began an hour earlier. I made a mental note to find a round of antibiotics in the medical tent and order a tetanus shot. I smiled to myself, grimly. I guess a hole in the foot is better than a hole in the head.

NINE

DON'T GET COCKY

"The only man who never makes mistakes is
the man who never does anything."
—Theodore Roosevelt

SOME DAYS IN the desert blend in my memory, and I try to sort them out the best I can. I remember some ops clearly, while the details of others become blurry as the years pass.

Some things remain crisp and clean in my mind's eye—things I could have lived without but carry with me as lessons I will teach my children.

We searched so many compounds for contraband, weapons, bomb-making materials. I couldn't tell you how many. In a compound in Tway Village we found a garbage bag full of videotapes. There were dozens. We played one of the videos to determine whether it held sensitive information and found it contained footage of beheadings. Al Qaeda in Iraq was beheading Iraqis, military and civilian alike, who collaborated with the coalition forces. They filmed the beheadings for distribution.

It was the most savage thing I've ever seen.

By mid-June, our op tempo was in overdrive. We had started off slow with the Army and Corregidor, but once we got back to Sharkbase, we really started establishing ourselves in the battle space. The head shed kept us wound pretty tight, like a dog fighter who beats his dog to make it mean. We were working 24/7, save the occasional meal and few hours of sleep. Coming off a twenty-four- or forty-eight-hour sniper overwatch, we'd have a little time to refit before going straight into a DA mission, often for high-value targets. Any days without an op were filled training Jundis or on the range, keeping ourselves sharp.

There's something about momentum. A unit's performance in combat can become a self-fulfilling prophecy. The more you win, the more the higher-ups want to send you out to kill bodies. We had developed a reputation for efficiency, and our skills were in high demand from commanders all over Ramadi.

After successive sniper overwatch missions with the Appalachian boys from the Guard, I was ready for a breather. Jonny was ready to call his woman. As our trucks pulled into Sharkbase, I looked forward to some chow and sleep after seven days of continuous ops. After breaking down the vehicle's heavy guns and putting away all the platoon gear and my own equipment, I had enough time to wash the stink off me, change into some PT gear, and grab some chow. I thought I'd be getting a well-deserved night's sleep.

The war had other plans.

Back in our tent, Marc, Spaz, and Bob were already racked out. I was about to do the same when Tony popped into our tent.

"We've got an op. HVT. Op order in ten mikes. This is a big one," he said in his clam-chowder accent.

"Roger that," I said. Sleep is a crutch.

In the mission planning space, V briefed the op. V was our task unit's senior enlisted advisor and a salty, tatted-up Frogman with chest and back hair like a sweater. He'd been in the Teams for almost twenty years and was amped to get after this mission. His op order was a quick PowerPoint. Our mission planning and prep had become like reflex, and the mission was a hostage rescue, one of our specialties as Teamguys. As V briefed the details, I fed off his energy. I was amped, too.

"This is a high-value individual being detained by AQI," V said. "There are at least five well-armed military-aged males in the target building. Expect a fight. Get in there and hit 'em hard and fast. Leave no room for error. Get the target and get out. Your target is the son of Ramadi's chief of police. Everyone in our AOR will be watching this one, and if we do this right, we will win some serious points with the locals—all that hearts-and-minds shit. Time to earn your paycheck, gents."

The mission was nothing new under the sun at this point. This was the muj's MO. They kidnap people. They torture and terrorize people. They murder people. And sometimes they make the whole thing into a propaganda video. Nobody deserves that fate. I wanted the mission, and if we were lucky, we'd get to shoot all the thugs in the process. One of the important details of our mission was that we were to facilitate the rescue operation with the Jundi's SMP. Given the high visibility, the head shed wanted to give the appearance of the Jundis having the lead. If successful, it would be a big publicity thing for them. In reality, we were doing the heavy lifting, as always.

The target building was a stand-alone house. There was an abandoned school about two hundred yards west and another building about three hundred yards south of the target. At our vehicle-staging point, our overwatch team rolled out to set up in the southern building. Chris was behind the scope with Biggles, Chucky, V, and a few straphangers (augmentees from outside our platoon) providing security for our assault team. If any squirters tried to make a run for it during our approach or after the bullets started flying, Chris and our machine gunners would light them up.

I was on the assault team, holding at the vehicles and waiting for the launch. I looked over to the turret on Vehicle 2. Guy stood rigid on the twin 240s. I could tell he wasn't amused with the fact that he wasn't on the assault. Teamguys are fiercely competitive in general, and no one wants to be left out of the action. Everyone wants to be first through the door on target, first to pull the trigger, first to deliver the punishment. Guy was no different. I waved at him and then promptly flipped him the bird. The sting resonated through the humidity.

"Moving," Squirrel passed over inter-squad comms, and the patrol moved out. We started moving toward the target in a dual-column formation, one squad on each side of the street. The assault element was twelve SEALs and about five Jundis. I still believed the Jundis were more of a liability than an asset, but this mission meant a lot to them. *Sweet Christ, it's hot,* I thought. The temperature had jumped about fifteen degrees a few days before and just stayed there. Dead of night, and I was dripping sweat. My Oakleys were constantly fogging up, and the dense air amplified the smell from the shit creeks and the river. Ramadi in the summer was a perpetual state of full-body swamp ass.

We stacked along the side of the structure, and Bob moved up to place the strip charge on the door. When he hit the breach, it was loud as hell. The sound ripped through the neighborhood. It felt like it should have woken anyone within a few hundred meters, and it jolted my adrenaline as I moved into the house and started clearing. It happened fast. The house was a simple two-story deal with about eight rooms total, including the kitchen. As we cleared, I was in the zone. My senses were wire-tight. Around every corner and in every room, I expected hell and was ready to shoot it in the face. But there wasn't a single bad guy in the building. It was empty.

Our Intelligence, Surveillance, and Reconnaissance assets had eyes on the building up to the point of our launch, and their intel said five bad guys minimum. The lack of resistance inside the house meant the bad guys had to be on the roof. They were waiting for us up there, and they were going to hit us with everything they had once we hit the fatal funnel. We moved up the stairs to the rooftop entrance and stacked. I was the lead man, and I was ready for the fight of my life. I fully expected to be the first man through that door and into a hail of gunfire. As a Teamguy, you're part of a culture that constantly emphasizes the mantra "It pays to be a winner." There wasn't a hint of hesitation in my body going onto that roof. I am the hunter; they are the prey. I will win. They will lose.

Bob gave me the signal, and I flung the door open and spilled onto the roof, seeing no threats in the green of my night vision. I continued on, peeling right around the back of the rooftop entrance while Bob peeled left. Bob turned the corner and held there. When I got around, I saw what Bob saw: an entire family sleeping on the roof. There were several women and children, and a few military-age males. One of the men got up, and Bob got to him first. The rest of the platoon flooded onto the rooftop behind us, and we subdued all the suspects.

I launched myself at one of the men. He began to wake and I noticed an AK-47 near him on the rooftop. With my weight on his back, I wrenched his wrists behind him and flex-cuffed them while another Teamguy secured the weapon. Around us, the rest of the military-age males were being flex-cuffed the same way.

Over intra-squad comms came the call, "PID." During the op brief we'd all studied a picture of the police chief's son to ensure no one accidentally shot him. He was there, on the rooftop, sleeping among the group. He was lanky with a big head and looked pretty scraggy in his black shirt and gray Adidas pants. He'd been roughed up a little but was otherwise unharmed. He looked nervous, but relieved.

After the mission and our enemy had been hyped so much, I actually felt a little disappointed that we hadn't fired a single shot. But our target was there and very much alive. Technically, the mission was a glaring success, despite killing zero muj.

Moose had directed the Jundis in the SSE, and I'd noticed a marked improvement in their performance. The women were scream-ing as we searched the house and detained the men. No doubt the ex-perience is terrifying for the women, and Moose and the Jundis had gotten very good at corralling the women and completing a thorough search quickly. They found a bunch of bomb-making material, and we detained four military-age males.

Watching our Jundis, I actually felt proud of how far they'd come. Sure, many of them were apathetic and treated their job more like a hobby than a profession, but we'd trained them well and could see them becoming better soldiers. Of course, they still looked like a bunch of desert pirates. They all wore the same chocolate-chip-patterned cammies, but some had black helmets while others had green helmets. Some had night-vision goggles. Others duct-taped flashlights to their guns. One guy carried an absurdly huge Crocodile Dundee knife. We had a guy named Akmed who always wore a Hoot-ers bandana tied around his head. I found this especially ironic, be-cause the odds of Akmed ever finding himself in a Hooters were slim to none.

One thing I could never understand was how the Jundis were al-ways checking out the women, no matter how old or unattractive. I turned to EOD Nick and said, "You see the way the Jundis are always checking out these old ladies? Fucking ugh, man."

"Yeah, bro," Nick said. "I get the impression these dudes would fuck a knot in a fence. I don't think they get laid much."

"Yo, how the fuck did these Iraqis sleep through us blowing the door off their house and then yelling like maniacs all the way up to the roof?" I asked.

"I have no idea, brother," Bob said, laughing. "I guess we just hit the hardest-sleeping muj in Ramadi tonight."

We saw some shit in Ramadi. I guess I shouldn't have been surprised by anything at that point. I just shook my head and laughed at the whole scene. Going back through it in my mind, I couldn't help but feel a little let down that the entire op had gone off without a shot fired. V had hyped it up so much, and I had mentally prepared myself for an epic gunfight with some very bad dudes. I'm confident the rescue would have been successful even if we had met resistance, but the outcome speaks to the unpredictable nature of combat.

When we got back to the detention center, it became clear what a big deal the rescue was. To us, the op was a mostly uneventful takedown. But the police chief's son had been missing for about two months, and the head shed put the SMP and their lieutenant front and center for a big photo op and press release. We got a quiet pat on the back, and the Jundis got the credit for a daring raid carried out with surgical efficiency. We didn't mind staying in the shadows because we could see how much the mission meant to the Jundis and the locals. It felt good. We did a great thing, and I was glad the SMP's lieutenant had his day in the sun. A product of the Iraqi Military Academy, he was a truly professional soldier who took his job seriously. The aftermath of that operation was a huge morale boost for the Jundis and many local Iraqis in general.

As the Punishers' legend grew, so did the demand for our services. Delta Platoon worked exclusively with the Army, but we were like freelancers, bouncing all over Ramadi in support of both the Army and Marines, often stopping over at Sharkbase only long enough for our head shed to iron out the next op's details and for us to refit. I went days at a time without showering or sleeping longer than a few hours' stretch just because our workload didn't allow it. When we did have the time to make an appearance at a chow hall at Camp Corregidor or Government Center, we could feel the eyes on us. We'd sit down to eat and pretend not to sense the soldiers and grunts glancing our way, whispering about the death-dealing SEALs in the back.

The work we did had a significant impact on the strategy in Ramadi and Anbar Province in general. Our mastery of sniper over-watches was highly effective in instilling fear in the enemy and deterring their movement and combat effectiveness. Direct-action ops were the surgical strike that we carried out when they least expected it. The combination of the two was a strong one-two punch in effectively hunting and capturing or killing the enemy. The insurgents feared us, and those who wanted peace were increasingly angered by Al Qaeda's brutality. There was a sense of cautious security among the locals as coalition forces pressed farther into the city. Village elders and sheiks began to support our efforts to rid the city of insurgents. We were increasing security and priming the region for the "surge" of 2007.

General David Petraeus's now-famous counterinsurgency strategy was summed up as "clear, hold, build." As Punishers, our job was to support the clear phase. We were the stick in the carrot-stick dynamic upon which Petraeus's strategy relied, and more and more battle-space commanders wanted our support in their efforts to change the dynamic in their areas of operation.

About a week after the rescue of the police chief's son, the Marines requested our support for an operation in the heart of Ramadi. Muj attacks had been frequent and bold in the area, and the Marines wanted us to try to disrupt the enemy's operations with sniper overwatches.

After our officers did their deconfliction dance with the Marine leadership, we headed out in Humvees for our first overwatch operation around Observation Post Firecracker, where the Marines were operating. Firecracker sits at a four-way intersection about a half mile north of Government Center in the heart of downtown Ramadi.

LEFT: Boat Crew 1 during Class 245 Hell Week.
Courtesy of the US Navy

RIGHT: Second Phase of BUDS.
Richard Schoenberg

LEFT: Marc, Biff, Biggles, and I during work-up.

LEFT: Our sniper group at Nellis Air Force Base.

RIGHT: Biggles.

LEFT: Coming back from a DA.

LEFT: Chucky and I preparing to go out on a presence patrol.

RIGHT: Marc Lee and me in the Stryker.

LEFT: With the Punisher logo on.

LEFT: Chris Kyle ("The Legend") and me in the hide.

LEFT: Painted up and ready to go on the final op of Third Phase.
Richard Schoenberg

RIGHT: Marc Lee.

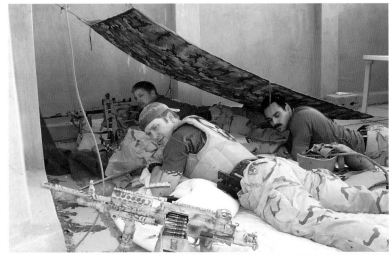

LEFT: Chris and I on the gun, with Marc Lee behind us.

RIGHT: Raising the flag north of Baseline Road.

LEFT: Leaving our mark on COP Falcon.

LEFT: The picture I took of Marc Lee on the way back from COP Springfield.

RIGHT: Moose and me.

ABOVE: Standing with the memorial we constructed to Marc Lee, Ryan Job, and Mike Monsoor.

LEFT: Seeing Chris off.

RIGHT: On the roof with one of my SMP Jundhis after a firefight. (Notice the holes in wall from incoming rounds.)

ABOVE: The only time Charlie Platoon got together for a picture.

LEFT: Chris and I at the awards ceremony following our Ramadi deployment.

RIGHT: Hanging out with Clint Eastwood in Morocco on the set of *American Sniper.* *Warner Bros.*

LEFT: Debriefing a take with Bradley Cooper and his stunt double, former Army Ranger Mike Trisler. *Jeff Habberstad*

When we arrived in country, the muj completely controlled the area around the OP. By June, American forces were clearing them out and had established a foothold.

Our team was Luke, our sister platoon chief Dale, Bob, Marc, Rex, me, and a couple of Jundis. Dale and I were the snipers, Bob and Marc were machine gunners, and Rex was our comms guy. We had a mutually supporting overwatch two hundred meters away and we were both tasked to get visibility on a particular intersection and negotiate targets accordingly.

We launched on foot from Firecracker and patrolled a mile to our target building. If I had to design a movie set for Dante's Seventh Level of Hell, I'd base it off that patrol into muj country. The sweltering heat registered as green haze in my night vision as I scanned the streets. Mongrel dogs barking in our direction seemed to reflect the malice of the city's heart. The smell of rot emanated from the piles of trash and refuse that reinforced the constant threat of IEDs. The angry heat coated my skin like the moondust our boots kicked up, and by the time we reached our building, sweat soaked every inch of my uniform.

Our target was a corner house on a big intersection about two hundred meters away. We expected a lot of activity coming in that direction in the morning. By this time, we had nearly perfected our soft-knock technique. The moments before we enter and secure a building are critical. Being outside with no cover leaves us exposed. The quieter and faster we can be on entry and set up, the longer we can go undetected in our hide. Our Jundis had gotten good at decreasing our wait time outside by getting us in quickly to search and set up. We were in fast, despite the angry protests of the women. There was no doubt we were occupying a muj house. It was full of women and children, and the women yelled endlessly. They did not want us to occupy their house, but business is business.

"Target secure," came across comms. The house was a large two-story with an open foyer and a spiral staircase up to the second deck.

Bob and Dale set up in a room with a window, looking north over the front of the house with a partial view of the intersection. I was in a room facing west, looking straight down the road at the big intersection. A table made for a nice stable platform, which I pulled a chair up to away from the window. I'd collected plenty of cushions from all over the house to make it as comfortable as possible, and I set up linens to hide my silhouette.

Most of the time, I was more careful, but the window had steel bars, which narrowed my line of sight on the target area below. The last thing I wanted was to see a muj through my scope and accidentally shoot the bars. I was willing to risk a little in order to have a better view. I guess you get greedy, maybe a little reckless when you start feeling invincible. Still, the hostile environment had my adrenaline up and pupils dilated. In those situations, you feel like a giant sense organ. You're just waiting for the hammer to drop, and you're ready to pounce.

"This is a good spot," Moose said as I prepped the hide.

"Clear view, just need some bad guys," I responded, soaking in the still of the night.

"Jobber, I'm jealous. You guys sit up here and do the killing, and I watch over the women and children."

"Well, Moose, just make sure none of them clack off a suicide vest while we're dealing some business," I replied.

Moose was solid on the job. He kept the Jundis and the locals quelled while we worked. We couldn't do our job effectively if the noncombatants were throwing a Dance Dance Revolution party during an overwatch. Because Moose was a former Jordanian Special Forces guy, I knew he missed the action. He felt this was his war just as much as it was ours. After all, he was a U.S. citizen.

After the call to prayer, the usual action began on the streets. When a family doesn't come out of their house in the morning, their neighbors know something's going on. The body language on the street was a whole lot of combat rubbernecking. The neighborhood women out dumping their dishwater—or whatever it is they dump in the road—were looking at our building. Reading the nonverbal cues, I filled in the dialogue as the women conversed: "Why hasn't Hiba or Muhammad come out of their house this morning? They're always outside." Of course, they know it's because the Americans are there.

I saw several peekers—muj surveilling our position—and cars kept driving up to the intersection, dropping one military-age male and then picking up another. Everything I saw through my scope looked shady. Everything does when you're operating in the enemy's den. After a while, the bustle died down and everything got quiet. People started evaporating from the street. That's when I knew something was about to go down.

It happened quickly. An RPG slammed into the wall of the house near Dale's position. The intense blast rattled my teeth and set off an intense ringing in my ears. The concussion rang my bell and threw me off for a second or two before I could scan for the source of the fire. Bullets snapped and cracked all around me. I could hear the machine gun, and then I'd feel the rounds cracking like a bullwhip repeatedly next to my head. Rounds were chewing up the window in front of me. My heart was pounding out of my chest as I tried to decide if I wanted to hold position or take cover. In a few short seconds, I'd gone from feeling like a zoo patron watching the animals in their cage to being the main attraction.

I lurched to my left and pulled my Mk 11 with me, sliding head-first into the corner of the room to my ten o'clock, hoping the wall was thick enough to stop 7.62 rounds. At almost the exact instant I dove away, a burst of rounds came in and stitched up the chair I'd been sitting in.

If I hadn't dove away, I'd be dead.

"Dauber, you good?" Luke called from the other room.

"I'm good! Still here!"

I waited for the opportunity to return fire, but I was pinned down. Before I could really think about how close I'd just come to dying, an RPG hit the side of the window and exploded—another earsplitting, heart-shaking blast. The deafening concussion felt like it sucked the air out of the room. After a couple of seconds, I looked up at the mangled hole where the window was and just lay there for a while. Being pinned down means the enemy's effective fire is suppressing all activity. There was nothing I could do. Rounds snapped and splintered the masonry all around. It was not a feeling I was used to, and I didn't like it. My instinct was to try to get back up and return fire, but the rounds kept coming in, intense and steady. All I could do was keep my head down and wait.

Luke low-crawled through the hallway to check on me; he was buttoned up as always with his helmet and body armor fixed tight.

"Dauber, what's going on?"

I pointed to the window, the table, the chair.

"I think I got shot at," I said, trying to laugh at the escape-and-evasion drill I'd just run against the Grim Reaper.

"All right. Well, get after it," Luke said.

"Roger that," I said. "Glad that fucking RPG didn't come into the room."

Bob managed to move around and get a clear shot out a window to return fire, and after about ten minutes, it all died down. I took another moment to acknowledge that I'd almost gotten seriously fucked up, and then I pushed it away. The rounds that shredded the table and chair I was sitting in had come incredibly close, and I found myself wondering, *How close is close? Close* was the answer I gave myself. *But almost only counts in horseshoes and hand grenades,* I thought, remembering another of our favorite mantras.

I can't imagine what guys in World War II had to endure when all they could do was sit in their fighting holes and wait out artillery barrages. Ramadi wasn't the European Theater, but there is a learning process a warrior has to go through in order to be consistently effective in combat. Even a Big Tough Frogman has to know when to take cover. You can't always hang your nuts out there. Sometimes you just need to live to fight another day. I thought about the sign from my early days in Iraq: COMPLACENCY KILLS. I hated to admit it, but a creeping complacency had set in. I thought about the contrast between the high I felt after the hostage rescue a week earlier and nearly dying in my hide site.

I slowly put my Red Sox cap back in my pack. I'd begun donning it in favor of my helmet on some of the overwatches. Begrudgingly, I acknowledged to myself that the chocolate-chip "B" hat, while cool, wasn't going to provide any protection to my dome here in muj country. I cinched the chinstrap on my helmet and put my web gear back on. I had gotten into the habit of sitting in the hide site slick because it was so damn hot. Oh well. The gear was going back on. I was willing to melt before I'd be caught with my pants down again. I'd keep my gear tight and be ready to grab everything and run at any time. Ramadi was not going to kill me. I would not let it. I got up and cautiously packed a dip. I moved the table, then moved the chair over and got back on the gun because that's what Frogmen do.

Marc joined me in the room.

"Damn, bro, muj lit this place the fuck up," he said.

"Yeah, apparently they can actually shoot," I said. "Who knew?"

"I guess every dog has its day, brother," he said. "Maybe this was God's way of saying, 'Don't get cocky.'"

It stayed quiet for the rest of our time in the hide, and Marc and I talked a lot. Something he said stuck with me. We had done some training at Nellis Air Force Base in Las Vegas before deployment. We all got hammered and hit the casino one night, and Marc went on an epic tear on the blackjack table. For a while it seemed like he couldn't lose, and every time the dealer started putting cards out, Marc would yell, "Everybody's a winner!" and we'd all yell and backslap.

"Maybe this shit's like Vegas," he said. "Sometimes you're flush. Sometimes you're bust."

"Truth," I said.

You have to know when to hit and when to stand.

TEN

OVERWATCH
AT BERNIE'S

**"The mind ought sometimes to be diverted
that it may return to better thinking."**

—Phaedrus

OVER THE COURSE of an operator's career, he learns to carry a wide range of gear, tools, and miscellanea. Ammo, rucksacks, rockets, downed men, you name it. He trains for every conceivable combat scenario and learns to adjust to those real-world situations no instructor could ever have imagined. He carries the tools of his trade: his weapons and his instinct.

Preparation is not reserved solely for work, however, and it habitually drifts off-duty and encompasses all aspects of a newguy's life. In Charlie Platoon, Biggles was awarded an extra piece of essential gear to be carried on him at all times: Laser, a four-foot-tall teddy bear.

I was relieved I wasn't chosen to carry the giant stuffed bear. So were the rest of the newguys. Biggles, however, embraced his companion and made him a part of all daily activities. He even took a rucksack frame and made a backpack for Laser so he could carry the bear around like an oversize toddler. When Biggles brought Laser along with him to the bars, no one could deny the favor he did us by providing a giant plush icebreaker. Laser was guaranteed to attract some attention. Biggles may not have had a choice about carrying Laser, but he owned it. And loved it.

We were at a bar when some chick asked Biggles what he was doing with a stuffed animal. He told her he was a Frogman.

"I still don't get why you're carrying a bear," she said.

"Girl," he responded, "you wouldn't believe the shit we have to carry."

SADDAM HOSPITAL, RAMADI, LATE JUNE 2006

Throughout the Battle of Ramadi, when wounded Iraqi police officers were taken to Ramadi General Hospital, members of Al Qaeda in Iraq cut their heads off. The Geneva Conventions stipulate that hospitals "may in no circumstances be the object of attack, but shall at all times be respected and protected by the parties to the conflict." The muj didn't care much for the laws of war, nor the laws of man. Throughout Ramadi, they were carrying out savage acts of brutality. The enemy we fought literally chained handicapped people to walls in basements or sawed off the heads of Iraqis who supported coalition forces, and they had been using the seven-story hospital just south of the Euphrates to treat their wounded and to fire on American forces in the area.

By late June, the Marines were pushing farther north, and they wanted sniper support for their operations to wrest the hospital from the insurgents and secure the surrounding area. Our mission was to conduct a forty-eight-hour sniper overwatch just north of the hospital. The most direct route to our target was via riverine insertion from the

Euphrates. This was a welcome change for us. We're Frogmen, after all, and there are no IEDs in the Euphrates.

We launched out of Camp Hurricane Point, a Marine base butted up in a corner of northwest Ramadi where the Euphrates meets the Habbaniyah Canal. The Marines had a Small Unit Riverine Craft unit, and we hitched a ride with them to our drop-off point. As I boarded what looked like a big camouflaged banana raft, I wondered, *Where the fuck are the Navy SWCC boat guys? Aren't they the special riverine unit of Surface Warfare Combatant Crafts that are supposed to take me to war? Why are the Marines driving me around?* Then again, I didn't complain. I liked working with the Marines.

"You're a former water taxi, Nick. Hop in there and drive us to the op," I said to EOD Nick as we watched the boats being loaded into the canal.

"Fuck you, Dauber," EOD Nick replied.

"Leave him alone, Dauber," Jonny cut in. "He's a tech now. He gets sensitive."

We newguys had zero authority over anyone in the platoon, but we made damn sure to give the support guys shit any chance we got. Nick was a good sport and always gave it right back.

"Go watch Charlie Sheen's *Navy SEALs* and keep telling yourself you're cool. I've got some work to do."

The SWCC guys are always there in the movies, but they apparently forgot to deploy to Iraq with us. So we rode banana rafts with the Marines.

The boats had a hard time getting out of Hurricane Point because the Euphrates's current was ripping. Eventually, the swirling current gave way to the straining hum of the engines, and we motored into the easterly flow toward our objective. The boats put out only a small wake as we slowly cut the oven-hot air, mosquito infested and miserably sticky like a Florida swamp in the summer. It was a short fifteen-minute cruise to our insertion point. Both boats nosed up to a small opening in the thick reeds and vegetation on the bank. I felt like I was in the Mekong Delta. I finally felt like an old-school Frogman, coming up out of the water. Check that box.

We hurried off and set security, and the boats quickly moved off to do some recon and false insertions. We stayed on the banks, motionless, listening to the frogs, and getting consistently more pissed off at the mutant mosquitos that bit us as we sat there pouring sweat. Finally, we got the signal to move.

Our target was a compound just forty yards up from the bank. We planned to use it as a staging point for our recon and eventual assault on the hospital. It had a huge wall around it, and there were three large houses.

We sent Squirrel over the eight-foot wall. Once on top, he discovered an eighteen-foot drop to the ground on the other side. "Oh shit," he muttered before climbing back over. He went back up with a rope, and we waited to climb over one by one. With the whole platoon waiting, I noticed how dead quiet it was. A fat mosquito buzzed up for a hearty drink of hot blood. Talk about terrorists.

Squirrel secured the rope and nimbly got up, over, and down the wall. *Fucking midgets,* I thought. Chris was next and did not move with the same dexterity and spring. A snicker came from someone on security as the old man disappeared from view. Each man slowly but quietly made his trip. We pressed through the open field to the large three-story house on the west side of the compound, lasers lighting up every dark space and open window.

We cleared through the three houses as quietly as possible, finding them completely empty. They were three-story structures with about fifteen fully furnished rooms in each. Most important, the two outside houses had air-conditioning, which meant we were really in the lap of luxury. My squad took up positions in the westernmost house. As we snooped around the house looking for the best spots to set up in, Biggles's guts announced pretty loudly the need to evacuate themselves ASAP.

"That fucking chili mac from the chow hall was a bad choice. I think it's trying to murder me," he whispered to me. "I gotta shit."

"Take your disgusting ass far away from me. I'm setting up here," I said, gesturing to the room I'd picked on the second floor looking west. "Whatever's going on in there sounds heinous."

Biggles had a reputation in the platoon as a serial shitter. He liked to leave little surprises in unexpected nooks and crannies of the buildings we operated from. He got a kick out of his self-appointed role as our resident shit-bomber. A few minutes after he disappeared, Tony was setting up in the room next to mine when he growled, "Whaat the faahhhkk? What the faahhkk is that smell?" I laughed hard, knowing Biggles had struck again. He'd quietly marked his territory right next to where Tony set up, blasting a disgusting chili-mac turd on the ledge in front of one of the windows. Biggles sat in the corner laughing and said nothing. The mad shitter strikes again.

I rolled out my foam mat, which stretched from my head to my thighs. It was about two in the morning, and I took off my web gear and body armor. We own the night, and the risk of attack was relatively low. I grabbed a few water bottles from my ruck and set them next to my mat. I pounded one and packed a dip. Then I drained another into my CamelBak so I'd have a piss bottle when the time came. In order to be effective behind the gun, the less time away from it, the better. The extra bottle prevented a trip to the head mid-hunt. I lay down on my mattress and arranged my trio of bottles strategically. From left to right: dip spitter, water, piss bottle. These are important details. You don't ever want to confuse the wrong bottle in these situations. Dale made that mistake when we first landed in Ramadi. I lay there, sucking up the air-conditioning while Chris took first watch. We traded time on the gun until the sun came up, sleeping during off hours. By six I was back on the gun, watching the rising sun spread out over our sector as the call to prayer stirred the city to life. Critiquing the singing voice of the muezzins at the morning call had become a favorite pastime.

"Is this guy sitting on a pineapple or something?" Chris said. "He's got a voice like a squeaky dog toy."

"Sounds like a drunk guy trying to sing Freddie Mercury at karaoke," I said.

"Good one," Chris said.

Queen was not the Legend's flavor of music.

Around eight, a loud burst of gunfire snapped us all to attention. I looked for the source and saw about five muj fighters about two hundred yards to the west, popping up and down out of the tall grass and shrubs like a Whac-A-Mole game, taking potshots at a Marine patrol across the river. They were all dressed in what was apparently the muj's standard uniform: Adidas tracksuit pants, sneakers, and a T-shirt or tank top. Most had short hair and ratty beards, and their obvious lack of training and tactical skill was so glaringly awful that it was almost impressive. Not only were they not shooting at us, but they had no idea we were there, which was a very unique and awesome position for us to be in. We'd set the perfect ambush for these guys without even meaning to. They had strolled right into the ideal kill zone. There's a saying: when life hands you lemons, make lemonade. As Teamguys, when Ramadi hands you a team of muj, make dead muj.

Luke gave the order to hold fire until the eight guys in our building could set up to engage. We would hit them simultaneously with a wall of lead. I watched them through my scope as Chris grabbed his gun and headed for the roof. All our guys scrambled to get into position quickly. Bob set up next to me with his Mk 48. A couple of the insurgents shot across the river while the others started setting up a mortar tube. As I waited for everyone to get set, my excitement grew with the thought of dropping the cleaver on these guys' necks. I remembered the night on the rooftop when Marc shook me out of my rack to help shoot the muj across the river. These guys were about to pay the man in full.

It took a minute or so to get in place, and then Luke gave the command over comms.

"Three, two, one, execute."

On the second syllable of *execute*, I squeezed the remaining slack out of the trigger on my Mk 11. I shot a guy in the neck and watched him crumple in a heap.

Never underestimate the neck shot.

I scanned for a second target and saw the life draining from the remaining fighters as Bob and the other gunners tore them up with a vicious onslaught of machine-gun fire while 40 mm "golden eggs" from Jeremy's M79 grenade launcher erupted loudly in massive dust plumes that swallowed up any life that might have remained. Within about three seconds, all five muj were dead, utterly ruined before they ever knew what hit them. Luke called cease fire over the radio, and all was quiet for a few seconds. Nothing moved from the dust below. Bob and I looked at each other with knowing smiles. I felt sated, like I'd just drunk my fill after hours of thirst.

"That was fucking awesome," I said.

"That might be the coolest thing I've seen yet," Bob replied, "besides the muj bus."

I looked out again at the muj lying dead. They lay out there all day in the summer heat, rotting. Better them than the Marines.

––––––––––––

At around two in the afternoon, I was lying on my back resting when I heard five shots come from the eastern house where the other half of our platoon was set up. There was about a half second in between each shot. Chris and I looked at each other. I got up and walked to the adjacent room.

"What the fuck's going on?" I asked Biff, our secondary comms guy.

"Jonny shot some guy who walked inside the compound, but he's not dead. They have to go get him."

"He shot five fucking times," I said. "How did he not kill him?"

Jason shrugged. "Asianvision."

"He's a sniper, right?!"

"Not today," Biff replied.

Because we actually adhere to the Geneva Conventions, and Article 12 requires we treat wounded combatants, Luke sent Jonny and EOD Nick to grab the guy and bring him inside. A couple of other guys and some Jundis provided security while Jonny and Nick ran outside and dragged him into their building. He was an old Iraqi man who had been pushing a wheelbarrow full of wires, bricks, and bomb-making materials. Jonny had been on his M4, watching the guy as he rolled up. He must not have zeroed his EOTech sight, because after five shots, Jonny managed to hit him only once in the shoulder and once in the left shin. He'd been using frangible rounds, which are designed to disintegrate when they come in contact with a surface harder than the bullet itself. When they hit flesh and bone, they behave very unpredictably. There was only a tiny hole near the guy's shoulder and not much blood. The bleeding was all internal. The round had taken a hard south turn and then hit some vital organs.

Luke, Marc, EOD Nick, and a bunch of Jundis gathered around watching as Jonny tried to save him. Jonny sweated profusely as he stripped the guy's man-dress down to find his anatomical landmarks. The guy's trachea started shifting, and Jonny had to do a needle decompression into his lung to try to save him. He sank the needle in, and a small whoosh of air came out when he pulled it. It took Jonny a minute to figure out the round had hit the descending aorta, and there was basically no chance for him. He died a few seconds later, and Jonny just kind of sat there for a few seconds, short of breath and sweating. Everyone was quiet.

Then the opening lines from Kansas's "Dust in the Wind" broke the silence: "I close my eyes, only for a moment and the moment's gone. . . ." Marc was singing.

Teamguy humor is dark because war is dark. Sometimes you need a laugh to get your head back in the game. All eyes turned to Marc, and we couldn't help but laugh.

"At least your singing is better than Jonny's shooting," EOD Nick said.

"Or his corpsman skills," Marc said. "I think you needled him to death, Jonny."

Everyone was laughing, but Jonny's somber look showed he was not amused, and he fired back, "Fuck all you guys," while packing up his med bag. Jonny was an excellent medic. He was more pissed about his shot placement than the futile attempt at saving the muj's life.

"I still gamble better than you, Marc. I'm Asian. It's math and I can at least count to eleven," Jonny replied. Laughter erupted.

Everyone stared at the body for a minute, realizing it couldn't just sit there in the middle of the hide site. Luke eventually made the call to put the body in the middle house—the one without air-conditioning. Because he had shot the guy, Jonny had to move him again. EOD Nick helped him, and everybody else went back to their positions.

The rest of the day was mostly uneventful. We didn't see the target-rich environment we'd been expecting from the Marines' assault on the hospital to our east, which started earlier that day. The head shed had hoped the assault would push a lot of retreating muj in our direction and we'd be able to take them out, but it didn't happen that way. The afternoon and evening were slow, and the biggest problem we faced was the need to conserve water for our second day of overwatch. Luke got on the horn and convinced the Marines we could do more good if we moved to the hospital that night.

Tony briefed us up on the plan. At midnight, we were going to move to another position inside the hospital and provide sniper overwatches there. The body was coming with us, and Jonny was going to carry him. The Marine leadership had told Luke he needed to clear out the buildings completely, and that included taking the dead muj with us and delivering him to the hospital. It really was the best thing to deliver him to the hospital and have a body to match the shooter statement. Nobody wants an investigation launched when some Iraqi civilian finds a body in a building with a couple of American rounds in it. And it wouldn't be beneath the muj to find a way to use it as a propaganda tool. Unfortunately for Jonny, the body had been cooking in the middle house for almost eight hours.

When it got close to launch time, we all consolidated in the eastern house, where I got a good look at the three-hundred-yard area we had to traverse. The seven-story hospital poked up prominently above the other buildings in the city to our south. Beyond our compound gate, there was an open field, stretching about two hundred yards to an east–west running road just before the hospital.

Right before we moved out, Tony told Jonny to get the dead guy and get ready to move. I swear I could hear the sound of Jonny's spirit breaking as he walked away to carry his prize. Under the cover of darkness, we left the house and moved tactically through the compound's gate with the first couple of guys pressing out left and right to set a footprint and hold security while the rest of the element rolled through. Jonny is a small guy and on top of his usual combat load, which includes sniper rifle and med bag, he had heaved the rotting muj onto his shoulder and was trying to run with him. The body was forcing Jonny's helmet down over his eyes. The poor guy couldn't see anything and was exhausted before we even got out of the gate. Ned, our third officer, gave Jonny a hand, and they made the mad dash through the field toward the hospital. I saw them in the middle of the platoon formation, awkwardly lugging the body, struggling to hold on to the guy's man-dress while their guns flapped all around.

"Dauber, give us a hand," Ned said.

"Fuck no," I said. "I didn't shoot that guy. I don't want anything to do with that. I'm not carrying that dirty muj."

When the patrol made it to the road, they stopped and put him down. Two hundred yards carrying almost two hundred pounds of dead weight was no joke, and as they sat there panting next to the muj, I thought about *Weekend at Bernie's* and almost laughed. The only thing missing was a pair of sunglasses for the dead guy. I know it's not really funny, but sometimes you just have to give in or go nuts.

We set security and pressed across the road, the dead guy tormenting Jonny and Ned the entire time. When we reached the hospital's perimeter, Jonny and Ned ran into yet another fuck-my-life moment. A wrought-iron fence surrounded the hospital, big spear-like spikes protruding about eight or nine feet high. We all had to get up and over that, and so did Desert Bernie. After a few of us got over, Jonny and Ned made a valiant heave, hoisting Bernie up and over feet-first, only to have his man-dress get caught on the fence. The fence pulled Bernie's dress over his head like a hockey player in a fight, and as he fell awkwardly against the fence on the other side, Bernie let out a death fart.

That was the moment I learned that a dead body farting is one of the most disgusting things you can ever smell, especially when it's a dead body that's been cooked for eight hours in a house with no AC in 130-degree heat. The smell was absolutely vile. I looked at Jonny and could tell it was almost too much for him. After shooting this guy, trying to save him, shepherding him across a few hundred yards of muj country, and then inhaling his death fart at close range, Jonny looked like he was ready to blow chunks. But he didn't. He held it together like a Frogman should.

"Want some Copenhagen?" I said.

He flicked me the bird.

We had done our duty with Bernie. We left him at the front door to the hospital and headed inside. The Marines said they needed help in the east wing, so we moved cautiously toward it. Even though the Marines had already cleared the building, we wanted to be careful. The hospital was huge, and the Marines had found a bunch of areas where the muj had been treating their people. We pressed into the east wing and set in our hide sites to provide overwatch for the Marines in the area. The fact that the place had so many windows meant better security for us because the muj didn't know where to shoot. We spent a day in the hospital, and Chris and Tony ended up getting one kill each. The Marines had assaulted the area in force, and met much less resistance than they had expected.

The next night, we left the same way we'd come. We opened the wrought-iron gate and headed toward the same road we'd crossed the night before. At the road, we set up security and moved tactically across. The road was on a berm that crested about ten feet above the hospital side and field to the north, and there was soft dirt on both shoulders. We set security on the near and far side, and the platoon moved across. Biggles and Tony picked up rear security, and as they began to cross, an Army unit shot at them. The soldiers had been holding security on the area and mistook Biggles for muj. He took cover, and we turned on our IFF markers (Identify Friend/Foe) to signal that we were friendly and could you please stop trying to kill us.

"Why the fuck are you shooting at us?" Rex barked into the radio at the Army unit.

I couldn't hear the response, but I have to assume it was something like "Whoops. Sorry." Thank God for poor marksmanship, I guess. We made our way back to the SURC-boat pickup, skipping the eighteen-foot wall, then to Hurricane Point and back to base. On the ride back to Sharkbase, we were all pretty tired, but Jonny looked like somebody had shit in his MRE.

"Hey, Jonny, are you going to head out to the range anytime soon?" Biggles asked.

"Why?" Jonny said.

"I was thinking you might help a lowly Pig gunner like me get better at shooting an M4," Biggles said.

"Carlos Hathcock couldn't help you, Biggles," Jonny said.

"Maybe help me with my medic skills," I said.

"Dumb Polack," Jonny retorted.

I joined in Biggles's laughter as we rumbled on in the back of Big Zev. I thought about Bernie and his wicked wheelbarrow of IED tricks. I looked to my left and heard Biff ragging Jonny about how bad he was at video games. Marc was smiling as he watched the banter. I was smiling, too. War can be terrible, but it has its moments.

"I promise you, Jonny," EOD Nick said above the hum of the diesel and groan of tires on the asphalt, "I'll drive the water taxi the next time we invade Vietnam." We all laughed. Even Jonny managed a chuckle.

ELEVEN

CHAINSAW MASSACRE

"A pint of sweat, saves a gallon of blood."
—George S. Patton

W E WERE ON our way to a land navigation exercise during work-up when Tony turned to me. "Dauba," he said nonchalantly, "you're on point. Get ya shit together."

"Roger that, Chief." Outwardly, I was calm. Inwardly, I was mildly panicked. Tony had just made me point for the entire platoon on our land navigation exercise, and I was a newguy. I was Charlie 13, as in "only take over if Charlies one through twelve are down."

We train for war. War is unpredictable. There was no reason why I might not step up and lead on the battlefield. I squared away my gear and led the platoon through the entire exercise.

"Stay sharp, Dauba," Tony said. "You gotta always stay sharp."

COP IRON, SOUTH RAMADI, EARLY JULY 2006

A year and a half before I landed in country, coalition forces launched the largest battle of the Iraq War in November 2004.

During Operation Phantom Fury, more than thirteen thousand troops from the United States, the United Kingdom, and Iraq isolated and surrounded the city of Fallujah. It had become a hotbed for the Sunni insurgency in Iraq's western province of Anbar, where Al Qaeda in Iraq set roots. The bloody offensive to wrest the enemy stronghold from the insurgents was fought house-to-house and block by block. It lasted more than six weeks, and when it was over the city was devastated.

The widespread destruction wrought during Phantom Fury led to a great deal of political backlash against the government of Iraq from the Iraqi people. After the insurgency fled Fallujah and dug its claws into Ramadi, the Iraqi government lacked the political will to launch a large-scale offensive to clear out the larger and more densely populated city. For that reason, General Richard Zilmer, who commanded the roughly thirty thousand American troops and coalition forces in Anbar Province, relied on a network of mutually supporting bases and combat outposts from which coalition forces could launch security and presence patrols. The long-game strategy was to clear and hold ground with the outposts spread throughout the city and eventually connect all the strategic dots.

After our adventures with the Marines north of Route Michigan, the Army requested us as forward support in a larger operation to extend the coalition footprint in southern Ramadi. The mission was to establish a command observation post, or COP (one of the strategic dots), at Ramadi's southern edge, about a kilometer east of the Habbaniyah Canal. With the newly established COP Iron as a foothold in the south, soldiers could establish a permanent security presence in the area and tighten the squeeze around the enemy.

Our head shed was always eager to extend our help into these areas for a multitude of reasons. They had a platoon of pipe hitters who were eager and capable of taking the fight to the enemy. Without Charlie Platoon's seasoned and levelheaded enlisted leadership to direct the course of operations on the ground, the head shed's demands would have been much more difficult to meet.

Our platoon chief, Tony, was on his ninth deployment. The Legend was on his third, as were Bob and Jeremy—these men were all enlisted. Luke, the ranking officer in the platoon, had done a three-month stint in Iraq before Ramadi, while Ralphie, Ned, and Guy were newguy officers—as new as me. It was really just a matter of simple math to show that experience levels favored the enlisted side of the house. Because of that, our enlisted leaders served as the vanguard in determining our success. Tony, Chris, and V were critical in the decision-making process when it came to choosing which missions were necessary and which were less so. On the officer side, Guy served as a levelheaded mediator and often had a better perspective from his angle at the TOC. In this particular case, the push to Springfield had larger, long-term implications. The call to move in came from the top.

Ramadi's southern edge was a very hostile environment. Other Special Operations assets had continually been shot off target there in the past. Our role in the operation was multifaceted. First, we conducted the main recon patrol to identify the best compound to strongpoint and use to establish a foothold. With an AC-130 gunship providing support from above, we patrolled on foot from a small outpost called ECP 3 about four kilometers from our target area. The recce (reconnaissance) patrol was pretty uneventful, just a sweaty walk through enemy territory to locate a compound to take over and build into a stronghold. We crossed the train bridge over the Habbaniyah Canal and skirted the railroad tracks along Ramadi's southern edge until we reached our target area. Tony and Chris had decided the most strategically advantageous compound was a building with a row of giant date palms surrounding the interior of its perimeter wall. Since the Springfield area was mostly residential buildings, the palm tree palace was the highest two-story building around. With our target building identified, we headed home to Sharkbase.

Two days later, the ECP parking lot buzzed with operators, Humvees, Bradleys, Strykers, and Iraqi tanks—all poised to pounce on the new COP we were going to secure. EOD Justin, our other bomb tech, the Legend, Guy, and I stared at a Jundi tanker struggling to control his vehicle. For a second, he looked almost cool, like some vato popping his hydraulics while cruising Hollywood. But the movement wasn't intentional. It was a result of the tanker's inability to drive his own tank, which is definitely not cool.

"No wonder they lost the fucking war," Justin said, rolling his eyes.

Without missing a beat, Guy chimed in, "Well, it doesn't bode well for the long-term future, either."

I nodded in agreement and spat out a Copenhagen dip. It was going to be a long, hot night. We were waiting to retrace our steps from the recce patrol two nights earlier. Our job was to secure the date-palm compound and set up a sniper overwatch and strongpoint position while the Army rolled in force with a bunch of tanks and armored vehicles. We patrolled in on foot across the train bridge, and then past the train station and on to our compound.

We brought our crypto-tech, Lurch, on this patrol. Lurch was able to provide situational awareness while we were on target. Lurch was about six-six and had played basketball at Maryland. He loved hip-hop and always had on a big pair of noise-canceling headphones. He is the only Navy crypto-tech I ever saw get a confirmed kill in Ramadi, when he took a shift on the gun during an overwatch mission and spotted a guy walking across the street with an AK slung on his shoulder.

"Should I shoot this guy?" Lurch had asked, hesitant. "He's got an AK on his shoulder, but I'm not sure if I should shoot him."

"He's got an AK, right?" Chucky said nonchalantly.

I was on my back, staring at the sky, sipping some water a few feet away.

"Yeah, but I'm not sure if—" The last bit of trigger slack that Lurch had been squeezing suddenly closed the distance, and a bullet cracked out of the gun, dumping the guy with the AK.

"Oh shit!" Lurch said.

I rolled over and looked through my binos. I saw the rifle next to a freshly dead guy.

"Dude, you shouldn't have shot him," Chucky said, fucking with Lurch's head. "It looks like he was just going for some groceries."

You could hear Lurch's ass snap shut. Then Chucky burst out laughing. Teamguy humor. Dark as always. First crypto-tech with a confirmed kill.

Lurch was all right.

The platoon began the slow trek to the target compound at 2200 that night. The night was ink black, minus the IR beam from the AC-130 gunship that glazed the landscape around us.

"Hey, Lurch," I said. "Know why I like patrolling next to you?"

"Because you love me?"

"Kind of. I love that you're a bigger target for the enemy to aim at."

"You're a dick," he replied. No sarcasm whatsoever.

"Leave him alone, Dauber," Guy piped in. "He's still struggling with the fact he smoked that guy getting groceries a few days ago."

Marc laughed as we stepped past the last Bradley and began the patrol to our date farm. We crossed the hundred-meter train bridge, circled under it, and headed east. Chris kept the patrol close to the berm to minimize our silhouette against the horizon. As we approached our target building, it became very apparent that I had neglected to adequately prepare for this op. It started as a slight headache and the realization I hadn't hydrated. The Copenhagen in my lip felt heavy and uncomfortably thick as my body looked for all the water it could get to cool down. By the time we reached our building, my head was pounding and I felt like a hot bag of shit that was ready to pop.

We sent the Jundis over the wall to let us in. Their training was beginning to pay off; we were in the compound within twenty seconds. Bob gave the main door a swift donkey kick, and we entered and cleared through quickly. The family consisted of an old couple in their seventies, two younger women, and their kids. The husbands—the military-age males—were missing. This arrangement was always suspect, and Moose started questioning the women.

"Where's your husband? Where did he go?" Moose asked in Arabic. He was always good at getting information from people quickly. He was even better than our intel assets when it came to questioning people and getting information. He was a truly top-notch terp and a solid operator.

The older woman was an invalid. She wore a black dress and was covered head to toe, save her face. While Moose questioned the younger women, the old woman went in the bathroom, where she lost control of her bowels. As she emerged, she began to crawl and writhe around on the floor downstairs like a half-crushed snail. She was like a human mop dipped in shit, painting the floor like a madman's canvas.

"This is fucking weird," Marc said to me.

"I've seen it all," Biggles commented as he pushed past to the roof.

The image heightened the feeling of nausea in my gut as my heart pounded heavy in my throbbing head. The world around me felt fuzzy, like I was moving in slow motion. I swallowed the residual Copenhagen and tried to keep my guts from ending up topside.

"Weird as fuck, and disgusting," I said, walking toward the stairs.

When I made it to the rooftop, I grabbed Jonny and made sure he saw my face, which was pale and sweaty.

"Jonny, you gotta do me a favor," I said. "I need an IV. I haven't pissed in hours. I have a crushing headache, and I feel like I'm gonna puke."

Jonny took one look at me and knew I was in a bad way. "Roger that, man."

The other Teamguys started blowing loophole charges and setting up their hides while Jonny hooked me up with an IV. With the catheter in my arm and the saline bag crudely hooked up above me, I took a knee next to the wall on the rooftop while Jonny went back to setting up his hide. I closed my eyes and continued to breathe deeply. In the quiet of the night, I cursed myself. I'd let myself become vulnerable. *Never again*, I thought. *Take a knee, drink a canteen of water, and stop being a pussy.*

It took about three minutes for the IV's saline solution to push through my veins, and when I stood up, I felt substantially better. I drank some water, popped four Motrin, threw in a dip, and got back to work.

Jonny looked over and laughed. "Fucking Polack meathead."

"If you're not smart, you might as well be tough."

"I see that works for you."

I had nothing. In this instance, he was right.

I looked through Jonny's loophole and saw the row of giant date palms obstructing the hell out of our view. This would not stand. Soon the Army was going to come rolling in with their tanks and armored vehicles, and we were supposed to cover their arrival. The area was rife with insurgents, and we couldn't provide effective overwatch without a clear view beyond the date palms. They were a perfect line of cover and concealment for any would-be muj assault force. The palms were going to have to go.

"Dauber, you done feeling sorry for yourself?" Tony asked.

I didn't think he had seen the IV.

"I'm good, Chief," I said.

"Good. Grab a gun and go with Chucky. You're gonna pull security for him while he cuts down those fahkin' trees."

It was standard operating procedure to carry a chainsaw and quickie saw on all our ops. Tony tasked Chucky to cut down all ten of the giants. At the time, none of us really thought about the fact that these date palms were probably at least one hundred years old, that they were probably somebody's source of food and/or liveli-hood, that they probably meant a lot to the people who lived there.

But this was muj country. The trees were coming down.

I grabbed an Mk 48 and headed downstairs to meet up with Chucky. As I approached, he jumped up and grabbed the chainsaw at-tached to the Alice pack frame, slinging it up on his shoulder.

"You ready to murder some trees, Dauber?"

"Let's do this," I said.

We headed outside, and I set up next to one of the trees to scan the area for any sign of bad guys. Chucky ripped the cord on the chainsaw and it buzzed to life, obliterating the quiet of the early morning and loudly announcing our presence to everyone in the area. As he tore into the first tree, sawdust spat toward me. Chucky, being a cheese-head from Wisconsin, was right at home on the saw. He really put his back into it as he pushed the chainsaw through the fat trunk of the mighty palm over the course of about a minute or two until the tree fi-nally made a cracking sound and fell hard to the ground, landing in a loud crash.

"Man, this is kind of like being back on the farm back home," Chucky whispered to me after his first kill. "Home, home on the range, Dauber."

"Try not to have too much fun," I said. "Every muj within a thou-sand meters knows we're out here now. Just hurry up."

We walked from date palm to date palm in the middle of night, and Chucky excitedly brutalized each one of the trees as if they were his mortal enemy. He wore just a T-shirt with his body armor and hel-met, and his shoddily drawn tattoo of a skull with scorpion legs almost looked like an octopus. The image of Chucky looking all wild-eyed and drunk on chainsaw lust in his T-shirt and body armor reminded me of Animal Mother from *Full Metal Jacket*.

"So, Dauber, how does the platoon corpsman forget to hydrate?"

Chucky asked after the third tree. "Isn't that, like, a pretty big no-shitter?"

"Yeah, man. What can I say, I'm too worried about your well-being to think of myself."

"Good to hear," he said, charging up the chainsaw for his next victim.

We got through all ten trees within about an hour and some change. When it was done, we looked at the gaggle of felled palms strewn about the compound, then at each other.

"Combat chainsaw," Chucky said proudly.

We nodded and headed back inside.

Back on the rooftop, Jonny and I traded time on the gun and didn't see much of anything in terms of targets or threats. It was, as usual, oven hot. Before 0800, the Bradleys, Abrams, and APCs began their slow drive over to Springfield. The push had come, but the day was otherwise a standard sniper overwatch where the enemy didn't want to play.

Eventually, I took a nap. When I woke I looked through our loop-hole and saw a Bradley Fighting Vehicle's main gun pointing right at us. The cavalry was all around. The next phase of building up the COP was already starting. Our job as tip of the spear was done.

Despite my brief bout of combat ineffectiveness from dehydra-tion, I felt all right about the op until word came over the radio that an ANGLICO (Air Naval Gunfire Liaison Company) Marine we'd worked with on previous missions had been killed when he popped up to return fire on a rooftop a kilometer from our hide.

He'd taken a round right to the head.

War has a way of pushing and pulling your psyche in different di-rections. Just as I was trying to put the dehydration out of my mind, Ramadi gave me another sobering reminder that the enemy is ev-erywhere all the time. You may not see him, but the danger is always there.

With all the armor in the area, we didn't even wait until nightfall to patrol back. We skirted the low side of the train bridge, and as we came around the bridge, I snapped a picture of Marc. He was carrying his Mk 48 in his signature style as if it were an extension of himself. He never wore a sling with his gun. Instead he just heaved it around with ease. The photo has always been one of my favorite pictures of Marc.

Securing COP Iron was a big deal for the Army. It was in a hairy part of Ramadi, and the Army was grateful for our help in making the op go smoothly. I read about the operation in *Stars and Stripes* a couple of days later. It was a good write-up, save the part where the Army said they used Navy SEALs along with Iraqi snipers. That made for a good laugh, since I'd never laid eyes on an Iraqi sniper. The whole thing was good press for the Army, and, more important, having a footprint in the southern end of the city was going to allow us to move through the middle and southeast. Just another op in Ramadi where both flora and fauna paid the price.

TWELVE

23 IN 24

"In war there is no substitute for victory."
—Douglas MacArthur

B EFORE 2006, THE best summer of my life was the single summer I spent in college. I was supposed to be in summer
school, trying to make up for my poor performance my first two semesters and earn enough credit to creep my way out of freshman year.
Instead, I played rugby, tossed horseshoes, drank a lot of beer, and
made the occasional appearance in an academic building. When the
summer ended, I was still a freshman according to the dean of students
at James Madison University.

Many people hear about the Battle of Ramadi, about what we did
there and the things that happened, and tell me they're sorry. Their
apologies, though well intentioned, normally make me angry. The
summer I spent in Ramadi was the watershed of my young adult life.
What most people don't understand is that I would give back that
summer in Harrisonburg in a heartbeat, but it's never occurred to me
to wish I hadn't gone to Ramadi.

COP FALCON, SOUTH-CENTRAL RAMADI, JULY 2006

After having a lot of success north of Route Michigan, the Army wanted to push farther into south-central Ramadi to establish a command observation post from which coalition forces could launch operations and further secure the district. The location the Army commanders chose for COP Falcon—as it would come to be known— was a compound at the corner of Sunset and Baseline Roads. Sunset runs north–south about a half mile east of the Habbaniyah Canal, and Baseline runs east from Sunset toward the Ma'Laab district in Ramadi's southeast. Our platoon was tasked as the main reconnaissance element for the Army's operation to secure Falcon. Our objective's proximity to the canal afforded another opportunity for a riverine insertion.

We started the op around 2000, trucking to Camp Hurricane Point under the cover of darkness to meet up with the Marine SURC-boat unit again. This was one of our few ops with no Jundis, and as the Marines nosed their boats into the water, our sixteen-man platoon piled in and packed it up tight. I took up a position with my Mk 11 toward the front of the boat. I had the suppressor elastic banded to my web gear to cut down on the length and weight of the gun. I slung one arm out of my ruck, sitting in a half crouch and pointing my gun out at the bank. Marc set up next to me with his Mk 48. He swatted at a mosquito on his neck.

"I really need to remember to bring bug juice for these riverine ops," he said.

"It doesn't really help," I said. "These mosquitos don't give a fuck. They're going to get theirs." I swatted at one buzzing next to my ear.

I packed a dip of Copenhagen as the boats rumbled to life and headed west on the Euphrates. We made the turn south down the canal and then passed under the bridge that extends Route Michigan into the city. The slow rumble of the engine cut the water smoothly as I watched the sleeping city pass grainy-green in my night vision. Our guns were equipped with Advanced Target Pointer/Illuminator/Aiming Lasers (ATPIALs), and they projected infrared lines of glowing green that danced around on the horizon. SURC boats are armed with two miniguns—one on each side—and a .50-cal on the back. Miniguns are six-barreled rotary machine guns and a pretty mean piece of ordnance. Our pace was just slow enough that the wind cutting past us provided no noticeable relief from the mid-July heat and sauna-like humidity. I spat toward the water and watched a line of dip spit fall on the boat's wall in front of me. The scenery changed from small buildings to reeds and palms, and finally to the structures that indicated we were entering the belly of the city. I rechecked the safety on my weapon.

We approached our insertion point in the city's south-central region, rumbling up toward a grove of trees and low grass. We hit the bank and exited quickly, fanning out and setting security. After a quick pause, we got into a single-column formation and moved out. Chris was on point with Biggles next in line, then Luke, Rex, me, and Marc. We moved slowly and stealthily, applying the same maxim we used while clearing buildings: slow is smooth; smooth is fast. We were in no rush to get there. No one is a fan of running to his death.

As we patrolled through the trees, I strained to see in the shadows, anticipating the muj who might be waiting to light us up. We reached an intersection and Chris gave the signal to halt. We took a knee and set security before moving across and into the city's ravaged streets. Chris passed back the signal to break into a dual-column formation. This provided cross-cover with each column watching its opposing rooftops. After a couple of blocks, the street narrowed and Chris signaled for us to funnel back to a single column. Suddenly, the smell of human shit smashed me in the face like a frying pan. About fifty yards in front of us was a canal of raw sewage. Shit creek. On one deployment, a SEAL buddy of mine actually fell into one of Iraq's shit creeks and was submerged in raw sewage for a few seconds. He became violently ill for several days.

Internally, I cursed the engineers who had conjured up the shit creeks, when the signal came back to freeze. Everyone silently took a knee. Several seconds passed and then three shots rang out from the front of the platoon. Then the signal came to move out with quickness. We ran, and I saw the first few guys make their way across the flimsy two-by-six that served as the shit creek's walking bridge. I rushed across carefully. Up ahead, Chris put three security rounds in a body laid out on the ground just off our path. He was already dead, but since there was an AK next to him, the Legend was just making sure. As I ran past, I looked down and saw a skinny muj in a blue tracksuit and tank top with a red and white wrap around his neck. His face had been mostly blown off, but I caught the sight of a giant pair of horse teeth, which I assumed were his front incisors. I could count at least three shots right to the (eyes-nose) triangle. An AK-47 lay on the ground next to him. Apparently, he was waiting to ambush another patrol as we approached. He had picked the wrong spot and the wrong time, to say the least.

Our target building was only about one hundred yards up, and I could see the eight-foot wall surrounding it as we approached the corner of Sunset and Baseline. We peeled left and right, stacking up on the wall to hold security while the rest of the platoon got in position. Marc and I hoisted Chris and Biggles up and over, and they unlocked the large main gate, which was big enough for a car to drive through. We flooded inside and Marc and I cleared to the left side of the building. It was about twenty feet wide and sixty deep. We busted through the front door and into an airy and empty front room. Our train swept through the building while a few guys cleared the half acre around the outside. Empty and clear. We all took a breath.

Those of us in the assault element headed to the rooftop to set up. We were all curious about what had gone down with the dead muj on our approach.

"Chris, what happened, man?" Jonny asked quietly. "Did you get a-fucking-nother one?"

"Hell no," he said in his Texas twang. "I saw the guy creepin', but my fuckin' ATPIAL shit the bed on me. Luke comes up; I'm like, 'Gimme a battery.' He's like, 'no.' And then he shot the dude."

"Gimme a fucking battery?" I said condescendingly. "In the middle of an op? Shit should have been squared away before we took off, man. Even the Legend has to PMS his gear, brother. Guess you let that one slip away."

"Well, how many motherfuckers you killed?" he said defensively. "Besides, you gotta let Luke get one once in a while. Officers need all the help they can get."

"Sounds like something the Myth would say," I shot back.

"Yeah, yeah, I got yer myth right here. By the way, Dauber, no more Copenhagen for you," Chris said.

"I guess you're right, Legend. I need to cut back. Don't want my grill looking like that Horse Teeth motherfucker you shot back there," I quietly quipped.

Chris smiled. "Fucking Dauber. Always some smart-ass shit to say."

"I love you too, Legend," I replied.

From the top of the building we could see clearly in every direction. The Army, with the recommendation from our recce patrol a few nights before, had specifically chosen the building for that reason. It was optimally located in that part of the city. I set up looking up Baseline Road to the north and attached the suppressor to my Mk 11. Chris set up facing east down Baseline with his .30-cal, and within a matter of minutes that lucky bastard shot a muj placing an IED at four hundred yards.

"Mother. Fucker," I mumbled to myself.

"Looks like you put some batteries in that weapons system," I said quietly.

"Yup," Chris said. "I think I got Horse Teeth's buddy."

We both enjoyed a laugh.

With our building secured and the surrounding area covered by SEAL snipers, it was time to call in the cavalry. Around midnight, the Army's main assault element rumbled down Sunset. At least thirty or forty tanks and Bradley Fighting Vehicles were rolling in force to establish a permanent presence around the newly christened COP Falcon compound. Things were about to get very boring. The Army's tanks and Bradleys surrounded the compound, locking down Baseline, Sunset, shit creek to the west, and the area to our south. We were suddenly smack in the middle of a highly protected security perimeter with nothing to do but sit there, sweating. Knowing we weren't going to get much action if we stayed put, Luke got on the horn with the Army to try to find us some work.

"Good luck finding targets with an entire armored division down there," I said to Chris and Jonny. "It's gonna take Luke a while to finish tickling the Army officers' balls. It's time for some rack ops."

"Maybe he could borrow some batteries from the Legend to power his radio and make the call," EOD Nick added.

Chris kept his eyes on his scope, clearly unamused by our banter.

By the time I woke up from a power nap, we had gotten the go-ahead to press forward and set up in another building outside COP Falcon's perimeter. Tony got everyone together and briefed the plan. Chris had identified a four-story apartment complex—perfect for sniping—about four hundred meters east on Baseline. We were going to patrol up, secure it, set up sniper hides, and kill any muj trying to ambush the COP. Another day at the office.

We patrolled out in a single column. At the edge of the Army's security perimeter, two tanks sat at an intersection, engines rumbling and guns trained to the north and east. The tank commanders' heads poked out from the top hatches like turtles from their shells. The Army's Abrams tanks use a weird type of fuel, and as we walked between them, I inhaled a hot blast of tank exhaust. It felt like Ramadi blowing a disgusting burp in my face—an angry breath from the rotten guts of a diseased city. We walked along crumbling sidewalks in the shadows of war-scarred buildings, and Baseline stretched before us into the distant blackness of the Ma'Laab to the east.

At the target building, those of us not in the assault team fanned out in a hasty security perimeter while the breachers moved into place. They quietly cut a lock on the compound's gate and assaulted in. The rest of us peeled off in trail. There were at least ten rooms on each floor, and we cleared the whole place quietly, calling our status over the radio as we progressed through. The building was completely abandoned, save the occasional prayer rug, bedding, and trash. Once again, I headed up to the roof with the other snipers. With the cover of darkness, we could stand up and get a good look over the wall around the rooftop at the real estate before us. Chris and I found a spot looking east that provided an unobstructed view of J Street for more than a kilometer. Chucky came up and blew two loophole charges in the wall on the east side and one on the south. Chris and I set up behind one of the holes looking east. EOD Justin set up with an Mk 48 on the hole to our right. Jonny set up looking south, and Marc, Spaz, and Ralphie set up watching the north. With COP Falcon behind us to the west, our six o'clock was well covered.

By seven in the morning, I had begun to develop a gnarly case of swamp ass. Marc had come by a few minutes before, and the reading on his Suunto watch said 119 degrees. Some people will tell you desert heat is dry heat. My ass on that four-story building would tell you those people are full of shit. Despite the heat, I had a view of about 1,200 meters in which to engage, and I was feeling pretty good about our position. Chris and I had set up a wood pallet to perch on and added some prayer rugs for support. I had a poncho liner strung overhead to block the sun and provide some protection for my Polack skin. Being in the middle of Indian country, I expected to get the jump on some unsuspecting muj. I was ready for some work.

The morning call to prayer sounded angry. It took me back to SERE (Survival, Evasion, Resistance, Escape) school, where I sat caged up in a box, listening to similar music, looking forward to being in this position. The street was a normal beehive of activity, but I'd seen nothing of interest since the sun breached the horizon. My focus hadn't flinched since I lased my reference points, checked my dope card, and packed a chaw. Behind the gun, a focused mind equals success. Boredom is the main cause of missed opportunity. Like in deer hunting, any subtle movement on my part might catch my prey's eye. My pool of Copenhagen spit began to threaten my prayer rug, but I ignored it. I remained fixed, scanning the street from near to far.

Then I saw him.

He was only two hundred yards away, and my scope provided a crystal-clear view. A middle-aged man with short, graying black hair, a widow's peak, and a thin beard walked out of his compound and locked the gate behind him. A crude satchel sagged awkwardly over his brown man-dress as he ambled my way.

"You got him, Dauber?" Chris asked.

I grunted an assent. He slid the satchel around to his front. The clear imprint of a 155 mm artillery round was unmistakable as I repositioned the cheek weld on my Mk 11. I felt the epinephrine pump through my arteries and hit the receptor sites like a freight train.

Ride the lightning.

Whether it's your first, third, or seventeenth kill, the excitement never fades. I controlled my breathing. The external temperature seemed to climb with my heart rate as he approached a hole in the middle of the road about 120 yards in front of me. The reticle began to settle as he crouched at the hole, pulled the IED out of the satchel, and dropped it in the hole.

As a professional warrior—a steward of the American flag—you operate under a strict set of guidelines. My rules of engagement were clear. Hostile action or hostile intent were the behaviors for which I could kill an insurgent. The presentation of the artillery round left no doubt. I felt the switch as my breathing deepened and my heart slowed even more. I felt every muscle in my body relax as I tightened the slack in the match-grade trigger of my Mk 11. The muj stood, looking up in my direction, and from behind a pair of binoculars, Chris said, "Dump him."

I hit my respiratory pause as the hammer dropping caught me by surprise. The bullet barked out of the rifle at 2,900 feet per second, tearing through the man's solar plexus. The kick from a suppressed Mk 11 is virtually nonexistent, so my reticle never left the target.

Snipers often talk about seeing the "pink mist" when we shoot someone. Pink mist is the spray of blood and matter exiting your target when your round impacts. This shot was definitely a pink-mist moment. I saw everything. His body buckled violently like a bear trap slamming shut. It looked almost like he kissed his toes before going down hard in a heap. I felt my senses go into overdrive as the adrenaline began to fire through my arteries again, and I immediately scanned for more targets. It was an easy shot. A blind man could have made it using a toilet paper roll as a scope. Regardless, it was a good kill and a great way to start our day on four-story.

It was a testament to our tactics and our ability to predict the enemy's response to our huge incursion into their territory. Knowing they couldn't mount a serious attack against COP Falcon's perimeter and a bunch of tanks and Bradleys, the muj settled for mining the areas just outside the COP's perimeter and trying to prevent the Army from pressing deeper into the district. The muj expected to see new American patrols pushing through the streets very soon. They were on a mission to mine the roads as much as possible, so stifling those efforts was pure satisfaction as a sniper. Each guy that I killed lessened the probability that an American soldier would be killed or maimed on patrol. I've seen the carnage from a 155 mm round that finds an American patrol. Preventing that outcome was incredibly rewarding. Knowing you're literally protecting somebody else in that way is a feeling unmatched by any other.

Chris's Texas drawl snapped me out of the zone.

"Why didn't you keyhole his eye?"

In my head, I said, *Are you fucking kidding me? The guy's dead. I just killed a terrorist. It doesn't matter where I shot him. He's fucking dead.* In reality, my grin flattened a little. What else could I expect from the Legend? Any other person making that comment would have drawn a snarky response from my twenty-four-year-old invincible ass. But Chris's acumen as a sniper was well established. I took his comment as a reminder to not get cocky. My rationale had been that center mass was less risky than a head shot, but Chris's words reminded me that there was always a tougher shot and there would be plenty more opportunities to take them.

I watched the muj's buddies as they threw ropes out from behind a wall, trying to get the dead man to grab on. Finally they came out with a white flag and collected up the body.

This exchange always killed me. They're collecting a muj, but they're muj, too. Because they have a white flag and no weapons, I have to watch through my scope and let them live. I have to do this knowing they would not extend me the same courtesy. Later, they will try to kill me. I will try to kill them first.

I sat on the gun for about another hour. I felt good, and my mind wandered to thoughts of newguy glory: I have three kills behind the gun—more than any other newguy. I just smoked this dude on J Street. This is going to be a great hideout. At about eight in the morning, I switched out with Chris on the gun and kicked back to take a nice rest and revel in the glory of my sweet kill.

Chris was on the gun for about an hour before he shot a guy. When he shot the second one a few minutes later, I was lying on my back, sweating buckets. I told myself maybe Chris was somehow bull-shitting me on the second one. I rolled over and grabbed the binoculars and watched Chris's sector for a while. After a few minutes, a muj with an AK-47 darted across the street at about three hundred yards. Chris shot him effortlessly. Every time I heard Chris take another shot and kill a muj, I'd think, *Fuck. Another one, really?* It's frustrating as a Teamguy because your competitive edge kicks in and you want to know how anyone can be that lucky. You want to be the one on the gun.

"Do you have a fucking AK painted on your reticle or something, you lucky bastard?" I asked sarcastically.

"Don't hate me because I'm beautiful, Dauber."

I just shook my head and grabbed an empty water bottle to piss into. When I was done, I tightened the lid and set the bottle next to two others, noticing the distinct progression in color from dark yellow, to even darker yellow, to amber. It was easily more than 120 degrees, and it was time to check on the guys in my capacity as a medic. The piss-bottle spectrum played out similarly at every position. Everybody looked beat down by the sun. *These guys are so dehydrated right now,* I thought. I told Luke we needed a water resupply if we were going to keep killing bodies on the rooftop.

Luke selected Marc, me, and Biff for a hasty resupply mission. At around eleven, we patrolled four hundred meters back to the COP, leapfrogging the whole way. We eagerly pounded two bottles of water each before filling a 120-gallon white cooler with ice and water. Then the four of us ran it back to four-story, heaving the awkward beast along through the streets, hoping speed would make up for our tactical disadvantage of being a patrol of only four and carrying a loaded ice chest through Ramadi in broad daylight.

Two of our boys waited at the door and two more popped out to hold security as we fumbled up to the building, running inside and dumping the chest heavily on the ground. We smiled as we sat catching our breath for a moment. The guys who were not on watch started trickling downstairs to grab cold waters. I grabbed several and delivered them to some of my guys on the roof. I set a couple of bottles next to Chris.

"You get any more?" I asked.

"A few," he said. "I counted ten total."

Four hours on the gun, and Chris had ten kills. I had one. Jonny had one, too. I just shook my head.

"Well, get your ass out of the way. It's my turn."

Chris and I had agreed to just leave his bolt-action .30-cal in place because switching out rifles was a hassle. We were about the same size, so our eye relief and shoulders matched up on the gun. From noon to two, I didn't see much. I took a shot at a guy at around eight hundred meters and missed. The midafternoon heat was brutal, and I was frustrated, so I gave the gun to Chris a little after two. He spent the next three hours behind the gun and shot at least seven more muj.

Son of a bitch.

"You know I hate you, right?" I said as Chris got up to switch out again.

"I know, Dauber. I'd hate me, too." He sat up and slapped me on the shoulder. "Don't worry, son. Someday your balls will drop."

Fucking Teamguys.

———

It was about five o'clock, and I was determined to find another target. I had to wait about an hour before a peeker obliged me. Peekers usually leave no doubt as to their hostile intent, but hostile intent is always more of an ethical hurdle for a sniper than clear-cut hostile action like the behavior for which I'd killed the man placing the IED. When you watch a peeker, in the back of your mind you're thinking, *If this isn't justified, I could really fuck myself.* Every shot has to be a good target, so you never shoot until you're sure. A curious little kid looking around a building after hearing gunfire nearby looks very different from a military-age male between sixteen and fifty trying to collect information. When somebody nervously creeps their eyes around a corner while talking into a cell phone, they're usually gathering and reporting information on American positions. Insurgents often used cell phones to coordinate attacks, so seeing peekers with phones always made us especially cautious. If someone was gathering intel on our position, we could shoot them. Those were our rules of engagement. The first peek around a corner is a try. A second peek confirms, and a third peek gets a round in the face.

At four hundred meters out I could see into a small courtyard with a couple bushes and some pillars on the front porch of a house. Behind the pillars, a bearded, black-haired man dressed in the standard muj attire of Adidas track pants and T-shirt was looking around one of the pillars with a cell phone pressed to his ear. I saw him look up in our direction, thinking we couldn't see him. He pulled back behind the pillar for a moment and then looked out again, still talking into the cell phone held to his ear. I thought, *He's either calling in our position to a mortar team, or he's working with another group to pull off a coordinated attack.* He disappeared momentarily and then looked out one last time, cocking his head and stretching his neck while holding the phone away from his ear. I settled my crosshairs just a little high at the top of his head, accounting for the 100-meter difference between my scope's elevation setting (300 meters) and the actual distance (400 meters).

Then I hit him.

The round tore through his right cheekbone and practically took his face off. I didn't see him fall because the kick from the .30-cal knocked my sight picture off, but I quickly tracked back on him in time to watch him buckle and fall on the sidewalk. Justin was looking out with binoculars through the loophole to my right.

"Can I get a witness from the congregation, Justin," I said to Justin. I didn't want to wake Chris. He hadn't slept since we landed to start our foot patrol to COP Falcon.

"Yeah, I got him," he replied. "He's fucking dead on the sidewalk. I think he looks better with that face-lift you gave him."

I cycled the bolt on the gun. I picked up the brass and put it in my pocket with the shell casing from the layup shot earlier. Easy money. I was feeling good again, and I went back to scanning for targets. We spent the entire day on that rooftop, dealing death. When we finally packed up to leave, Chris, Jonny, and I had racked up twenty-three kills.

"Battle is the most magnificent competition in which a human being can indulge. It brings out all that is best; it removes all that is base. . . . Duty is the essence of manhood." I thought about the quote from General Patton as I continued to scan the street for the rest of the evening. Whether the Legend thought my nuts had dropped or not was the least of my worries. I was in combat and that's all that mattered to me. I thought about the poor sons of bitches back in their college dorms, playing video games about the stuff we were doing on a daily basis. College felt like a lifetime ago and I wasn't looking back.

I was feeling extremely satisfied as we patrolled back to COP Falcon in the dark that night. Soldiers and vehicles distributed HESCO and Jersey barriers around the perimeter of the burgeoning COP as we approached, and about a block away from our main entry point, a wrecker truck was hooking up a mangled MRAP, still smoking from the IED blast that had chewed up its entire front end. The troop compartment with its V-shaped hull had worked like it was supposed to and deflected the blast away, protecting the soldiers inside. Nevertheless, the sight put a damper on the high I was feeling after a windfall day. I really did not want to die from an IED blast. One bad day is all it takes. When we walked inside the building we'd secured the night before, the Army was filling sandbags, the most basic defense we had against blasts. I gave Marc and Biggles a what-the-fuck look. We dropped our rucks and started moving sandbags upstairs. War never sleeps.

THIRTEEN

TWO-FOR

"And five of you shall chase a hundred, and a
hundred of you shall chase ten thousand; and your
enemies shall fall before you by the sword."

—Leviticus 26:8

A S LONG AS there have been guns, there have been men
trying to make long-range shots. While the term *sniper* was not
coined until the early nineteenth century, forms of sniping existed as
early as the Battle of Saratoga in 1777, when American rifleman Timo-
thy Murphy shot and killed British general Simon Fraser at a distance
of roughly four hundred yards. Sharpshooters became increasingly important as wars waged on over the next centuries, using their skills to
take out the enemy's most important assets.

In the United States, however, Americans were slow to accept
this form of killing on the battlefield, and at first grudgingly acknowledged it during wartime only. For its first two hundred years of existence, the United States did not train or develop snipers in peacetime,
due to the "ungentlemanly" nature of such tactics. Eventually, by

1 5 6   KEVIN LACZ

Vietnam, the necessity for well-trained snipers was clear and this thinking reversed.*

There are many rumors and myths about an officer's inability to attend Sniper School or to be a sniper, supposedly a holdover grudge from the days when snipers shot officers exclusively. I never met a sniper-qualified officer, but I'm sure it has more to do with the other duties an officer has that would keep him out of a sniper hide than with a regulation barring him from Sniper School. What I can tell you without reservation is that for only having started training fifty years ago, it sure didn't take the American snipers long to catch up.

COP FALCON, MID-JULY 2006

COP Falcon quickly became "COP Misery." The place earned the nickname as our leadership gravitated to it as the new front in the never-ending mission to rid the city of the terrorist infestation. After securing the initial compound, the COP grew steadily to almost a quarter of a city block. The Army set up HESCO and Jersey barriers all around the perimeter and carved out a huge parking lot right on top of shit creek. I couldn't help but appreciate the humor of that decision. What a perfect way to say "Welcome to COP Falcon."

Securing and building up the COP (aka clearing and holding it) was the initial phase of the push into the Al Hawz and Al Mualemeen districts in southwest Ramadi. Of course, the real strategic prize wasn't COP Falcon itself. The COP simply provided a base of operations for clearing the surrounding area of insurgents and holding all that ground indefinitely.

Basically, every unit in Ramadi was playing an elaborate game

---

* Michael Lee Lanning, *Blood Warriors: American Military Elites* (New York: Random House, 2002), 235–36.

of Whac-A-Mole, but our task unit had emerged as one of the fiercest hammers in the game. With plenty of moles to crush around the COP, our head shed was eager to keep us on the smash as much as possible. Falcon became the place Charlie Platoon went to find work, like the parking lot where migrant workers gather, hoping to be hired for a day's labor. The head shed would take us down there to link up with the Army or Marines, and we never had a hard time getting hired. The districts teemed with muj, and asking a ground commander if he wants to employ a SEAL platoon is like asking a gearhead if he wants to drive your new Lamborghini. Our officers were always eager to please and jumped on every mission they could get. The more we worked, the more we killed. And the more we killed, the better it looked. Our op tempo was pretty exhausting before COP Falcon, and it ratcheted up even more as the southern outpost became our primary base of operations: COP Misery.

Just getting from Sharkbase to Falcon and back was a risky operation, which we ran frequently. As a main artery road into the southern districts, Sunset was riddled with IEDs. Running from north to south, Sunset connected Route Michigan with Baseline Road. Route clearance was an endless mission for the Army engineers, whom we knew by the call sign "Dagger." The muj had mastered the art of the stealthy IED drop, and the sheer volume of the crude bombs and craters to drop them into created for Dagger an endless cycle that could have been aptly named Operation Groundhog Day. If Dagger had recently swept and cleared the route, Sunset's status was green. If Sunset was black, that meant the IEDs had returned like angry weeds, and the road was to be avoided. We had to plan our ops accordingly, and sometimes the work we found at Falcon was in direct response to IED attacks.

Early in our support of COP Falcon, the Army tasked us to provide sniper overwatch support while they extracted the remains of some tankers who'd been killed in an attack on Sunset. The possibility that the muj would drag the remains of the Americans off target and parade them around on Al Jazeera was very real. Our mission was to prevent that possibility until the Army could launch a full recovery. The mangled tank's hatch was still smoldering, and I realized that my war could be worse. We were crushing the enemy, doing a job we wanted to do. At least we had that. We could be shoveling shit in Louisiana.

A few days after the recovery mission, I found myself in a position to get some retribution for the soldiers killed in the tank. I was behind the gun on an overwatch in the southwest corner of the city when a man walked into the middle of the road about two hundred yards out and started digging. When someone has a bunch of equipment and is digging a hole in the road in Ramadi in the middle of the day, it's pretty obvious why they're doing it. I was fairly certain shooting him would be well within the rules of engagement, but I made the mistake of asking an officer to confirm the man's status as a bona fide bad guy. Our assistant OIC, Ralphie, was in the room when I saw the guy. Ralphie was a likable guy we used to razz for being a baby-faced beanpole.

"Hey, Ralphie, see what he's doing? Legit?"

"Let me see," he responded before getting on the gun. I watched him adjust the scope, thinking he was just getting a better look. I tried to calm the itch in my trigger finger and be patient when the loud crack of a shot rang next to my ear. I looked up and saw the muj, unscathed and sprinting away in a blur of assholes and elbows. Not only had Ralphie taken the shot himself, but he'd missed badly from just two hundred yards.

"What the fuck, dude?" I said.

"He was a bad guy."

"Well, why didn't you fucking hit him?" I said, incredulously. "Gimme my gun."

Looking through the scope, I scanned the area and saw a bullet hole in a telephone pole off to the right of where the muj had been.

Ralphie had jerked the trigger and missed badly. *Keep it to the Power-Points,* I thought. Our retribution would have to wait.

In mid-July, the Marines cleared an area around a college campus about a half mile north of Falcon and a few blocks west of Sunset. There was a lot of IED activity on the roads around the campus, and we were tasked to provide overwatch support in the area and help the Marines hold the ground they'd taken. We left Falcon on foot around midnight and patrolled up Sunset. The fact that the route was green for our convoy from Sharkbase a few hours earlier brought me little comfort as we patrolled up the scarred and malignant avenue. During the day, the area was a bustling commercial district, and the wide street accommodated overhangs from markets that hummed with activity. At night, the markets slept, locked away behind wrought-iron gates that collected ominous shadows.

Chris slid to the side of the concertina wire that blocked the vehicle entrance of COP Falcon on Sunset Road. The patrol began its movement northward in silence with head count passed visually from the rear. I pointed the neon green of my infrared laser into the blackness behind the gates, ready for any ambush that might materialize. We had trained our eyes to pick up the slightest movement. We pressed up Sunset to the target building like a leopard stalking an antelope, moving from cover to cover, not a sound audible.

As we neared our target building, the markets tapered off, giving way to an appropriate battlefield landmark. On the right side of the road, a massive cemetery sprawled out toward the east. The mausoleums, tombs, and gravestones offered numerous places to hide and cast dark shadows across Sunset. The fact that graveyards at night carry a certain psychological connotation goes without saying. Knowing that Charlie Platoon personally added to the tally of inhabitants of that graveyard was pure satisfaction.

What a lot of people don't know is that a very bloody battle was fought in an Iraqi cemetery during the Battle of Najaf in August 2004. I had read a detailed account of the battle between Marines from the 11th Marine Expeditionary Unit and Shia insurgents from Muqtada al-Sadr's Mahdi Army in the Wadi al-Salam Cemetery—one of the largest and oldest cemeteries in the world. The Marines ultimately killed hundreds of insurgents when they assaulted through a tight maze of catacombs and tombs filled with Mahdi Army fighters. Four Marines were killed, and dozens were wounded in the assault. While it's fair to say the Marines handed the Mahdi Army their asses in that cemetery, a graveyard is still not my ideal setting for a firefight. There are far too many places for the enemy to hide and catch you by surprise, and cemeteries are often deemed "exclusion zones" for artillery or other indirect fires. Muj rarely did everything I wanted them to do, though. When you hunt the enemy, you go where he goes.

Our target building was inside a small compound directly across from the graveyard. It was very compact. The platoon quickly locked down the intersections as we sent the assault element to gain entry. Moose and the Jundis did a soft knock and got us inside quickly. In a matter of forty-five seconds, the "target secure" call came across comms. As we corralled up the family, we discovered they were pleasantly "un-muj-like" compared to some of the other families we'd interacted with. In fact, they were fairly accommodating. They quickly welcomed us into their house and turned on the AC. Instantly, a cool blast of climate-controlled air hit me.

Air-conditioning. God is great.

The only man in the house was in his fifties or sixties, and his haggard, sun-beaten face reflected the harsh nature of life in Ramadi.

We cleared through the house and unscrewed a few fluorescent lights along the way. Operating in darkness was always to our advantage. The family seemed to be among those in Ramadi who believed we were there doing good things. The woman of the house brewed us some chai, probably the result of some coaxing by Moose. We set up in the house's superstructure to do some work.

I sucked up as much AC as I could before heading to the roof to set up our sniper hide. The rooftop was wide open with a lot of clear space and a three-foot-high brick wall around the perimeter—not much cover, but it offered a superb vantage point to the north up Sunset and the west over the cemetery and University Road.

"What do you think, Dauber?" Chris asked as he looked up Sunset.

"Well, the muj won't have to drag the carcasses far to the cemetery when we're done here," I said.

The Legend stifled a cackle in the stillness of the night. "Fucking A, Dauber. Fucking A."

The Legend picked a spot on the northwest corner of the wall for the breachers to blow a loophole through. When we blew holes on the rooftops of inhabited houses, we normally left the family some cash to have it fixed when we patrolled out. Chucky rigged a standard loophole charge, and when it blew, an entire section of the wall crumbled.

"Chucky, why you blowing down the fucking roof, man?" Chris said. "They're gonna know we're here now."

"Man, fuck you guys," Chucky said. "Don't blame me; blame that piece-of-shit wall."

"Well, fuck," Chris said. "We can't stay up on the roof now. I guess we're gonna have to go downstairs in the AC."

"Oh, don't throw me in the briar patch, boss," I said.

Chris and I headed down to the second floor and sniffed out the luxury penthouse suite of sniper hides. The room had a plush queen-size bed whose height aligned perfectly with a curtained window facing east. The window provided a clear view down a busy street for at least a mile, and I could look down on the cemetery to the right. We pushed the bed away from the front of the window and moved some furniture around to help break up our silhouette. We set a bedroll toward the edge of the bed and gloved it up to rest the guns on. Lying prone, we could position our guns at optimal height. There were no bars on the window. We had a clear shooting lane, and the curtains cut down on our silhouette. The AC was blowing strong, and we were ready to deal all day long and then some.

Chris packed a Copenhagen, sent some my way, and took the first shift on the gun. Then I took the two-to-six block. With the exception of the time that Luke lit up Horse Teeth on the assault COP Falcon, the nighttime hours were usually uneventful. At those times, Copenhagen chewing became incessant. I wiped my dip-stained fingers in my eyes to chase the sleep away. I strained into the darkness, hoping some muj made their way across my view. Unfortunately, a few cur dogs and feral cats were the only ones who patrolled the garbage-riddled streets that night.

I gave the gun back to Chris at six and tried to get some sleep. The call to prayer droned in the distance as I struggled to fall asleep. I sat up next to Chris and watched the sun rising in the distance. I picked up my Leupold binoculars and watched as the morning sun breathed life into the streets again.

"Eight hundred meters," Chris said.

"What?"

"That's where I'm watching—eight hundred meters. That's where you see the most activity right now, isn't it?"

I brought the binos back up. There was no doubt. The busiest part of the street was eight hundred meters out.

"Yeah, you're right," I said.

"No shit. This ain't my first rodeo, you know."

I stayed on the binos, hoping to suck up all the trade secrets the Legend was willing to give out.

"Two guys on a moped. You see 'em?" he said. "Looks like they're carrying something."

I found them in my binos. Two military-age males in standard tracksuit-and-sandals muj attire, riding a moped. Just a second after I located them, I saw the passenger drop something in a hole in the road and then drive on without missing a beat.

"You see that?" Chris asked.

"Yeah, dude on the back dropped something in a hole," I said.

"Yeah, a backpack. I'm gonna shoot 'em."

Chris and I tracked the moped for several hundred meters, waiting patiently as they meandered between parked cars and pedestrians, slowly closing the distance between themselves and death. I sat watching through binos, waiting for the hammer to fall. Sniping is a voyeuristic practice. You always know the person you're about to kill has no idea it's coming. You're watching them up close, and then you drop the hammer before they ever know what hit them. These guys were thinking they'd just had a highly successful bomb-laying mission and were probably feeling pretty good about themselves. In my mind, they were a train wreck in slow motion. They grew bigger and bigger in my binos: 700 meters, 600, 500, 400 . . .

At about 200 meters, I heard Chris say, "All right," before taking a deep breath, and then the crack from his .30-cal. The moped was a mere 150 yards out when I saw the pink mist explode from around the two men—a perfect center-mass shot. The driver's head dropped lifeless like a rag doll, and his hands fell from the handlebars. The moped started wiggling out of control, and I could see that the second guy wasn't moving at all—no diving for cover or jumping off the bike. He just piled up on top of the driver, obviously lifeless, too. The wiggling moped crashed into a small wall and fell over. Neither passenger moved, and a pool of blood started forming on the ground around them.

"Good kill," I said from behind the binos. I put the binos down and looked at Chris. "Dude, that was fucking awesome! You just smoked two dudes with one bullet!"

"Yeah, I guess the taxpayer got his money's worth with that one,"

Chris said smiling, eye still on the scope. "Two birds, one badass piece of American lead."

"Two more for the Legend. What are you at now, like sixty? Seventy?"

"Something like that."

"Better watch out. If you fart too hard, them lucky horseshoes will fall out. Nice shooting."

"Yeah, that was a good one," Chris replied.

"I guess that makes up for Ralphie's miss," I said.

"He sure killed that PowerPoint presentation for this op, though," the Legend said with a chuckle as he resumed his scan.

About a block over from the moped crash, a Marine patrol had a clear line of sight to the intersection where the muj went down. They'd heard the shot, and from their perspective, all they saw was this moped with two dead guys, wiggling out of control and crashing into a wall. They had no context of the hostile action we'd witnessed when the muj dropped a bomb in a hole eight hundred meters out and casually drove on. The Marines knew our location but didn't have a line of sight to our building.

Luke came up to our room to get the usual report after a kill. Whenever one of our snipers shot somebody, our OIC or chief would take a report and annotate the details, ensuring all our shots were justified under the rules of engagement. We had to document the shots we took, filling out "Shooter Statements" after every engagement where hostile force was used. These documents involved the time, location, caliber of rifle, what the enemy action was at the time of the shot, and general atmospherics. Early on in our deployment, whenever a sniper would shoot somebody, other Teamguys would come to the room or roof wanting to know what went down. By this point in the deployment, we'd been smoke-checking so many guys that a bad guy getting dumped just became commonplace. The only people who still came asking for the story were those who were duty-bound to do so. I felt a strong urge to tell everybody in the platoon about the awesomeness I'd just witnessed.

"What do you got?" Luke asked.

"I shot two guys on a moped. Killed 'em both with one bullet. The passenger dropped an IED in a crater at eight hundred meters. Dauber saw the whole thing."

"Roger that, Luke," I said.

"Roger that," he responded.

While Luke took his report, Rex's radio came alive downstairs in the house with chatter from the Marines asking for an explanation: Why did these two dead guys just coast into a wall? They don't have any weapons on them. They weren't doing anything outside our ROEs. Luke explained the situation to the Marines, but they insisted on sending a patrol to inspect the hole. Chris and I weren't in the loop for all this. We didn't expect anyone to doubt what we'd seen and question the validity of the shot. With our sniper overwatches, we had thwarted coordinated attacks on Marine patrols on many occasions. In this instance, we were being proactive. We had just stopped an IED before a Marine patrol drove over it. Chris and I kept scanning the road for a potential counterattack.

The muj were sneaky. The going rate Al Qaeda was paying for digging an IED crater in Ramadi was two hundred dollars. Dropping an IED into a hole earned twice as much. The IED business in Ramadi was literally booming. For dirt-poor Iraqis, freelancing as IED droppers often meant the ability to buy food or add a few more goats and chickens to their flock. The muj were clever enough to drop the IEDs, throw fishing line across the street to drag the pressure pads into place, and then fake a broken-down vehicle so someone could connect the device in twenty seconds or less. To the untrained observer, it was easy to miss the nefarious nature of this behavior, but we were dialed into the enemy's tactics. Any time you're hunting the enemy, you have to think like them, and we Teamguys had gotten exceedingly good at this.

After Chris dumped the duo, the street where they'd dropped the IED buzzed with activity. The foot and vehicle traffic around the site obscured our view, and we were unable to maintain a constant visual on the IED crater. I'm sure some aspiring capitalist picked up the IED and took it home so it could fight another day.

When we got word the Marines were sending a patrol, we focused up on the area where the muj had dropped the IED. The road was flooded with activity, and we watched three Humvees approach the hole eight hundred meters out. They set up a security perimeter and inspected the hole. Unsurprisingly, there was nothing in it. Chris and I knew what we saw, and we saw the passenger on the muj moped drop a bomb in that hole.

The lack of evidence was a sticky point, and it caused some friction between the Marines and our leadership. There was an investigation, and the judge advocate general (JAG) paid Chris some special attention. Fortunately, my shooter statement corroborated the fact that lethal force was justified, and that was the end of it. Everyone in the platoon was irritated by the lack of trust. We weren't in the business of killing innocents, and as professional soldiers, we were very surgical with our use of force. For us newguys, this event marked a baptism into the politics of war. There is a stark dichotomy between Special Operations and the Rear Echelon Motherfuckers (REMFs). From a purely statistical standpoint, the REMFs thought we were operating with carte blanche. To them, shooting two guys on a moped probably seemed too incredible, but the hostile action the muj had committed was undeniable. The REMFs would try to make life difficult for us, but to the Marine grunts and Army ground pounders I chewed Copenhagen with in sniper hides and COPs, we were putting the fear of God into the enemy. That was the only validation I needed. One team, one fight.

We knew what was at stake if our actions caused the deaths of innocent civilians. The media would crucify us, and Leavenworth would become home. Winning the hearts and minds of the local populace was an important part of the overall mission in Ramadi, and you can't win hearts and minds if you can't protect the innocent while you kill the bad guys. Truthfully, the threats of the media and Leavenworth were not what kept me honest behind the gun. I wanted to kill bad men. I did not want to kill innocent ones. The investigation pissed me off. I knew what the fog of war was, what the risks were when I pulled the slack from the trigger. I also knew that not every American who had ever donned the uniform deserved to. I knew about Haditha, about My Lai, about atrocities committed as far back as Atlanta in 1864. I also knew my personal motive for being there was for killing terrorists, period. So though I understood somebody might see a shot or engagement from a different perspective, it didn't take the sting out of their questioning our actions or integrity. Fortunately, the more dead muj you stack up like cordwood, the more conventional troops on the ground appreciate it and help protect you from the bullshit. To those of us in the mix, the struggle was constant, and creeping death was a heartbeat away.

Twenty-four hours later, I watched the ink dry on my shooter statement in the platoon hut at Sharkbase. I reread my words, making sure not to omit any pertinent details. The devil is in the details. In this case, two muj dropping an IED with the intent to kill Americans and coalition forces. "Two military aged males carrying an IED device on a moped . . . IED crater . . . effectively engaged with .30 cal . . . Targets eliminated." My shooter statement corroborated the fact that lethal force was justified, and that was the end of it. I had signed statements prior to this, and there would be more to come. The Battle of Ramadi was hitting the fever pitch of summer.

I thought about the Legend's poise when he engaged the easy riders. The man was a machine. In sniping, there are minor details that can determine whether there is success or total failure. Any clown can pull a trigger on a range, but a vigilant eye and a clear mindset are necessities on the battlefield. Robert Heinlein said, "There are no dangerous weapons. Only dangerous men." For a few months now we'd been meeting Ramadi's most dangerous men, and we hammered them as if that desert city were the anvil on which we struck. I stood up, my shooter statement in one hand as I slung my rifle over my shoulder. I needed to head back to my tent and recharge, but I was feeling hungry. Only not for food.

I let the weight of the weapon on my side comfort me. It was a gnawing that grew daily in the desert, quenched only by the squeeze of the trigger and the blood of my enemy. I took a deep breath and headed out into the bright Iraqi sunlight. *Maybe "hungry" is the wrong word,* I thought. I nodded to myself, trudging through the moondust toward my tent. *Dangerous,* I thought.

I feel dangerous.

FOURTEEN

THE MAILMAN DELIVERS

"We have met the enemy and they are ours. . . ."

—Oliver Hazard Perry

PHOTOJOURNALIST RICHARD SCHOENBERG followed BUD/S Class 246 through the entire journey from indoc to SQT graduation. When it was over, he sorted through his thousands of photographs and published a coffee-table book called *The Only Easy Day Is Yesterday: Making Navy SEALs.* I'm twenty-one in the photographs, my hair bleached from the sun and salt, my face masked in youth and fatigue.

When my son was old enough to realize that some of the pictures were of me, he pointed me out. "What are you doing there?" he asked. He was three years old.

"I'm trying to be a SEAL," I answered.

"It looks hard," he said.

"It was."

He thought for several moments, his face a mess of concentration. "Could you do it again?" he asked.

It was my turn to think for a moment.

"Yes," I said. "Yes, I could."

SHARKBASE, MID-JULY 2006

Doc Crispin was an old Frogman. Pushing fifty, Crispin had been in the Navy about as long as I'd been alive. After enlisting as a corpsman and completing BUD/S in the late 1970s, he did one four-year stint on active duty and then transitioned to the Navy Reserve. There he completed his weekend-warrior training requirements for more than twenty years until the Navy called him up for active duty in the Global War on Terror. With the wars in Iraq and Afghanistan in full swing, the frequency of deployments had started to put a strain on Naval Special Warfare, so the Navy tapped old salts like Crispin to shoulder some of the burden. He left his successful practice as a chiropractor in middle America to train up and deploy with us, and his age and worldliness made him the old man of SEAL Team THREE. He was a Frogman, but he was a Frogman well into middle age. Having arrived in the Teams after the Vietnam War, Panama, Grenada, and Desert Storm were the conflicts of his era. He was as new to the War on Terror as I was.

Since Crispin was a recently activated reservist, our leadership found him best suited for administrative duties back at Sharkbase. He became our trusty mailman, making the trip from Sharkbase into Camp Ramadi every day to pick up our mail. He was also our rear-echelon corpsman. His presence on Sharkbase meant I didn't have to deal with anyone's trivial aches and ailments during the few periods of downtime I had back in the rear. You've got jock itch? Negative, Ghostrider; the pattern is full. Go see Crispin. For anything relating to back pain, Crispin was a guru. Guys popped in frequently to see the old man for a quick back adjustment—Doc Crispin's Frogman-in-combat special. My own back received an adjustment or two from the grandpa Frog. The old man was a fixture at Sharkbase. For the most part, he had settled early on into the monotony of life inside the wire. He seemed to thrive on routine, and he could often be seen making his nightly walk from the homey tent that housed his de facto medical practice to the plywood shower house where all the Teamguys and other operators washed away the filth and stink of combat. With his middle-aged-doctor glasses and his little shower towel and toiletry bag tucked neatly under one arm like the morning newspaper, Doc Crispin would slip into his flip-flops and head to the shower box.

Like all of us, Crispin strived to avoid contact with the toxically organic slime that coated the thin sheets of vinyl hanging as partitions between each shower. The water we bathed in smelled like a juicy government contract whose corners had been liberally cut—like some retired trucker from Arkansas had pumped Euphrates water into the giant bladder feeding the showers, thrown in some iodine tablets, said a few Hail Marys, and then moved on to suck out the shitters. Showering in Iraq was kind of like being one of the uninfected survivors in *28 Days Later*. You had to be always on alert for the possibility of someone angling the showerhead next to yours in a way that launched the scum-sheets toward you in a biological-warfare ambush. The slow-draining ecosystem that pooled menacingly around your feet was one thing, but you were even more wary of the bacterial-supervirus mutation fermenting on the dividers a few inches from your skin. Nobody wants to catch the Rage Virus. Never touch the goo partitions. I remembered studying the Civil War in high school, reading about the hundreds of thousands of soldiers who died of disease, largely because of poor hygiene. *Some threats on the battlefield change,* I thought. *And some don't.*

After returning from an unremarkable but blazing-hot twenty-four-hour overwatch in western Ramadi one night, I changed into PT gear and flip-flops and headed to the shower box. Doc Crispin was there and in the midst of his nightly routine.

"Hey, Dauber, how's it going? How's that back of yours?"

"Been good, bro. Thanks for lining me up."

"You guys been dropping the hammer out there. Kill any bad guys lately?" he said before unsheathing his toothbrush from its little plastic scabbard. Who actually uses those things?

"Not lately. I can't complain, I know you're not gonna rack up the numbers on them mail runs," I muttered.

"Well, Daubs, it's war. Back in the 'Nam days, you never knew when you'd get the chance to engage. Always ready, bro," he said non-chalantly.

He squeezed out a neat line of toothpaste and started brushing his grill. I turned my focus to the showers and disease prevention. Getting clean and hitting the rack were the only things on my mind. By now, I was accustomed to our task unit commander's dogged quest to keep us employed and the unpredictability of our relentless op tempo.

Our tactical operations center (TOC) was a beehive of key leaders and support staff, constantly monitoring the blue force tracker and video feeds from our Intelligence, Surveillance, and Reconnaissance (ISR) assets, and communicating with our guys on the hunt while working simultaneously to coordinate new ops. Whenever we finished an op, another one wasn't far behind, and opportunity often knocked at less-than-ideal times, like when Dauber wanted to sleep after a twenty-four-hour overwatch. We had gotten to the point where we just left our guns on our trucks because it didn't make sense to pull them off in case we needed to pull out fast and hit a target. We just put the dust covers on and called that good.

I made my shower a quick one, headed back to my tent, and fell asleep. The dream was just getting good when Tony stormed in, still dressed out in full cammies. I'm positive I never saw Tony in PT gear.

Rest and *relaxation* didn't seem to be words in his vocabulary. I'm pretty sure he made it a point to never be seen sleeping or eating, especially by newguys. Sleep and chow were crutches, and Tony had no use for crutches or any other signs of weakness. I never saw him take Motrin, but I'm sure he ate it by the handful when no one was looking. He was like an ancient Spartan throwback—an impenetrable one-man phalanx of hard-motherfuckering.

"Get ya shit. We're PLO'ing in five minutes," he said saltily.

I sat up, shook the dream off, and banged on the wall to make sure Marc was awake. His angry "What?" echoed my feelings and assured me he was conscious. We threw our gear on and headed to the mission planning space.

Luke gave a lightning-fast op order: bomb maker in north Ramadi . . . high-value target . . . time sensitive . . . capture/kill. Time sensitive meant we were going after another high-value target and we had a short time window to get him. We had already racked up plenty of raids on HVTs, including some of Zarqawi's lieutenants, so this op was nothing outside the norm, but we needed more men to man the turrets in the convoy. Luke finished his order and launched us to the trucks. Doc Crispin the Mailman secured his chinstrap, grabbed his M4, and headed out. He'd been tapped to man the .50-cal in the front truck on the raid.

"You ready for this, Crispin?" I asked. "The last time you fired a fifty must have been back in 'Nam, right?"

"Something like that," he said. "I think I'll be okay. Like riding a bike, right?"

"I guess so, bro. Gotta be careful on those bikes, though. Wouldn't want you to fall and break a hip," I shot back. Jonny chuckled as he threw his med bag in Vehicle 2.

Crispin smirked and climbed up into the turret of the front truck. He began his prep of the .50, situating his ammo cans and checking the gun's IR laser in his night vision. I watched him go through his gear checks as methodically as his shower routine. The Mailman was ready to roll.

The convoy rumbled to life, and we headed out in a hurry. There was no time to pick up any Jundis. Rousting them out of bed at two in the morning and getting them mission ready would have taken the kind of time we didn't have.

There's nothing quite like rolling out for a direct-action raid. The thought of screaming to a target building in the middle of the night, all jocked up in assault gear with some of the meanest dudes on the planet, intending to capture or kill a high-value individual while he sleeps in his bed and has no idea you're coming, never failed to fire me up internally. Inside the truck, however, the atmosphere was always eerily mellow when you consider what we were headed out to do.

From the driver-side rear seat, I looked over at Chris. The Legend's eyes were glued to the navigation computer, passing directions to the convoy as Chucky hammered away at the throttle of the 1152B Humvee. I looked over at Bob across from me in the backseat. He was quietly taking in the landscape as we burned up the night. Playing off his cue, I closed my eyes for a quick nap, waiting to hear the five-minutes call over comms.

"Five min," Chris passed over comms and I snapped awake. The thirty-minute drive had passed by in a blink. As we rolled in, I noticed how poorly lit the neighborhood was. Streetlights were nearly nonexistent, and there was an occasional light on in a few houses here and there. We drove down a long alleyway with eleven-foot walls on each side, and my immediate thought was, *Why the fuck are we in this alleyway?* Alleyways are the fatal funnels of urban convoys. Alleyways are never ideal, but Murphy's law can rear its head at any time once you leave the wire. You can do map studies of an area until your eyes bleed, but you never know what you're going to get until you arrive. I knew Chris would have never planned to park us in an alleyway, but Ramadi continued to present us with situations that materialized differently than we planned for. We just had to read and react.

The plan called for a roll-up assault to the target building in order to minimize our movement on foot to the compound. We were hitting two simultaneous targets, one beyond the wall on our left side, and one beyond the wall on our right.

"All stop."

The command came across comms as the vehicles halted. The assault force quickly disembarked from the trucks and moved into patrol formation. We split into dual columns instinctively, one squad on each side of the street. I was assault team 1's lead on the right side of the alley. I had the Legend, Squirrel, EOD Nick, Ralphie, Bob, and Marc carrying the ladder behind me. Our objective was house 1. Vehicle 1—the Mailman's vehicle—pushed ahead to set security for the assault force as we made our way over the walls and into our respective compounds.

As I led the patrol up to the ladder set point, I saw an unarmed military-age male milling around at the end of the alleyway. He appeared briefly in a splash of scant light from a house and then scurried out of sight.

"I've got one guy at the far end of the alleyway," I said quietly into my PRC 148 MBITR radio before climbing up the ladder.

"Roger that," came back as I reached the top of the wall and peeked over. Clear, as far as I could tell. I cradled my M4, rolled over, and slithered down the wall, hanging for just a second before dropping the last three feet. I popped up on a knee and scanned with my laser. I was in a corner of the yard about twelve feet from the building. We had planned to breach the front door, but it turned out to be at the other side of the house. We would need to go completely around the building first. Read and react.

Uncle Bob came over next and picked up security to my right. I stayed focused on everything to the left while the other guys dropped one by one into place behind me. It took no time at all to get all nine guys over. I got the signal to go.

I was designated to be the first man up to the breach point. It was my job to set security for the breacher so he could place his charge. Unlike previous targets, this would not be a simultaneous breach and we would not be communicating over comms to the other assault force. We needed everything to go off as quickly as possible, so we were just supposed to blow it whenever we were ready. Speed, surprise, and violence of action were the plan.

Once I got the signal, I moved up and around the first corner of the house to my left, assuming the rest of the element was behind me. There was a car in a carport that I needed to clear to get a line of sight on the front door. I was moving steadily toward the car when Chris reached up from behind me and pulled me backward. I froze and took a knee, holding forward, looking for whatever threat Chris might have noticed.

For a minute or so, I waited, scanning. I saw nothing. When Chris gave me the signal again, I moved around the car toward the front door. My intention was to reach it and hold security while Bob came up from behind me and set the C6 strips to blow the door open. I thought about the time we lost moments earlier and wanted to make the breach point quickly. I moved with a purpose.

I was within about six feet of my target when an explosion went off, knocking me backward with a blast of hot air and unexpected momentum. "Fuck," I muttered, trying to determine what had just rung my bell so hard. I shook it off as Chris jumped past me into the open door. I followed him as the rest of the element materialized around us. Somehow, the breach charge had been set before I'd reached the door.

Later, I would find out that in the fog of war my assault team had split in half, with Bob and three guys hooking around the other side of the house to set the breach. Chris holding me back by the car had been him realizing we were alone. He'd given me the signal when he thought they'd caught up. "Once more into the breach, dear friends" gained a whole new meaning for me. If I'd been a few feet closer to the blast I could have gotten blown up.

Shattered glass from the door crunched beneath our boots on the foyer's slick tile, and my right foot rode one piece like an errant Rollerblade into a merciless angle that sent me hard into the marble. The unmistakable breeze through the crotch of my pants reassured me that I had just blown out yet another pair of cammies. Doc Crispin's old ears probably heard that rip all the way in the turret. Old Murphy was laying down his law in full force on this raid. I jumped up quickly, still slipping all over the place like Gumby on roller skates. I cleared through the house. A long hallway with several rooms on either side was to my front. I knew by that point of my deployment that the hotter it was, the more likely the muj were to be sleeping on the rooftop. The room clearing went fast, and, as expected, they were all empty. We headed to the roof. Same shit, different day.

We busted onto the roof, and Bob peeled around the entrance straight toward an angry Iraqi in a full-on bull rush. Bob put him down with a highly effective left hook and the rest of us swarmed on him. Bob could have shot the guy and been well within the ROE. A man charging like that could be on his way to clack off a suicide vest and meet his virgins. Successful direct-action raids are determined by split seconds. The rest of our squad poured onto the roof behind us and secured two other men, slamming them to the ground and flex-cuffing their hands so tight they couldn't move. There were several women and children, all of them very upset by the sight of us putting masks over the men's heads and marching them downstairs.

Moose corralled the women and children downstairs as we dragged off the detained and searched the premises. The place was an IED factory. We found a cornucopia of bomb-making material. Intel had hit a home run with this op. The guy who caught Bob's left hook was the bomb maker we were after and apparently had a lot of product on-site. One of the other guys was his son, and one was his neighbor, who turned out to be an accomplice. We loaded up several trash bags full of evidence and intel and then waited in the foyer until the ground force commander was ready for us to consolidate on the vehicles.

As we waited, I stepped outside and looked at the car in the carport. Vehicle-borne IEDs were a major threat in Ramadi and a favorite muj tactic. I pulled out the old CRKT tactical knife and slashed the car's tires.

"You're a born Frogman," Chris cackled as I moved back to the foyer.

"Thanks, Legend."

"Great job, Dauber," Uncle Bob said. "Make sure all the heavy weapons are cleaned when we get back, Meat. But seriously, good job."

Newguy shit. *Gotta love it,* I thought.

After a five-minute wait for assault team 2 to finish business, we got the okay to move. We broke out of the building and headed to the ladders with our loot bags while pushing or dragging our prisoners along with us. The women stayed on target. We hustled over to Big Zev and loaded up our bad guys, about to make a clean getaway on another highly successful snatch mission. That's when the .50 barked to life on the front vehicle.

The chug-chug-chug of the .50 got everyone's attention. Usually, you'll hear "Contact front!" before somebody opens up like that, but Crispin wasn't wasting any time. A hundred meters from where I'd seen the guy in the alley on our approach, eight muj loaded up with machine guns and RPGs had been maneuvering around, trying to get into position for a hasty ambush. Unfortunately for them, we had night vision and they couldn't be sure where we were because the alleyway was so dark. Meanwhile, our ISR eyes in the sky were tracking their approach, and Crispin had them dead to rights with his laser and .50-cal. The Mailman unleashed on our would-be ambushers, cutting all eight of them to shreds with ruthless efficiency in a matter of seconds. I listened to the .50's rhythmic chug-chug-chug and hustled our cargo onto Big Zev. As I climbed into the truck, Crispin came over comms. "Eight military-aged males with RPGs and PKCs down 150 m in front of Vehicle 1." His voice was as calm as if he were about to cut his toenails. "Check," came back as the trucks began to roll.

With the assault force loaded up, bad guys detained, intel in the loot bags, and eight muj lying in the dust, we backed out of the alley, turned around, and headed home. The chatter started up on our radios immediately, the voices disguised.

"Crispin, you motherfucker, I busted my ass through that house and didn't shoot anyone, but you sit in the truck and kill eight dudes?"

"You never go out on ops, and the one time you do, a bunch of muj jump in front of your fifty-cal."

"That's how it's done, boys," Crispin said.

"Bitch, you physically can't even walk on ops because you're so damn old."

We were all cracking up and giving Crispin an endless barrage of giddy shit-talk when Tony shouted into the radio, "Lock it the fuck up!"

Our comms went quiet for about thirty seconds, and then guys started disguising their voices:

"Fucking Crispin."

"Old man ain't lost a step since 'Nam!"

"Or WW Two."

"I guess the Mailman delivered."

"Yeah, I wish the post office was that fucking efficient!"

The solid two minutes of salty Teamguy ridicule tapered off. The rhythmic sound of the diesel engines, the occasional "Tails up" call from Tony, and Chris's directions took over. I looked over at Bob as he peered out through the ballistic glass of the vehicle. I leaned my head back and dozed off.

The hilarious irony of the whole situation had us all laughing our asses off because nobody had yet had a chance to really think about what had gone down. The muj Crispin mowed down were about to lay waste to our patrol. If they had gotten set up and initiated an ambush with a well-aimed RPG in that fatal funnel, our patrol would have ended much differently. When Crispin got his BTF moment, he rose to the occasion, lining up and knocking down a whole squad of muj like he was shooting bottles at a carnival. He probably saved a bunch of our lives that night, and for his actions, Crispin earned the Bronze Star.

The convoy ambled lazily up to the Prisoner Detention Facility on Camp Ramadi, full of men content with a successful night's work. I couldn't resist taking one more potshot at Crispin.

"Putting that bicycle back up for another twenty years, Doc?" I asked. "Maybe next time you deploy I'll have a kid in the Teams and you'll have a couple new hips. You'll be killing muj in your seventies."

Doc stepped down out of the truck and nodded toward my pants. "Maybe," he said. "Looks like you're good to go in that department." Doc grabbed his gear and walked off while the rest of the squad howled. In the excitement, I'd forgotten about my blown-out crotch and my fully exposed nuts.

I gave in and laughed, too. The old man got me.

But he still had to get the mail.

FIFTEEN

PATROL TO CONTACT

"In battle it is the cowards who run the most
risk; bravery is a rampart of defense."

—Sallust

WITHOUT FAIL, ANYTIME I visit a classroom to talk about my experiences in the SEAL Teams, a hand shoots up and a child asks me, "Were you ever afraid?"

I always give the same answer:

"All the time."

Anyone who tells you he was in the kind of shit we were in and was not afraid is either lying or has something wrong with his head. Fear is your basic human response to a dangerous situation; it activates your fight-or-flight mechanism. There's a complicated physiological explanation I could give you, but the point is that fear is your friend. It lets you know to wake up and pay attention.

Fear is not the enemy. I did not want to die in Iraq, so naturally situations that presented the possibility of being shot, blown up, or otherwise injured scared me. Fear was a given. It was one of many emotions I experienced there, in addition to fury, exhilaration, relief, delight, despair, and apathy. Fearlessness wasn't necessary, and fear is not the polar opposite of courage. What mattered was how we managed that fear in order to overcome it. It was what we did in spite of it.

———————

Sitting on the edge of his rack in our tent on Sharkbase, Marc Lee looked perturbed. After four months of living and working together nearly constantly, I'd gotten pretty good at reading him. You eat, sleep, sweat, and kick ass right next to somebody for that long, you're going to figure him out. We newguys had the nonverbal communication down. We transmitted information in silent subtleties: the eye-roll, the eyebrow raise, the what-the-fuck brow. It's not exactly a secret language. The cues mean pretty much what you'd expect, and Marc's were no exception. If anything, his spoke a little louder than the rest of the newguys'. He was the kind of dude who always seemed to tell it like it was, and for that, everybody respected him.

"I talked to Guy," he murmured.

"About what?"

"About that shit we discussed the other night."

I was picking up what Marc was putting down. "These daytime presence patrols ain't what we're supposed to be doing," he said. "Figured somebody should say something. Running us ragged all night is one thing, bro, but having us walk down the street in muj country in the middle of the day? That's not how we're supposed to do business. Not exactly what we trained up for."

I recalled a conversation we newguys had held during a routine game of Halo on Xbox a few nights before. I couldn't recall who had first brought up the topic, but we had all agreed that daytime presence patrols with Iraqi Jundis weren't exactly the type of business we had planned, or trained for, for that matter, to conduct in Ramadi. The general consensus among us was that we were already crushing the enemy. Why put ourselves in a vulnerable position with some new job?

"Yeah, man, it's bullshit. I don't like it, either. So what did Guy say?" I asked.

"He said he'd talk to Jocko about it."

Jocko was our task unit commander, and his job was to keep us in the business of staying employed. Fortunately, laziness wasn't commonplace in the Teams and we were always willing to work. When Jocko and our other officers sat in on the Army's morning briefings at COP Falcon or Camp Ramadi, they looked for ways to add value to whatever the Army was doing—employment opportunities. The HVT missions, DAs, and sniper overwatches weren't exactly drying up like the banks of the Euphrates toward the end of July, but Jocko and the officers had decided to feed their combat addiction with any ops they could get for us, even nonconventional ones. What little free time we had they used to plug us into the big-Army rotation around the COP. Charlie Platoon's success was becoming addictive, and the higher the body count rose, the more the leadership wanted to add to it, no matter the risk.

As a newguy in the Teams, you generally do whatever you're told, and if you don't like something, you just suck it up and do it anyway. But when we got word we were going to start doing daytime patrols with the Army, the general attitude among the newguys and some of the other platoon members turned pretty sour. In Ramadi, the tactic for conducting a presence patrol was pretty straightforward. Basically, we were supposed to walk down the street in the middle of the day until somebody shot at us. Then, we would try to kill them. If we needed help killing them, we would call in the Army.

"Well, I'm sure we'll hear something back soon," I said aimlessly.

"Yeah," said Marc.

"It's all right, bro. I'm sure the bullshit will figure itself out," I replied. "Teams and shit."

Sunset was green on the morning of our first daytime presence patrol, and I rode in the turret of Snake Eyes (Vehicle 1) on the convoy from Sharkbase to Falcon. We had picked up the Jundis prior to our departure and the convoy meandered through the serpentine barriers of Camp Ramadi.

I waved to the guard as we lurched forward from the line of departure.

What the hell?

I was at a loss for words since the op brief earlier that morning. Guy's request to rethink our strategy hadn't made a dent in the new mission outline. Charlie Platoon was being volunteered to do presence patrols in and around COP Falcon with Jundis, in an attempt to reinforce to the local populace that we were here to stay.

I didn't like it. A SEAL's biggest advantage is surprise. For months we'd experienced tremendous success kicking down doors and rolling up bad guys in the middle of the night, swift and deadly. We'd laid up quietly on Ramadi's rooftops, picking off IED planters and peekers who threatened our Army and Marine brothers and sisters. In both types of scenario, we controlled the action. There is none of that on a presence patrol. I angrily packed a Copenhagen as the convoy rolled out onto Michigan. I pursed my face tight and sent a giant juicer down into the cab. *Fucking presence patrols.*

The drive was uneventful, and as we snaked through the serpentine arrangement of Jersey barriers at the COP's entrance, I looked down at the Army guard holding back the razor wire to let us through and gave him a nod. He nodded back. *At least they don't have us pulling guard duty,* I thought. We parked our vehicles at the Shit Creek Welcome Center, and then the officers headed off for their meeting of the minds or whatever it is they do while the rest of us went looking for chow. We found a field-mess setup of green mermite containers full of Salisbury steak with peas and gravy.

Biggles looked down disapprovingly at the containers that held the grade-F, prison-quality food. "Only the best, for the best."

"Biggles, man," Marc said, between mouthfuls, "I don't know what we'd do without you."

"Well," Biggles said, "for one thing, you'd have to cradle two machine guns with them giant biceps, Marc."

"If you got 'em, use 'em. If you don't got 'em, hit the gym."

I chuckled along with Biggles, Jonny, and Biff.

Jonny looked around. "A misallocation of resources if I've ever seen one," he said.

"Careful, man," Biggles said. "That's a pretty big word. Don't hurt yourself."

"Shakespeare wasn't Asian, Jonny. Stick to numbers," Biff joined in.

"I get it," I said, catching my fellow medic's tone. "Patrolling until one of us gets a slug in the grill is a misallocation, but Mr. Muj wants to meet some virgins. I'd say we arrange the meeting."

A round of distracted chuckles echoed through the group. I tried not to get too caught up bitching because I knew we all needed to get our heads in the game, but the unrest wasn't unfounded. I wasn't exactly thrilled about our new job. We were preparing to patrol down J and K Streets, the same place Chris, Jonny, and I had killed twenty-three bad guys in twenty-four hours. We'd have a sniper overwatch, but we'd be otherwise extremely exposed compared to the way we normally operated. I remembered a wise saying in the Teams: If the guys ain't complaining, something is wrong. I tried to trust that since we were all complaining, we might be headed out to do the right thing.

Daytime ops require even more hypervigilance than nighttime ops. Because we own the night, you can be a lot more liberal with your movement then. In the daytime, moving from cover to cover was necessary. *Dauba', where the fahk you gonna go when you get shot at? Stick to cuvah.* Tony's words echoed. If the enemy starts spraying, you want to have something to dive to. I rechecked my med bag and gear, making sure all systems were intact.

As our launch time drew nearer, I remembered Tony's words during work-up. "This shit'll keep you alive, Daubah," he said with poker-face eyes. "Head on a fahking swivel," he said in between Copenhagen spits. "And wear some fahking sunglasses. It makes you look fahking mean and the muj have no idea if yah lookin at 'em or naht."

We huddled into the Teamguy annex of COP Falcon as we got the op brief a little before noon. The house reeked of body odor, Copenhagen, and the stale stench of dried sweat. The ventilation was poor at best. Ralphie would lead my element when the platoon split into two squads. Squad 1—my squad—was going to patrol east for about a mile down K Street while Squad 2 mirrored Squad 1's movement a block south on J Street. We were going to patrol to contact, establish a strongpoint, and either kill the enemy or call the Army to help us kill the enemy or get us out of a jam if the situation called for it. *Get after it,* I reminded myself.

We launched around noon with Squirrel running point, Ralphie as OIC, followed by Marc, Biff running comms, EOD Nick, me, and Chucky in the rear. Sprinkled here and there in among us were a bunch of Jundis in their usual pirate outfits.

I felt a certain amount of pride in the Jersey barriers that had been erected on the western edge of COP Falcon as we started the patrol west down Baseline. COP Falcon had begun to take shape as the coalition footprint pressed into the moondust of southwestern Ramadi. We'd come a long way in the last month or so since Horse Teeth took one to the brain housing group. More work to be done.

The sun beat down on my neck as we passed the head count up to the front of the patrol. I flipped my collar up, readjusted my sling, and moved tactically to the doorjamb of the nearest building. I scanned the rooftops of the uneven hodgepodge of Middle Eastern architecture. It was an insurgent's advantage up in that network of wires, uneven walls, and clusterfuck. I scanned over my EOTech optic at the adjacent rooftop.

Head on a swivel.

The muscle memory Tony instilled during work-up took over as I moved with purpose from cover to cover, hugging doorjambs while scanning for my next position or strongpoint. I had to make sure Chucky and the Jundis could always see me. Line of sight in a daytime patrol is very important. I didn't need another accidental discharge in my direction from the Jundis. We walked for about three-quarters of a mile, and I started to think maybe we would reach the end of K Street and turn back without a single muj trying to engage.

After we crossed a small intersection two-thirds of the way down the one-kilometer stretch of K Street, I could see the brick wall at the end. I patrolled on the right side of the street and realized the long wall shielded a mosque on our right side, two hundred meters up. *Fuck,* I thought. Mosques were terrible places to hang out by. The muj loved to hide out inside and attack coalition forces from within, knowing we got our asses chewed—or worse—for shooting at the religious buildings. I'd rather walk across shit creek than do a daytime presence patrol around a mosque in muj country. Squirrel looked back to assess the squad as he carefully sidestepped the giant pile of trash in front of him. That hum of expectation ran throughout the patrol. *It's coming,* I thought, carefully scanning my sector. *Where are you, fucker?*

I didn't see him before I felt the heat of the first ten rounds come screaming down K Street toward the patrol. A military-age male with a PKC nosed out at our twelve o'clock position and delivered a healthy dose of lead. For all my daytime-op acuity and muscle memory, I somehow earned an enemy ambush at the exact moment I was passing by the huge wall around the mosque. I had no cover or concealment, aside from some skinny telephone poles about thirty yards away and a shit creek of human waste three feet to my right. Diving into raw sewage for cover was not an option in my mind.

EOD Nick and Squirrel opened up with their guns immediately at the patrol's twelve o'clock position as a second muj with a machine gun opened up from another mosque 150 yards away. The rounds whipped the air around me with a furious snap-snap-snap-snap-snap-snap-snap-snap.

Incoming fire is one thing Hollywood always messes up. When you're firing it with your weapon, it's a loud bang. When it's coming at you, however, it snaps like a bullwhip. Nick and Squirrel dumped rounds at the enemy as the rest of the patrol sucked into the surroundings like ticks on a deer. The unmistakable concussion of an RPG impact reverberated from the wall to my left. I had no choice but to seek cover from the telephone pole, melting into the microterrain as best I could and scanning the adjacent rooftop for possible threats.

A few yards away, Ralphie stood pressed against the side of a building. He called for a center peel and then pointed to me. "You!" he yelled loudly, making eye contact. "Strongpoint that fucking building!" He pointed to a building directly across the twenty-meter-wide, PKC-wall-of-lead-saturated K Street. We needed to get off the X (point of contact), out of the fire, and attempt to secure a building to lock down a fighting position in a strongpoint. Ralphie had realized the coordinated attack and understood the gravity of the firefight. If we didn't get into a building and suppress the effective enemy fire, we were screwed. Chucky and I had the rear of the patrol locked down; we just needed to find a building that worked.

The withering enemy fire continued from down K Street. Squirrel dumped the rest of his magazine and sprinted down the side of the road opposite to me. Biff picked up his field of fire with a steady fifty-round burst toward the enemy. The telephone pole that I was tucked into tight provided little cover. Several of my squad were between me and the muj engaging us. I needed the peel to move so that I could start shooting, too.

Just as I was about to get up to move, EOD Nick ran past me. He sprinted toward the rear of our patrol on my side of the street, his faded yellow Asolo hiking boots tearing up a wake of dust behind him. Suddenly one boot connected with the other and launched him skidding into shit creek. As he flew face-first toward the river of shit and wastewater, he held his rifle skyward in the high port position. I stepped away from the last place of cover with a smirk and made a mental note to compliment him on his exceptional muzzle discipline. I saw his face as he emerged from his fecal predicament, his web gear smeared with shit, and could already predict that he would not appreciate my sarcasm.

I had to sprint forty yards across the street. Another burst from the muj's PKC came down the street, sending the unmistakable bullwhip sound right above my bean. As I ran, I thought about Nick going face-first into raw sewage and laughed out loud. Sometimes you need to throw your nuts in your back pocket and move. Nick's stumble brought some comic relief to the tense situation. Inadvertently, Nick had managed to distract me from the enemy onslaught that snapped and crackled on either side of me. I sprinted across the road toward our strongpoint with a point to make my 225-pound frame as small as possible while Chucky peeled in behind me. He ran past me and continued on to the door of the compound while I stopped and held security on the second-story balconies and windows of the building behind the eight-foot-high, heavily graffitied wall.

We needed to get in fast, so Chucky decided to kick in the metal door. He delivered the kick with gusto, his right boot high in the air when it connected with and opened the door. He was so enthusiastic that Chucky, who's about 220 sans gear and about 280 with it, fell flat on his back from the shift in his center of gravity and the weight of his ruck. He lay there, faceup on the little ramp that led to his blue, sheet-metal nemesis. I saw my opening. I moved quickly to the doorway, eager to get inside and clear. I laughed audibly and made sure to make eye contact with Chucky before stepping on his chest plate on my way inside.

There is nothing funny about a firefight in the street, but watching your buddy land like an upside-down turtle going into a compound door does provide a little levity.

If somebody falls on an assault, your job is to get in that door. Speed and surprise are critical, so you do whatever is necessary to get in, even if that means stepping on your buddy's chest.

I began to clear the courtyard by myself as Chucky staggered to his feet and fell in behind me. The Jundis flooded toward our building in pulsatile bounds and into the courtyard with its protective walls. The rest of the element stayed in the street to deal with the contact from the mosque and the end of the street. Chucky and I moved past a car in the open courtyard and the Jundis joined the train before we entered the house. In the first room, a scared-looking man got in my way, and I threw him into a corner with the rest of the residents, already cowering. No weapon. The Jundis reflexively took to the business of restraining them as Chucky and I continued moving through the house and quickly got to the rooftop.

We could see the firefight developing on the street below, and the last of our guys were coming across K Street to strongpoint on our position. As far as I could see, we had no casualties, and so I settled into my God-mode POV, scanning the mosque and adjacent streets below for targets. Chucky engaged the far end of the alley where the contact had originated.

About two hundred yards out, I saw a single muj try to flank us. He carried an AK-47 with an olive-drab weapons holder slung on his shoulder.

I took a knee and steadied my M4, using the three-foot wall as a stable shooting platform. I put the dot of my optic sight center-mass with a slight lead to compensate for his movement.

Exhale.

Pause.

I fired three shots and the target crumbled. It was like poking a puck into an empty net from just outside the goalie crease.

"Chucky, got one. He's down, two hundred yards," I said as I went back to scanning.

"Roger. Reloading."

Chucky knelt behind the wall and pulled out another hundred-round box of ammo for his gun. I picked up his suppressive fire toward the mosque and street as gunmen darted behind points of cover.

With Chucky back in the mix and his Pig keeping heads down, we held on the rooftop until all enemy fire stopped. I watched as Ralphie entered the compound hollering "Last man!" to Marc Lee at the entrance of our building. After a brief lull, our sister squad on J Street came under fire. Like clockwork, they executed the same type of strongpoint drill and took no casualties.

On the rooftop, Chucky, Marc, Squirrel, and I had a great vantage point from our two-story building. To our north, Squad 2 was 150 yards away locking down J Street and parts of Baseline. To our south, the mosque was silent. To our west, and the origin of the contact, no one moved. I trained my sights back to the muj I had shot—still no movement.

I looked to my right and left. All of us were covered with sweat and dust. Thankfully, EOD Nick had kept himself and his shit-covered clothes downstairs instead of coming up to the rooftop. No one spoke, but all heads moved on a swivel, the Punisher skulls visible on each helmet. We waited in silence for our next movement, soaking up the experience.

Ralphie got on the horn with Squad 2 and determined a coordinated linkup on K Street. The Army was sending Bradleys and Abrams tanks to support the patrol back. Squad 2 would set security on the ground and leave the Legend and Biggles up on the roof. Our squad would patrol up and together, and we would make our way back to COP Falcon.

I looked over at Marc and Chucky as I tightened my helmet strap and loaded a fresh mag.

"Well," Marc said.

"Mission success," I replied drily. "We patrolled to contact."

"Lighten up, boys. Charlie one, muj zero this go-round," Chucky said.

Marc laughed. "I'm sure Nick enjoyed this op."

"It could always be worse," I replied.

Back at Falcon, I noticed Jonny sitting on his cot next to Biggles, Biff, and Marc. Jonny had been running point for his squad when a muj machine gunner had let loose on him, pinning him down for a few minutes. He was damn lucky to get out of it without getting shot.

"Fuck," Jonny said with a look of disbelief. "That was gnarly . . . and not in a good way."

"It was," replied Biggles as he started twisting his hair in his habitual way.

I packed a dip and stared at the wall.

"It could be worse," I said. "Nick literally ate shit when we started our center peel."

The tension quickly faded as Marc Lee began recounting the story of EOD Nick. I grabbed a few boxes of 5.56 mm ammo. I relaxed back onto my cot, jamming rounds into the empty magazines, listening to the description of Nick's face and rhetorical questioning of why is Jonny point if he can't see.

Teams and shit . . . Teams and shit.

SIXTEEN

UP THE GUT

"Problem solving is hunting. It is savage
pleasure and we are born to it."

—Thomas Harris

I WENT TO AN all-boys Catholic high school in a quiet central
Connecticut town. I was not the wildest kid, nor the tamest—in
many ways I was your typical teenage boy. Our sleepy town didn't offer
much in the way of weekend entertainment, so my buddies and I spent
a lot of time driving the back roads, waiting for graduation.

We were in my buddy's SUV late one Saturday night when he hit a
deer. He pulled over quickly to assess the damage to his car, which was
considerable, but I wanted to check on the animal.

A large doe lay in the road. She was alive, but badly hurt. At least
two of her legs were broken, and it looked like her back was, too. She
wasn't going to make it. "What do we do?" my friend asked. "Call the
cops?" I shook my head.

"Nah," I said. I pulled out my pocketknife and knelt by the deer.
My younger brother got out of the car and stood over me, nervously

shifting his weight. Before he could speak, I sank the blade into the doe's neck and slit its throat.

We waited while it died, making sure she was done before we climbed back in the vehicle and headed for home in silence. Finally, my buddy spoke. "Why the fuck did you do that?"

I shrugged. "Somebody had to."

COP FALCON, MID-JULY 2006

By mid-July, Ramadi was effectively in a coalition rear-naked choke-hold. The Army and Marines were pressing the western third of the city while the 1st Battalion of the Army's 502nd Infantry Regiment closed in from the east. The tightening vise concentrated the muj in the beaten zone between. The summer of 2006 brought the fight for Ramadi deep into the bowels of the city, where the Punishers pressed the offense.

About two miles east of COP Falcon and just north of Baseline Road, a triple-stack IED had killed another four Marines. Seeking to disrupt muj operations in the area, our leaders coordinated a sniper overwatch operation at an abandoned four-story apartment complex a few hundred meters from the site of the IED attack. Nothing puts fear in the enemy more than a smile you can feel from a mile. The mission was a full-platoon op—all sixteen Teamguys, our two EOD techs, a couple of straphangers, and about a half-dozen Jundis.

Charlie Platoon stepped off at 2300 from Falcon, and all the new-guys were glad to be operating in the darkness where we belonged. I looked around me at my brothers: Rex to my front, Marc Lee behind me. Having been on so many patrols together, we could read each other's thoughts through night vision. Everybody looked tuned in to the environment—alert and ready for anything. *This is what we're meant to do,* I thought. *Silent and deadly.* We own the night. My senses were sharp.

The Legend took his place as point man in our dual-column formation. Our route took us through the tightly packed neighborhoods north of Baseline—an endless patchwork of Iraqi residences, narrow streets, and dark alleyways. The houses and their yards provided plenty of cover and shadows, but a maze of poorly constructed hovels, shanties, and marketplaces allowed no direct route. The target building was just two miles away, but Chris had to stop several times and recheck his GPS. The buildings made it difficult to acquire satellite connections. It didn't matter how diligent you were with a map, how thorough your recon, or how lucky you were. A dog in the road or someone looking out their window could blow your cover. We moved like a bloated accordion in the stifling heat, covering about a mile and a half in two hours.

Half the fun is getting there.

Chris was a great navigator. I'd never really seen him get lost, but he once let a padlocked fence kick his ass after navigating into it during a big reconnaissance exercise back in the States. We easily could have all just climbed over, but Chris was dying to use the new lockpicking skills he'd learned in secret-squirrel school. He pulled out his lockpicking kit, turned his nods on fine focus, and spent about twenty-five minutes failing to pick the lock. Someone finally put him out of his misery and cut the lock with bolt cutters. Because Chris was the Legend, we always offered him no quarter when he stumbled or had difficulty. Chris loved being the Legend, but in those moments where his fallibility was laid bare, he just kind of bore it. Teamguys have to get their shots where we can, and Chris was no exception. He was going to take some shots when we got to the target. I looked toward the tail end of our patrol at Tony pulling up the rear security. Tony was something of a comfort to me there in the back. He was always ready, holding his gun tight, looking around, scanning for threats and his next point of cover, looking behind him every five seconds in true Frogman fashion.

We reached the four-story apartment complex a little after 0200. A couple of machine gunners pushed past the front door and picked up security at the end of the building while the point shooters fanned out to cover all threats high and low. Chris moved up to the front door with an entry team of Jundis. One of them quietly cut the lock on the door, and the Jundis began their clearance.

The front doorway opened up into a lobby from which hallways jutted out on each side and stairs sat straight ahead. We cleared through the entire ground floor, avoiding the littered refuse from an apartment community that had obviously deserted in a hurry. The assault train flowed stealthily through the crevices and hallways, passing updates quietly over comms. It took almost fifteen minutes to clear the fifty-room structure.

Tony posted a team of Jundis in the foyer, and the snipers headed for the roof to begin the hunt. With plenty of space to set up and a view of multiple intersections, choosing the angles that provided the best return on investment was crucial. It's not like fishing, where you can get up and move if you're not catching. Once the loopholes are blown, that's your real estate.

Chris and Tony decided to split sniper assets and utilize the roof and the third floor. Spaz and Squirrel took the real estate to the north. The view to the west was limited by a morass of dilapidated buildings and zigzagging streets. We left a few machine gunners and EOD Nick to pick up that angle. Chris, Marc, and I found a room on the third deck with a window looking toward a big intersection with Baseline Road three hundred meters southeast. The view gave us a wide field of fire into muj country and the intersection where the Marines had been ambushed with the triple-stack IED. The window had some bars and curtains, and we set up in the darkness several feet back.

Tony and a few other guys set up in the adjoining room looking straight east, and the rest of the platoon filled in positions to the west and north. The north side of the building was physically adjoined to a market whose roof aligned perfectly with the second floor of the complex.

"Have a little trouble with your GPS tonight, Legend?" I said to Chris.

"Safe in, safe out, Dauber."

"Home, home on the range . . . Legend," Marc said.

"It wasn't my best performance," Chris said. "But I got us here in one piece. Don't bitch."

Marc and I smirked at each other. He was right.

Chris took the first shift on the gun as the twilight opened on the horizon. Marc and I set up in the back corners of the room, shedding our body armor and lying on our backs, trying not to melt in the suffocating staleness of the hot air inside the building. The daytime temperature was averaging about 120 around that time, and the nights didn't give much relief, especially with the lack of airflow in the city. In that type of environment, you can't really cool yourself down. All you can do is drink water and try not to think about how miserable the heat is. I felt like a hound chained to a post with no relief from the elements.

Around 1100, the muj said good morning with machine guns and a few RPGs. Lying on my back sipping water, I watched apathetically as the rounds came in, hitting the wall above and behind me. I rolled over toward the corner of the room and kept sipping as I slipped into my armor and kit. I'd been shot at so many times that I was pretty tuned in to the drill. If nobody's hit, and you don't have a vantage point to engage, there's not much you can do but take cover.

I low-crawled toward Marc's room, knocking my own piss bottle over in the process. I found him wide-eyed with a HOLY FUCK! look on his face. An entire belt of PKC fire had impacted right around him.

The enemy fire wasn't super-intense, but it was sustained in a way that kept our heads down for a while. Chris, who had been a few rooms away checking on the other snipers, wiggled on up next to me. "Isn't this great?!" he said.

"You bet," replied Marc. "Time to unleash some BTF on them."

I gave Marc a wink.

The machine guns on the rooftop opened up. I looked up and then at Marc. I gave Chris a tap and bolted out and up the stairs to the rooftop. Staying low, I hurried to the roof's east wall, looked over, and saw a bunch of muj scurrying like cockroaches down on the street. Biggles was on a sniper rifle. His Mk 48 sat just next to him. "Biggles, let me use your gun!" I said, grabbing it hurriedly as I put my M4 down. I ran and planted my shoulder on the wall before popping up to spray some 7.62 music down on the corner. The heavy bolt had slammed home, but there was no round seated on the feed tray, no primer to strike, no chain reaction that sends some American lead toward the enemy. Basically, the gun malfunctioned.

Chucky and Bob were engaging effectively with the Pigs to my left as Ned, our third officer, and Jeremy fired 40 mm rounds down on the south side of the wall. I ducked down behind the wall and applied immediate action: charge the weapon, safe it, open feed-tray cover, sweep the linkage, load the belt of ammo, seat the round, slam home the cover, and switch to fire. I jumped back up from behind the wall, letting loose and missing some muj about 250 meters out. I burned through the first hundred-round drum, shooting the bushes and cars the muj disappeared behind. Then I popped the feed tray, swept the links, loaded a new drum, slammed the cover, and popped up again. A small camera on EOD Nick's helmet recorded the scene as I let loose with about another fifty rounds on the muj positions. Looking through my ACOG scope, I couldn't confirm any dead guys, but nobody was moving from behind the bushes or cars I'd lit up.

"Dauber, great shooting, man," Biggles said. "Glad you were able to get that weapon system up and running in time to almost shoot some of the bad guys."

"Nice malfunction there, Dauber," said Chucky. "Too bad you missed the turkey shoot."

"You shoot a machine gun like a corpsman, Daubs," Uncle Bob joked.

Chucky and Bob got after it. They had their guns talking to each other in a perfect my-turn-your-turn rhythm. EOD Nick and Justin took sporadic shots here and there, and Ned continued to launch golden eggs in the general direction of any hostile movement. We all enjoyed the opportunity to pour out some aggression, and I stayed up top for a while, shooting at the enemy in anger, messing around, cracking jokes, and talking shit.

"Guys, check this out," said EOD Nick. He pointed to the wall behind his position. Just above the bedroll he'd been using as a pillow, a gang of bullet holes sat staring at us. Some of the muj machine-gun fire had come through the rooftop wall and impacted just above Nick's head.

Just another day in Ramadi.

One of the best parts about being a newguy, which always sucks, is that you have other newguys to suffer beside, to laugh off the type of stuff most people only ever have to consider in abstract terms. An old salty operator once said, "Men, it only sucks while you're doing it," and I eventually grew to understand that those words are about glory bought by suffering.

After thirty minutes, the enemy fire was suppressed. I crawled toward the rooftop exit and headed back to my sniper position. Marc was on the gun, and Chris was laid out on his back, spitting sunflower seeds listlessly into the space around him. Chris was notorious for just not having any fucks to give about where his spent seeds landed.

He wouldn't even turn his head or make any effort to steer the trajectory of the shells spewing out of his mouth. He was just like the rest of us—dirty men doing dirty work, killing bad people. He spat a seed lazily, and it did sort of a backflip and landed on the Punisher skull painted on his armor. He made no effort to remove it. I shook my head in mock disapproval. Fucking Legend.

"Hey," Marc said from behind Chris's .30-cal, "I've got a peeker, three hundred yards."

"Well, you know the deal," Chris said. "Three strikes, you're out."

"He's kind of moving around in the same area and looking up toward our position," Marc said. "I think he's peeking."

"Well, is he or isn't he?" said the Legend. "How many times has he peeked?"

"I think that was seven or eight," Marc said.

"Well, send him to Allah," Chris said sluggishly.

"Lights out," I said. "Dump him."

Marc closed his left eye and looked back through the scope. He aimed center-mass, exhaled into his natural respiratory pause, and pulled the slack out of the trigger. The bullet exploded out of the barrel and hit lower than Marc had intended, tearing through the man's intestines and turning his insides into a mangled mess of poisoned flesh. He flopped down hard in a heap.

"Nice, Marc," I said, moving to pat him on the back. It was his first kill.

"Nice job, Marc," Chris said.

Marc stared through the scope, scanning for a moment before he opened both eyes and said, "Dude, that was cool," in a voice just above a whisper.

"It's about time you got on the board, Marc," Chris said. "It's fuckin' July after all."

"Yeah, maybe I'll catch up to your numbers now, Legend."

Chris turned and gave me a look that said not a chance in hell, newguy.

"Marc, you've got one more confirmed kill than a lot of guys in the platoon, but you're about seventy behind Chris," I said. "I wouldn't bet on catching him."

Luke came into the room and said, "Whatta ya got?"

"Military-aged male peeker at three hundred yards. Gave him about eight chances before I shot him."

Chris and I confirmed Marc's account.

"Roger that," Luke said and then walked out.

Marc looked back through the scope and watched the guy he'd shot, still alive and in a lot of pain, writhing around near the corner of the intersection, trying to get up and failing. He held his gut and tried to wiggle away, but his insides were too torn up to muster the core strength to move himself. This routine continued for about thirty minutes, and Marc just sat there watching the man's suffering and slow death.

"That's fucking gnarly, man," Marc said solemnly.

I had to agree. It was pretty gnarly. The man's guts drained slowly onto the street around him, and he tried to worm away toward safety or a quicker death, whichever he could manage. But he got nowhere and just kept not dying instead. "Fuck, man," Marc said. "That's gnarly. But they don't give a fuck when they kill our dudes."

"Amen," I replied.

Marc took his first sniper kill a lot differently than I had. He remained fixed, staring at the shit show below. When the guy finally died, his muj buddies came out with white flags and pulled him back around the corner out of sight, a blood trail staining the ground as they dragged him away. Marc got off the gun and gave it over to me.

I don't know if Marc had feelings about that kill. I do know that peekers were cogs in the evil machine we worked day in and day out to dismantle. I shot them. The Legend shot them. Marc shot them. Peekers reported our movements and locations to other muj, who planted IEDs or engaged us outright. Peekers were a problem. The peekers had to go.

My shift was extremely uneventful. Not every minute on the gun is an action movie. When I finished my watch, I was in desperate need of a dip. I was notorious for running out of Copenhagen and bumming way more than is reasonable before even the most generous Teamguy will tell you to pound sand. You know you've hit rock bottom when your most reliable donors suddenly cut you off. I was always bumming Copenhagen off Chris, and apparently, I'd finally reached the point where Chris was fed up and tired of being taken advantage of. I had to find a new benefactor, one who wasn't yet aware of my MO as a shameless dip moocher.

I headed back up to the roof and crawled over to Biggles.

"You're out of dip, aren't you?" he asked knowingly.

I nodded. "Yup."

"You're pretty hard up, aren't you?"

"I'm asking you, and you chew Berry Blend. You know I'm a Copenhagen man."

Biggles handed me his can of Berry Blend Skoal, and I scooped out a chaw and packed it in my lip, immediately regretting it. The Berry Blend tasted far worse than I remembered. I didn't even make it back to my room before I dug it out of my lip and slung it to the ground. "Shit is fucking disgusting," I said to myself. I knew I couldn't let Biggles see the wasted dip. There were two things he loved dearly. One was his girlfriend Kelly, and the other was his Berry Blend Skoal.

Back in our room, I turned my attention to dinner. I pulled out my MRE of spaghetti and slipped the meal packet into the heating element. I poured some water in, folded the plastic container over, and set it down to cook.

At 2300, Tony told us to start breaking down our hide and sanitizing the area. "Muster in the lobby downstairs in thirty minutes." We all tightened up our gear and packed away our trash. Everything we brought in always had to be packed out, shit bags and piss bottles the exception. When in muj country, we left those as a parting gift.

As everyone trickled down to the lobby, EOD Nick and Justin were on the roof, scanning our exfil route one last time for possible IEDs or other dangers. The streets were quiet, and Nick was about to call it all clear and head downstairs when he looked straight down at the front entrance of the complex. Sitting conspicuously against the front door was a big, fat 155 mm artillery round. Traceable from the stumpy phallus to some unseeable end across the street was a command wire, which a muj trigger team was, no doubt, eagerly waiting to detonate the moment we walked out the door.

"Luke, this is Nick," he said over comms. "I've got a command-wired IED at the front door. Get everybody back upstairs."

The muj had been pretty slick in planting it. The firefight earlier in the day had been a diversion. They kept our heads down while an IED team set the huge bomb.

Tony pulled the platoon back to the second floor and the north side of the complex, where the adjacent market's rooftop butted up against the building. If we could get through the wall and onto the roof, there was a stairwell down to the market, where we could exit onto the street and into the darkness. First, we newguys had to bust through the wall.

Marc, Biggles, Jonny, Biff, and I took off our body armor and started hammering. After twenty minutes we had about a three-foot hole. We put our gear back on, and Spaz and I followed Tony and the Legend out onto the roof, setting security for the guys who poured onto the roof behind us.

Spaz and I followed Tony and Chris to the wrought-iron gate forty meters ahead. I shined my IR light through the gate's bars at the stairwell below and the market entrance. Out of the corner of my eye, I saw Spaz walking several feet to my right. He turned around and looked at me.

Then he took another step and disappeared straight down in a blur.

On our night vision, the market's stone roofs and fabric shade structures at the edges read the same. Spaz mistook a shade structure for rooftop. He fell right through and twenty feet down into the middle of the market.

"Fuck!" I said in a hushed tone. This was very bad.

Chris rushed over to see what happened. He could see Spaz lying motionless below. I opened the gate and rushed down the stairs toward the gate that opened into the market. It was locked. A chain and padlock taunted me. "What the fuck, dude!" I whisper-yelled toward Spaz. No answer.

"I need bolt cutters," I said into comms.

"They're in the rear of the platoon," Tony said. "It's gonna be a minute."

"Check. Tell them to hurry."

I stared at Spaz's motionless body just ten feet from me.

"Spaz, you all right?" I said, still trying to whisper loudly enough to where he'd hear me. "Spaz, you all right?"

Everyone on the rooftop fanned out and held security on every conceivable avenue of attack, but nobody could see into the market. If any bad guys were in it, nobody in the platoon could see or shoot them. The 155 mm round was in the back of my mind. The muj were out there, not too far away, waiting for us to exit the building. We couldn't afford to alert them.

"Spaz! You all right? Spaz??"

After what felt like an eternity, the bolt cutters came up from the back of the platoon. Uncle Bob cut the lock, but we still couldn't open the gate. *Fuck, this is not good,* I thought. There were about a thousand ways this could go south.

"Spaz, you okay??" I heard a groan, and my ears perked up. Then I saw him move. Moving is good—alive and he's not paralyzed.

"Spaz, you all right?" Bob hissed at him. He sat up and slowly came into consciousness, taking stock of his situation and groaning painfully. "Spaz, come open the gate. We need you to unlock the gate, bro," Bob coaxed.

He stood awkwardly, keeping his right arm hung motionless by his side. The impact had been so powerful it broke off the buttstock of his gun. It lay on the ground where he had been. His rifle dangled awkwardly from his shoulder and the three-point sling it was clipped to. He hobbled over slowly and worked the gate with his left hand until it finally opened.

The squad quickly fanned out into the market and set security while I assessed Spaz. If he hadn't been wearing his helmet, there's a good chance that fall would have killed him. He'd landed on his right elbow, which was completely messed up. I ripped his cammie sleeve open and saw that his elbow was swollen, but not grossly disfigured. Not much to do two miles from the COP. I slung it up as best I could and got him ready to move.

"Daubah," said Tony, "carry his fahkin' gun and watch his fahkin' back for Chrissake." We took off.

After just a few steps Spaz said, "Gimme that fucking shit," gesturing to his gun. "I'm not a pussy." Maybe he didn't want to look like a pussy, or maybe he just didn't want a newguy carrying his gun for him on an op. Spaz's attitude toward the newguys had not eased even months into the deployment. Either way, he had decided I wasn't carrying his gun back to the COP. I handed the gun over silently and stayed close to him for the patrol back.

Behind the entire platoon, still on the rooftop of the apartment complex, Nick and Justin dropped a quarter block of C4 with a five-minute timed fuse down onto the 155 round. The C4 was a disruption device for the IED. Nick and Justin wanted to leave nothing salvageable for the muj. It took just a few minutes for the platoon to skirt the market and circle back west toward Falcon. We were well on our way home when the C4 blew.

The walk back was uneventful, and the Legend found a new route, applying the old-school safe-in, safe-out mantra and taking no chances with a potential ambush. At Falcon, we sent Spaz back to Camp Ramadi to have his arm looked at. Then it was time to wait around for the next big mission. We headed into our BTF building and started peeling off our gear.

"That one was close," I said to Jonny.

"You bet," he replied back.

"You bet," echoed Biggles. "Luckily Nick and Justin were on point. It's about time EOD proves its use," he said with a smile.

Nick couldn't help but smile. He knew that one was too close for comfort.

"Muj had their shit locked with that one," Nick said. "But seriously, can we critique Marc's accuracy with the sniper rifle?"

The banter quickly enveloped the crew. It felt good to be back at COP Falcon in one piece, despite Spaz's lawn dart impression from twenty feet up. Fortunately, he suffered only a large contusion and bursitis from the fall.

If EOD Nick and Justin hadn't discovered the IED before leaving the rooftop, the massive bomb likely would have killed us all. In the world of Special Operations, there is no extra weight. Each individual serves a crucial purpose that adds to the team's effectiveness. The EOD guys in our platoon were worth their weight in gold, day in and day out. Nick and Justin did their job well, and they literally saved all our lives in that apartment complex. We treated Nick like the hero he was.

After a while, my thoughts drifted to how the muj had kept our heads down while planting the IED. Those motherfuckers.

Jonny looked at me. "I don't give a fuck," he said coldly, seeming to read my mind.

"I don't give a fuck, either."

Our enemy deserved no quarter.

SEVENTEEN

IWO JIMA GAMES

"When snatched from the jaws of death,
tooth marks are to be expected."

—Hal Story

H ELL WEEK IS secured on Friday morning in a scene of quiet
reverence. My class came over a berm on the beach and face-
to-face with an American flag flapping in the wind. As we stopped and
surrounded it, the commanding officer of BUD/S got on the bullhorn and
announced we were secured, congratulating us on our accomplishment.

We slapped each other on the backs, took knees, and waited to
hear the words of encouragement from each of the instructors and officers who had gathered to see us secured. I was well past the point
of exhaustion and their words began to trail away, but I fixed my eyes
firmly on Old Glory, and she did not waver.

COP FALCON, LATE JULY 2006

I carried an American flag on every patrol in Ramadi. The Stars and
Stripes always stayed close to my heart, folded neatly and stored in my

body armor between the hard and soft plates. Carrying the flag into battle is a centuries-old tradition whose formal origins were mostly abandoned with the evolution of warfare in the twentieth century. Our National Ensign still flies today in war zones above all military bases and outposts, but Old Glory goes out into the fray only when someone carries her into battle as a reminder of what we're fighting for. Pilots often carry flags with them on bombing runs or other missions. I don't doubt that other troops in Iraq carried our flag close to their hearts like I did. As service members, we are stewards of the flag and everything it symbolizes, and you never know when you're going to need to fly the colors high in combat. For that reason, I carried my flag as if it were a required piece of gear. I was never sure how or when I might need it. After four months in country, I figured I'd probably end up flying it over Sharkbase for a day and then fold it up and give it to my parents or something.

Little did I know, Ramadi would provide a much better use.

The head shed had decided to hybridize our ops. Instead of just splitting the platoon into two squads and patrolling to contact during the day, they sent one patrol on a sniper overwatch to provide cover for the other squad's presence patrol. The plan was that when the squad patrolled to contact, the overwatch element would light up the muj, engaging them. I was in the overwatch squad with Luke, Chris, Tony, Jeremy, Marc, Biggles, Rex, Spaz, and augmentees from SEAL Team EIGHT. The op tempo in Baghdad wasn't optimizing EIGHT's skill sets, so they came to Ramadi to bolster our operations. The platoon from EIGHT was solid, and they blended well into our day-to-day operations.

Willie was EIGHT's main sniper. Like Marc, he also looked Iraqi and caught a lot of jokes to that effect. He had a few kills and was known for catching an unlucky stray round in the back inside the Green Zone* in Baghdad. The stray bullet's force was minimized by its

---

* A roughly four-square-mile area in Baghdad that housed the Coalition Provisional Authority. It was heavily fortified and one of the safest military bases in Iraq.

long trajectory, but it lodged in the meat of Willie's back for a superficial wound. The docs pulled it out, and Willie went back to work.

We took a building just north of Baseline about a mile east of COP Falcon. It was a nice corner house a few hundred meters west of the apartment complex where EOD Nick had saved us all from an inglorious demise. It provided a limited view of J and K Streets across Baseline to the south and a nice long view down the streets to the east, north, and back toward Falcon to the west. With 360-degree coverage, our sniper ambush was set to catch any muj trying to get the jump on our patrol.

Our breachers blew four loopholes in the four-foot wall. Marc and I set up on the rooftop looking east. We had a good angle looking down the road about four hundred yards. Willie was one floor down, directly below us looking out a window to the south. Chris looked east through a loophole on the roof, and Tony had a loophole looking north.

In addition to the augmentees from EIGHT, our task unit chief, Pepper, joined us on the op. He was a well-seasoned Frogman from Texas with several deployments under his belt who added to the wealth of experience of our enlisted leadership. Pepper was a mobility and tactics guru whose sound advice, as an ordnance rep, I sought frequently. He was a legend at Team THREE for his role in the initial invasion of Iraq and the charge into Baghdad. He covered the west. I shaded myself with my poncho liner tied to some rebar protruding from the roof's wall, and Marc and I started our rotation on my Mk 11.

As usual, we didn't see much of anything during the night, and the morning was mostly uneventful. Around eleven, we got the call on comms that the other squad had launched its presence patrol from Falcon. A few minutes later, a single shot rang out from Willie's position downstairs.

"Willie, what are you shooting at?" Tony called over comms.

"Some guy," Willie replied. "Looks like muj."

"Well, did you hit him?"

"No."

"Well, why not?"

"Well, he's just standing around looking shady, so I sent a warning shot over his head."

"What the fuck?!" Tony barked. "You're a fucking sniper! You don't fire warning shots!"

Marc and I burst out laughing. A fucking warning shot.

"Really, Willie?" Chris said over comms. "Is that how they do it on the East Coast? You Team EIGHT guys send warning shots?"

"Yeah, Willie, great idea, man," Luke said. "Give away our position for a warning shot."

Willie didn't need any more critiquing; he got the point.

"Roger that," Willie replied sheepishly.

It took a while for our presence patrol to make their way down J Street and patrol to contact, but when the contact came it came with a vengeance. The muj opened up on the patrol with what sounded like an insane amount of fire. I heard AKs, PKCs, and RPGs going off like Armageddon a few blocks to the southwest.

"Jesus Christ," Tony said. "Anybody got a line of sight on that contact?"

Nobody did. We couldn't engage.

"Well, shit," Chris said. "What do we do now?"

"I've got a flag in my body armor," I said.

"Well, shit yes, let's run it up. Draw some attention away from that patrol." Chris got off his gun and crawled over to my position. I took the flag out of my body armor while Chris found a big aluminum pole. He grabbed the flag and tied it to the pole.

"Let's fucking hoist it," he said.

Marc pulled out his little video camera and started filming the historic event while Jeremy joined Chris and me as we hoisted the flag up, flying it high on the rooftop in the middle of muj country.

We all crouched there beaming over what had to be one of the most America-fuck-yeah moves in the entire war.

"We just Iwo Jima'd this shit," Chris said, crouching behind the wall with a shit-eating grin. AP photographer Joe Rosenthal's famous photo of U.S. Marines raising the flag on the summit of Mount Suribachi during the Battle of Iwo Jima is among the most iconic photos ever produced. The image is seared into the American consciousness as a symbol of our unbreakable will and fighting spirit. We Punishers felt it was completely appropriate to fly Old Glory high above an enemy stronghold in the same tradition of so many proud American warriors whose legacy we inherited.

It took a few seconds for the muj to catch on, but when they saw the flag, they responded accordingly. Our game had worked. To say we drew their fire is an understatement. We drew their wrath. The muj unloaded hate at our building, and I've never felt so good about taking intense enemy fire.

Our guys on the ground had reacted perfectly when they took contact. They strongpointed a building, and one of the guys saw our flag and managed to take a picture of it when the muj turned their attention our way. From our building, we still couldn't see our attackers, so we just stayed low and waited. After a while, the fire died down. We took the flag down, and I folded it back up and stowed it between my plates. I carried that flag throughout the rest of the deployment and all the way back home. Eventually, I framed it with a little engraving summarizing the story of our Iwo Jima reenactment, and gave it to my parents as a Christmas gift.

Our Iwo Jima stunt had all of us feeling confident, and Tony decided to commemorate the occasion by tagging the rooftop wall: "Charlie Platoon 100, Savages 0." Our feeling of invincibility was at its height. We took pictures of Tony's tag and dreamed up more ways to entertain ourselves with the monotony of war.

"Gimme that wooden dowel," I said to Marc, pointing to a three-foot stick. I took a sheet and tightened it around the dowel like the base for a torch head. I drew some eyes, a nose, and a smile on it and then put some sunglasses on it. I finished it off with my helmet.

"Looks like a head, right?" I said. "Let's see what this does."

I named him Wilson. I hoisted Wilson up and kind of crawled back and forth, goading our enemy to shoot at him and entertaining myself and my brothers. To tweak that famous quote from Rick James, boredom is a helluva drug. Nobody shot at Wilson, but after a minute, I kind of smartened up. I looked at the wall and realized that it was only a few inches thick and the right weapon and concentration of fire could quickly render the whole situation very unfunny. They didn't have to get a head shot. A well-aimed RPG could really fuck me up. *Man, this is a dumb idea,* I thought, pulling my dummy down and putting my helmet back on. I settled back into a tactical mindset and sat down next to Marc.

"This is kind of a waste," I said. "I hope the guys on that presence patrol did all right."

"Right? This machine gun is aching to run."

"I hear ya."

Tony told us they had called in the quick reaction force, and the Army sent a bunch of armored vehicles to pick them up. Fortunately, no one was hit. We stayed the rest of the day without incident and patrolled back that evening.

Pepper was in front of me as we walked back. I watched him and I could tell he was smoked. His cammies were soaked through with sweat, and he walked pretty heavily. At one point, Marc gave him a pull from his CamelBak. Pepper looked like a man who was severely dehydrated. I knew that feeling well, and I kept an eye on him. At an intersection, he walked off the sidewalk to cross the street. As he looked back toward me, he must have caught his boot on a rock or some rubble, because he fell flat on his face. I saw him go plank—from a straight 90 degrees to a 180 in a heartbeat. He hit the ground hard right in the middle of the street. I saw it and realized he was probably as bad off as I had suspected. *He's gonna need an IV,* I thought. Pepper was a Big Tough Frogman for sure and got right back on his feet, but the rousting began immediately. The rest of the patrol back, the chatter over comms was merciless.

When we got back to COP Falcon, I looked around at our guys. They looked beat to shit. Despite our messing with Pepper, his condition was understandable. We were all smoked. Jonny and I gave Pepper an IV and we got him on a convoy back to Sharkbase for some more hydration. The rest of us went to our SEAL house on the COP to trade stories about what had gone down. When I walked in, the smell of man-ass, stale sweat, and spent meal packs hit me hard. Disgusting. The rest of the newguys were already sitting around bullshitting. I slid my helmet under my cot and plopped down. Biff was in the corner, still sweating balls with the fan on him.

"You hear what happened to Biff?" Marc asked.

"No, dude. I just hooked Pepper up with some IV awesomeness." I looked at Biff. He looked haggard and exhausted with a fuck-all look. "Biff, what happened, man?"

"Not again . . ." he said, exhaling deeply and kind of shaking his head. He paused for a second. "I got shot in the fucking head, man. After we strongpointed the building, I got to the roof, and when I peeked over the wall a round nailed me right in the NVG mount. Knocked me on my fucking ass. I just saw this huge flash of light. Fucking rung my bell. Fucking pissed me off. I was so pissed I jumped up and went cyclic. Unloaded about two hundred rounds over the wall and somehow forgot to shoot the gun right-handed." He lifted his right bicep. It was burned black. Biff was a natural southpaw, and the Mk 48 isn't built for lefties. The ejection port spits brass out the right side of the gun, and Biff had managed to spit two hundred rounds of burning-hot brass straight into his bicep without skipping a beat.

Combat rage is a helluva drug, too.

"That's pretty fucking gnarly, man," I said.

"Yeah, bro, too close for my comfort," Biff replied. "Ralphie also took a few rounds off his armor."

"Shit's getting pretty close, man," Jonny said. "I mean, we lost a Jundi the other day, and another one got injured. There was that close call with the IED house, and now Biff takes one to the helmet. We're hanging out there like dog's balls." A small squad from Charlie Platoon had gone on an op a few days before with a group of Jundis. They'd taken fire and two Jundis had been hit, one of them mortally.

"Well, no one makes fun of a dog with large balls," Biggles replied.

"Like the one that was humping your leg the other night at Shark-base," Marc replied.

We all laughed. Cutting up with my brothers never got old.

EIGHTEEN

KYK'ING ASS

"The strength of the team is each individual member.
The strength of each member is the team."

—Phil Jackson

I RECALL A PARTICULAR hazing incident during work-up in Niland, California. I'd gotten myself completely taped up from head to foot by the older guys and dumped into a rack. No newguy is ever thrilled with this situation: getting bum-rushed, tackled, and wrapped in duct tape is one of the most uncomfortable, and most common, hazing rituals Teamguys have. They left me there.

I lay there, alone and pissed off, while they went back to their drinking. A few minutes later, the Legend crept in to make sure I was okay. He didn't untape me, but he asked me in his Texas drawl, "Hey, buddy, you okay? Just checkin' on ya." I grunted an assent and he crept back out of the room, chuckling his unmistakable laugh. That was just like Chris. He'd never want anything to happen to any of his guys, but he sure wasn't going to let us out of paying our dues, either.

I waited there for about an hour until they came back for me. I ripped off the yards of tape and acknowledged, begrudgingly, that no matter what kind of shit we pull on each other, we're still family.

————————

SHARKBASE, LATE JULY 2006

Biff had the look of a desperate man. Teamguys aren't prone to panic, but it's fair to say he was freaking out a little after we wrapped up the op brief for another mission with the Marines up around Firecracker. Everybody was jacked up and ready to hit it, but Biff was nearly at his breaking point. As a radio operator in the Teams, he was responsible for a highly sensitive piece of gear called the KYK-13, and at the moment we were supposed to launch into the fray, Biff had to report that he was unable to say with any certainty where the cryptographic key loader for his radio was. He had lost the device that kept our comms secure.

I quickly understood why Biff had looked so pale and worried. The KYK-13, although mostly outdated now, is a device the National Security Agency developed for the transfer and loading of cryptographic keys for our long-range radios. In enemy hands, the little metal box with its crude knobs and switches could have some pretty hefty implications for our operational security within Ramadi and pretty much all of CENTCOM. The likelihood that the muj would be able to use the KYK was low, but the potential for disaster was still there should it fall into the wrong hands.

Our priorities immediately shifted. Without the KYK, we couldn't launch for the scheduled operation. We communicated our situation up the chain, and finding the KYK became our new mission. We started on Sharkbase, searching our compound thoroughly. Nothing. Tony took Biff aside like a disappointed father.

"All right, where do you think it is, Biff? When was the last time

you know you had it?" Tony asked like a parent asking a child who'd
lost his favorite blanket.

"Falcon," Biff said. "I had it when we were on Falcon."

We all jumped into the vehicles and headed down to COP Falcon. Rolling down Sunset, I thought about how awful it would be if
our forced audible literally blew up in our faces. I felt sorry for Biff,
who had situated himself firmly atop the shit lists of many people, including himself. We were being pushed so hard that nobody was unaffected. At this point, anybody could have lost a piece of gear.

This was a platoon issue, and I just hoped we could find the KYK.
At COP Falcon, the gate guard pulled back the concertina wire to let
our convoy pass, and we zipped into the parking lot, quickly mus-
tering up to search the COP. We gently ransacked our SEAL house
and found nothing. Then we combed around the entire compound,
looking for a six-inch olive-drab rectangle in the middle of the night.
Nothing.

"I honestly cannot remember where it was," Biff said after Tony
returned to his interrogation. "I might have put it on the roof of the
truck and forgotten it there."

"So it could be pretty much anywhere between here and Sharkbase?"

"Well, it would probably fall off early."

Luke decided we would take a small foot patrol up Sunset and
look for the KYK along the road we'd taken back to Sharkbase about
twenty-four hours earlier. The odds of finding it weren't good, but the
stakes were too high not to try. Patrolling up a heavily IED'd road at
night was, to put it lightly, less than ideal, and Luke picked Chris, me,
and Marc to accompany him on the tiny four-man patrol. The group's
small size would optimize our stealth and speed. The plan was to patrol north on Sunset for about a mile and then turn back. If we got into
trouble along the way, we'd call in the rest of the platoon as a quick reaction force.

"The op's simple," Luke told us. "We'll go up, walk the road, and come back. If we don't see anything, we don't see anything and that's it."

Chris took his usual spot on point for a dual-column formation. Luke was staggered ten meters behind on the opposite side of the street. I fell in behind Chris in the same crisscross pattern with Marc in tow with the big gun on rear security behind Luke. The poorly lit streets kept us cloaked in darkness, providing plenty of concealment as we moved slowly, scanning the cratered and debris-laden streets through night vision. Looking for a small green object in the all-green world of night vision is not ideal. Needles and haystacks come to mind. Regardless, you never know when you might get an opportunity to BTF.

Further complicating the already difficult task, we had to vigilantly keep an eye out for IEDs and other threats. I saw what looked like a command wire running into a crater.

I noticed a suspicious cluster of wires and signaled to Chris, alerting him to the potential IED. We stayed away from using comms around IEDs since the muj had perfected their booby-trap techniques. I didn't want to detonate the fire team by ignorantly mistaking a command wire when it was a cell phone base station. That's EOD's job. Better safe than a grease spot in Ramadi.

I threw an IR ChemLight next to the spot, marking it for Dagger to sweep up when they came through. Then I saw another potential threat, and another. I marked them all until I ran out of IR Chem-Lights, trying to keep my distance at the same time. I stayed calm and completely tuned in to my surroundings.

The hasty patrol had me feeling alive. It was a nice change to get out of the conventional routine and do some real Frogman work. We had to walk this full patrol and do our best to find the lost KYK. If we didn't find it, we'd turn around and that would be it. Losing a KYK is nothing to take lightly, but the risk-return ratio wasn't going to hold together beyond the mission we were already running.

About halfway to the building where Chris had shot the two guys on the moped, he halted the patrol and took a knee. Carefully, he raised his M4 and lased a target about one hundred meters ahead.

"Hey, I got a guy moving with an AK, creeping around in the shadows," Chris said over comms. "He's moving west."

"Bird-dog him," Luke said. Marc and I didn't need further instructions.

The hunt was on.

We popped up and moved to the shadows.

Chris ran up about twenty meters and knelt at the corner of a building, raising his M4 toward our muj prey. Luke popped up and bounded past Chris, twenty meters on the opposite side of the street. Marc and I followed. The four of us moved like an accordion.

"Military-aged male moving tactically with an AK. Turned west off Sunset, eight hundred meters from the COP," Luke called back to Falcon, reporting our position to the platoon as we made our first turn in pursuit of our prey. We activated our IFF markers. We didn't need the conventionals lighting our asses up like they had on the hospital op.

The Legend pressed our hasty stalk as we zigzagged methodically through the darkened city blocks to track and outmaneuver the muj. At every turn, Luke reported our position back to the platoon at Falcon. We played a game of read and react, responding to each other's movements and picking up fields of fire reflexively. At each intersection, we flowed straight into our crossing drill, picking up security and then peeling back into columns and bounding ahead. Speed was vital as we mirrored the muj's movement. He moved stealthily between city blocks and could have been on his way to any kind of attack on coalition forces.

Adrenaline fine-tuned my senses to every aspect of my surroundings. I thought more of noise discipline than of an ambush or IED attack as I ran over trash and debris. The thick darkness of the poorly lit streets provided a tremendous advantage, and we stalked the muj for about four hundred meters, scurrying from shadow to shadow like a fox on a chicken farm. As we passed the faint, intermittent light from surrounding buildings, my heart rate spiked.

Our movement reminded me of *Call of Duty* on Xbox, like watching myself stalking in a first-person shooter. Hunting the guy with such efficiency amped me up. I just felt we were going to catch him and he had no idea what was coming. I could feel the unspoken competition between the four of us, urging us forward as we each willed ourselves to shoot first. As he moved on a street parallel to us, Chris pushed us ahead and led us into an alleyway to cut him off. The Legend took a knee and waited. Marc, Luke, and I did the same, picking up 360-degree security. As if on cue, the muj popped around the corner, moving straight toward Chris at less than one hundred yards. The Legend lined up his IR laser center-mass and dumped three rounds in a tight cluster. The suppressed shots in quick succession split the near silence of the white noise blowing off the Habbaniyah Canal to the west.

Say cheese, buddy.

The guy never knew what hit him. Chris might as well have been a ghost in the alley's shadows, waiting to send the muj to his virgins. If the guy saw anything, it was a couple of quick muzzle flashes piercing the blackness and then making it permanent.

The Legend's Texas twang came over comms. "He's down, one hundred yards."

Marc and I looked at each other. We were both panting from the run. Even through NVGs, I could see Marc and I were thinking the same thing: *That was fucking awesome.* Chris had led the hunt on the most badass rundown I'd ever seen. There was something exhilarating about the unscripted nature of the engagement and the way we'd reacted so perfectly. We had started off on a glorified FOD walk and ended up hunting down and killing an armed insurgent. We stayed in the shadows for another ten minutes, waiting for another armed insurgent who never appeared.

It was one of the cooler things we'd ever done. We left the dead muj where he lay, turned around, and patrolled back to Falcon. The conventional forces would pick up the body later. We moved quietly back to the COP, high on victory, anticipating an ambush that didn't materialize.

At the front gate of COP Falcon, all the guys stood by, waiting for us. They pulled the concertina wire out of the way.

"What the fahk did you get into out theya?" Tony asked.

"We just ran some savage down," Chris said. "Couldn't find the KYK. But we did find some dude with an AK. I smoked him."

I relaxed as Biff pulled the concertina wire back into place behind us.

"Dude, that was fucking cool," I said to Marc. "Can't beat working in the dark."

"Yeah, that was cool," Marc replied. "That's the type of shit we're meant for. We own the night, brother."

"Fucking Legend," I said, turning to Chris. "How come you always get to shoot the bad guys?"

"It's the lucky horseshoes he's got stuffed up his ass," Jonny piped in.

"Well, it's a good thing you remembered to put fresh batteries in your ATPIALs this time, Legend," I said.

"All the things I do for you, and this is what I get in return, Dauber? Hating on my kill count?"

"Well, I gotta take my shots where I can, Legend. You're pretty good at killing muj. Let's just hope we don't come to a fence where you need to pick the lock."

"Tell me again how many kills you have, son?" Chris said, pulling out his shit-talking trump card.

Biff's unlucky incident had kept us off a Marine operation in north Ramadi that some skeevy Devil Dog had named Operation Rug Muncher. I had been very motivated about the possibility of serving in Operation Rug Muncher, but losing the KYK ended up being fortunate for the platoon as a whole. Going down to Falcon to patrol an IED road was a pretty comical and potentially disastrous mission, but Ramadi coughed up a bit of combat serendipity in the form of an armed muj to hunt down and neutralize. Adding another kill to our tally lessened the sting of losing a KYK, but at the same time, we still lost a KYK. It was never recovered and a new crypto-load had to be done to ensure that if the KYK did fall into enemy hands it couldn't be used against us.

Of course, nobody expected that Biff's mistake would lead to some much-needed rest for the platoon, but that's what happened. The head shed seemed to recognize that Biff's gaffe might have been related to our op tempo. They could see guys were tired. We needed a break.

———————

With slightly fewer ops for a few days, we had a little more time to indulge in the comforts of camp life. Everyone had his habits, and by July we were well established in our routines. When we had any time off, we liked to blow off some steam.

The tent I shared with Marc, Spaz, and Bob had one of the more reliable AC units, so on a rare true night off, we'd hang a sheet and watch a movie. Contraband liquor, carefully repackaged into mouthwash or Gatorade bottles and shipped via care package by our buddies stateside, was an important ingredient for movie night. *Patton* was a staple at these gatherings. We lit cigars and spoke the opening monologue along with George C. Scott; we all knew it by heart.

Tony could often be found in my tent binge-watching *The Sopranos*. His obsession made me chuckle, because he was like the mob boss of our platoon. Not only did he share the same name as *The Sopranos'* main character, but he had a ruthlessness toward the enemy tempered by a charm and tactical efficiency that made him impossible to dislike. Not unlike the Tony of his show, he really cared for his guys, even when he was being tough. In the military, there are men you have orders to follow, and there are others you follow because you know they will keep you alive. I'd follow Tony into hell.

I tried to work out when I could. Marc was a good lifting buddy. There was a gym on the veranda of Sharkbase, and we would have had a great view of the Euphrates if they hadn't erected ballistic sheets to deflect incoming sniper fire. We'd lift when we could, but our op tempo meant we weren't always consistent. At least once a week we ran a three-mile loop past the guard shack on Sharkbase. We'd run along the river road and past the Ranger compound, cursing the heat and the dust.

In a short lull in late July, guys like Marc and Jonny took full advantage of the Internet and the chance to call their ladies. Most of the rest of us had gotten used to limited contact with loved ones back home and subscribed to the if-it-ain't-broke school of thought. We were still in Ramadi, after all. What did I have to say? I sent sporadic, heavily edited emails home to my family.

Rarely, a couple of guys would watch a movie on a computer or hang out alone. I watched *Jeremiah Johnson* with Biggles at the end of July, right before starting the ops hard again. He had never seen it and it was one of my favorites.

The trouble with slowing down is that after going at a certain pace for so long, taking a little break feels like just waiting for something to happen. In the desert, life continues one way until it doesn't. You go and go and go until one day you don't, and then your hands itch for your rifle and your chest aches for your body armor. You grow so accustomed to the sound of mortars every day that you realize they're the standard, and when your day starts without an explosion, you don't feel right until one goes off. When life outside the wire becomes normal, even life at the camp seems incompatible with the mindset you're in.

The break didn't last. A few days later, we were right back at our previous op tempo. To be honest, it was probably ratcheted up a notch to make up for lost time. We hit the city hard, like a firing pin on a .30-cal round. I settled into a cold and composed acceptance of the situation.

I'm not going to die in this desert.

NINETEEN

MAN DOWN

"The bravest are surely those who have the clearest
vision of what is before them, glory and danger alike,
and yet notwithstanding go out to meet it."

—Thucydides

YOU KNOW THE moment when momentum turns against
you in a fight. I got in a bar fight once with a professional football player and that moment occurred for me when he bit me solidly
in the cheek. As he sank his teeth deep into my flesh, liberally breaking
the skin, I dug my thumbs into his eye sockets and pushed. He relaxed
his jaw, but he proceeded to kick my ass.

The following Monday, I showed up at the platoon with a black
eye and a festering human bite wound on my face. Tony looked at me
hard for a moment, his eyes narrow. I waited for his retribution, whatever form it might take. Finally he asked, "Didya get arrested?"

"No, Chief," I answered.

"Good. Stay outta trouble with the cops, Dauba'. I can't help you
there. Get ya shit. We got work to do."

Sometimes it's just a matter of being reminded not to try to go it alone.

August 2 was a bad day.

We'd been going heavy. Really heavy. The list of close calls loomed as we ratcheted up the risk factor of our missions. Instructor Torsen's words of wisdom rang true. "If you motherfuckers think this is bad," referring to Hell Week, "wait until you get downrange. War is relentless. There is no stop, no quit, no Bell. Suck it the fuck up." COP San Quentin, a Johnny Cash reference, had become the newguy name for our miserable southern home. We hated every inch of it. In the heat of that Iraqi August, I felt the words of Led Zeppelin's "When the Levee Breaks" swell within me. Something was growing.

The brass excelled at keeping us mean, and coalition casualties reminded us why we needed to be. Despite losing a Jundi, we were getting results. We were winning the war of attrition. Muj casualty rates were overwhelming compared to our own. The flood of coalition forces into the heart of the city was breaking the back of the insurgency and laying the groundwork for the Anbar Awakening, brokered during the surge. It was time to break the levee. Our operations north of Baseline left no doubt the muj were massed in the area, and their IED attacks killed and maimed troops regularly. The Army wanted to go for the muj's throat, and we were the junkyard dog they wanted for the mission.

A cordon-and-search operation is exactly what it sounds like. You cordon off an area, allowing no one in or out while you search every building within the perimeter. Hopefully, you find an enemy weapons cache or other insurgent contraband, or you find a bunch of bad guys and neutralize them. Fortunately, the area we were headed to was the enemy den. We expected to hit pay dirt. Big Army was ready to roll in force on the area we'd been softening and flush the rats out of hiding. They tasked us to spearhead the push.

We left just before dawn, all of Charlie Platoon and a few shooters from Team EIGHT. We were without Spaz and Bob. Bob had taken some shrapnel to his knee on a patrol and was sent back to San Diego, and Spaz's elbow was still on the mend from his fall through the shade structure at the market weeks before. We brought ten Jundis to help with the clearances. The neighborhood with the apartment complex—the one that had nearly entombed us a couple of weeks earlier—was our target. We were ready to shake the hornet's nest, knock it to the ground, spray it with fire, and stomp on any survivors.

The Legend took point in our lead squad, with Marc, Biggles, Jonny, Tony, and Luke. The second squad was Ralphie, Ned, Biff, Squirrel, me, and Scotty from Team EIGHT. The Jundis pulled up the rear. As we left Falcon, we stretched slowly into our dual column and settled into four months of muscle memory. I vividly remember looking to my right and left that morning at the men around me and thinking, in spite of the heat and the danger and the arguable absurdity of operating into the daytime hours, *There's no other place I'd rather be right now.*

Baseline was crystal clear in the morning darkness, and we flowed smoothly through the green-filtered streets, our lasers scanning methodically. Our Jundis—scruffy pirates that they were—had tightened up substantially after four months of intensive training and combat operations. Despite having no night-vision goggles, they moved like professional operators, reading and reacting. No one smoked a cigarette as we left Falcon. They understood the area we were headed into. I looked at Hassan, as much of a meathead as I'd ever seen. He and the rest of our Jundis looked impressive. They had come a long way. Marc,

Bob, Spaz, and I had trained them hard for countless hours, and seeing the results in action made me proud.

The lead squad turned north off Baseline and funneled into a single column on the east side of the street. Our trail squad took the west side with the Jundis. Two blocks up, Chris's squad split off and cleared through a building, setting up a sniper overwatch on the rooftop to cover our squad and the Jundis as we cleared and searched houses. The Army, with its Bradley Fighting Vehicles and Abrams tanks, set blocking positions all around the city block. Once the Army closed off any escape routes and prevented potential coordinated attacks, we were cleared hot.

As we approached our first building, the pirates, with their sledgehammers and ladders, looked like a gang of hooligans, eager to break into buildings at our command. Surprise was our advantage, so a soft knock was preferred. Moose and our Jundis had really mastered the technique, and we got in fast and cleared through quickly.

Slow is smooth; smooth is fast.

We glided through the houses cautiously, expecting to meet resistance and to find guns and bombs, but the first few houses left us empty-handed.

In the fourth house, I made my way to the roof with Ned and Biff and took a knee. *Maybe this won't be so bad, after all,* I thought. We'd been out in muj country plenty of times before. We'd been in plenty of shit.

A single shot cracked in the distance, and I jerked my head in the direction of the sound, as if by sheer will I could ensure the safety of my Teammates.

Silence for a beat.

Then a Teamguy's Mk 48 opening up in an angry spray of aggression. As a sniper, I knew that silence after a shot too well. Over squad comms came the call we told ourselves we would never hear, yet somehow expected eventually: "Man down," Luke called. "Biggles is down." I looked at Biff, my eyes widening.

"What the fuck?" I said to Biff and Ned. Biff just looked at me, mouth open.

"Fucking chill," said Ned. "We'll figure it out. We don't know what's going on."

We hurried to the rooftop's wall on the side facing Biggles's building. A mess of date palms and scrub brush obscured our view of the opposite rooftop, but I could hear Marc's gun spraying rage. He burned through the first hundred rounds and reloaded in a blink of an eye. Marc was in machine mode.

With a clear view of the ground around the building, we scanned for flanking muj. Over comms, I heard Luke initiate Biggles's medevac. The Bradleys and tanks were closer to the regular infantry units that were hitting other buildings in the area, but the medevac came quickly. A Bradley roared up to Biggles's building, spun into a perfect 180 turn, backed up, and dropped the ramp in front of the door. A moment later, the Legend burst out of the building, gun at the ready, providing cover. Behind him in the doorway, Biggles leaned heavily on Jonny. Biggles's face was heavily bandaged. His body armor and helmet were gone, and his upper body was covered in blood from the wound to his face, but he stood on his own. *Alive and walking.* My heart settled back into my chest. Biggles and Jonny rushed toward the Bradley while Marc's Pig blasted in the background, and a few more gunners added to the music.

"Fuck, dude," I said, exhaling and scanning the surrounding streets. The walking was a good sign, but I felt powerless.

The officers went back and forth over inter-squad comms, trying to figure out our next move while the rest of us kept the watch. Biggles getting hit had us all uneasy and hyperalert. He was the first Teamguy to be seriously wounded in our platoon.

We had practiced man-down drills until we puked. Everyone

knew what to do and when to do it. The drills had etched themselves into our muscle memory just like clearing rooms. But there's no practice that prepares you to see your buddy's face half removed from an enemy round. In moments like that, you push everything else aside and stick to what you know. Read and react. Muscle memory and training. We took positions on our building's second floor, trying to stay clear of the windows while scanning the streets below for an enemy soul to extinguish.

Finally, we got the plan. Chris's squad, now missing Biggles and Jonny, would absorb several of the Jundis and lead the patrol back to Falcon. Squad 2 would follow behind with Tony and me picking up the rear-security mission.

The Jundis could feel the tension. They had come to understand the brotherhood we all shared. Biggles was loved by everyone in the platoon. The tough bastard had a smart-ass joke for every occasion, and we all leaned on his ability to make the best of any situation. When he got saddled with all the shitty jobs, he did them without question because that was his style. Everybody knew how hard he worked to get through BUD/S, and when he got wounded, it scraped us raw. The Jundis saw a side of rage from the platoon they had never seen before. They were squirrelly, like nervous horses, ready to stampede.

Luke announced the first squad's departure, and Chris stepped off to lead them into the fray, absorbing half the Jundis into his squad. Squad 2 and the rest linked up behind them, and Tony and I covered their six, picking up an exhausting Frogman-peel rhythm while the patrol pushed hard toward Falcon. With Tony set, I'd check my flank, turn inboard, and sprint past him to the next covered position and call "Set." The leapfrogging kept us running the entire way back. We struggled to keep up with the fast-moving patrol and even lost contact from the main element as Chris took a left into some side streets toward Baseline. We were running our own version of the Mogadishu Mile from *Black Hawk Down*. Before we knew what had happened, it was just the two of us, running our asses off through muj country.

"Whe' the fack did they go?" Tony said, panting as he ran past me.

My adrenaline surged as I knelt at a corner, heart pounding out of my chest. Tony called "Set" fifty meters past me. I turned reflexively to check my flank and peel. As if on cue, a muj materialized out of a door in the alley directly in my line of fire thirty yards out. He had a manicured chinstrap beard and blue shirt, and he was running with an RPG raised in the same fuck-all-banzai manner that seemed to be a muj calling card. He was obviously excited, thinking he had the jump on us, but I turned mechanically and found him perfectly placed in my EO-Tech reticle. His eyes ballooned up wide in surprised horror as he saw me lock on to him. He knew he was dead. I didn't even have to think. As he fumbled to react, I fired two shots into his dumbstruck face, putting him to rest with a perfect double tap to the T-box. With his brain stem likely severed, his knees buckled under him, and his torso folded down onto his legs in a perfect child's-pose—ass up, head down like he was praying. I scanned the area and locked on to the compound the muj had come from. I grabbed a frag grenade, pulled the pin, and chucked it over the wall before peeling toward Tony. "He's down," I panted as I sprinted past him.

"Nice shootin', Dauba'!" Tony said. His compliment took a moment to register as I continued to scan for threats. No sarcastic overtone, no wiseass admonishment. Just a compliment.

"Slow it down, point," Tony said over comms to let Chris know they were pulling too far ahead of us. He pulled the pin on a smoke grenade and lodged the spoon under his boot. He stepped off the grenade, cleared his flank, and peeled as smoke billowed up behind us. "Pop smoke, Dauba'," Tony said as he ran past. With Tony set, I popped a smoke grenade and peeled as we made the last turn onto Baseline. Tony threw one last smoke after mine, and we ran harder to catch up to our guys. We headed south at the end of the block and saw the Jundis. We turned down Baseline and had a full view of the platoon. The Bradleys and Abrams had set a corridor for us, and the platoon funneled into their perimeter.

At the last intersection before the COP, I popped up and ran all the way back to the Jersey barrier at Falcon's entrance. I turned and planted, holding until Tony ran past me. "Last man," he called. I checked my flank and turned reflexively. Just beyond the Jersey barrier, a tank sat with its turret pointing straight over my shoulder. I was too wasted physically from the run back to feel stupid.

I tried to laugh as I walked past the tank, but its thick exhaust overwhelmed me. While the rest of the platoon had jogged back to the COP, it felt like Tony and I covered the mile-plus in about four minutes. The patrol melted into a blur of adrenaline and distorted time. Trying to catch my breath, I swallowed a big gulp of tank fumes. My head felt like a roasting tomato that was ready to burst. The ingestion of tank exhaust fused with a wave of thoughts that sent my body autonomic: Biggles getting shot, the platoon's collective gasp, sprinting in bounds, shooting the muj, chucking grenades, my body on fire with adrenaline.

I bent over to puke.

After a few heaves, I stood up and composed myself. I took a swig of water and threw in a dip. I looked at Tony. He looked about as smoked as I was, but I could tell his thoughts were on something other than himself. Like the rest of us, his focus had turned back to Biggles. Tony said nothing as he walked past me and headed into our tactical operations center with the officers. The rest of us plopped down in front of our SEAL house and tried to process everything without the adrenaline blur. Marc sat next to me on the ledge. Chris sat near the door with Biff and Squirrel, and everyone else sprawled out on the grass nearby. Nobody spoke. Most of us were lost in our thoughts, staring down at the ground or closing our eyes to try to rest. I had never seen our guys that way before. We were all waiting for word on Biggles's condition.

Biggles. *Ryan.* The pulse of the platoon, the eternal smart-ass, the mad-shitter. Biggles, the newguy who dared to mad-dog our task unit commander—a mixed martial arts enthusiast—and got choked out for our amusement. He was fearless and hilarious—a great friend and an all-around Big Tough Frogman. All of us were lost in thought, but Chris seemed especially crushed. The Legend, hard as he was, was very compassionate and had a soft spot for newguys, especially Biggles. He got up, walked inside the SEAL house, grabbed some boxes of ammo, and vacantly began to reload his mags. He acted on reflex, like his body was working to get his mind off Biggles and back into the war.

"All right," I mumbled to myself, getting up to follow Chris's lead. Inside the house, I grabbed another grenade and several boxes of ammo and then returned to my stoop with Marc. I handed him a couple hundred rounds of linked ammo for his gun and started jamming my mags.

"Jesus," Marc said.

"I know," I said, pushing a round down. "This fucking sucks."

"Fuck," Marc said listlessly, shaking his head in disbelief.

Fifteen minutes later, Tony, Luke, and the other officers came out of the TOC and approached the platoon for a brief.

"Biggles took a frag to the right side of his face," Luke said. "The round hit the wall, skipped off the feed tray of the Pig, then hit him. The good news is he's alive and stable. They're taking him to Charlie Med, and from there, he'll fly to Balad and then on to Germany. Remember, he's alive. Now, ISR kept eyes on the area after we left, and they say the muj are scurrying around all over the place. We think we know which building Biggles was shot from, and we're going back in with the Bradleys to get some payback. It's time to finish what we started."

Marc and I looked at each other. As I looked around the platoon, I saw a lot of guys looking down or furrowing their brows. The tension was palpable. The close calls had already caught up with us, and we were about to double down on our hornet's-nest gamble. No one was especially eager to go back out, but we just sort of grudgingly acknowledged the order.

After a moment, Chris and Tony got up to get their gear together. They started jamming mags and retaping grenades. The rest of us followed their lead.

One more run.

TWENTY

ALL STOP

"Never take counsel of your fears."
—Stonewall Jackson

I REMEMBER BEING ABOUT five years old and staring at the kerosene stove in my parents' basement. "Don't touch that," my mom warned me repeatedly. "It's very hot." I know I heard her: she must have told me a hundred times not to touch the stove. Still, I wanted to see for myself, so I held my hand out to the side of it.

She was right. It hurt.

I don't know why I had to touch it again, but it was like I just wanted to see what would happen to me if I defied her warning. I held my hand out again, this time longer. It burned me and I screamed.

I don't remember the pain, but I remember the mix of anger, concern, and disbelief on her face as she bandaged my hand. "Why would you do that?" she asked. "Why in the world would you go back and touch it again?"

COP Falcon, August 2, 2006

It took a few minutes to flip our collective switch from demoralized to calculated blood rage. It's a reflex as old as war: they kill yours; you kill more of theirs. As the Klingons say, "Revenge is a dish best served cold."

Whatever went on in the TOC was decided by the head shed. Lord Tennyson's "The Charge of the Light Brigade" came to mind: "Theirs not to reason why. Theirs but to do and die." I'm certain Tennyson was talking about newguys with that stanza. Who were we to question an ancient reflex? Maybe it was finally time to have the stand-up fight we'd been wanting—to meet the muj on their own ground and hand them their asses. As Luke briefed the plan, Tony stood next to him, looking hard and mean as ever. Tony, the man who most epitomized the BTF persona, looked ready for a fight. He had the biggest combat balls in the platoon, and possibly at Team THREE, so if he was ready to get into the mix, I could make myself be, too. His deadpan visage at Luke's side pushed my mind into offense mode as images from the previous hour flashed in my thoughts: Biggles, bloody and stumbling. His disfigured face. The muj whose face I made a hole. It was barely nine in the morning.

Looking back on the mission our head shed cooked up, I've often wondered what the statistical breakdown is of satisfying versus unsatisfying outcomes from a retaliation mission. Seems like a good research topic for a military historian.

How often does it work?

At the time, that type of quantitative calculus wasn't a priority. We had business to handle.

A frontal assault. Violence of action. That was the plan. Luke broke down our new squad assignments, and the Punishers joined the mechanized infantry. The Bradleys, with their ramps dropped like thirsty tongues, swallowed us up into chalks. Luke, Chucky, Biff, and EOD Nick joined Marc and me in the first track. Marc and I took the last two seats, mirroring each other just inside the vehicle's mouth. As the ramp retracted with a hydraulic whine, I watched the shrinking geometry of morning light on Marc's face. The ramp locked and sealed us in, and for a moment I felt the familiar threat of claustrophobia. I shook it off and looked around at my brothers. Biff sat to Marc's right. EOD Nick was next to me. Chucky was near the driver and Luke opposite him. Marc and I locked wide eyes for a nonverbal conversation. *We're really doing this. We're going back out there.*

Adrenaline electrified my cognitive reflex. I remember the mech grunts cranking heavy metal for the assault. The driver hit the throttle and tore out of Falcon, sending Marc and me into a hard lean on the back end. On my internal soundtrack, or maybe in real life, Metallica's "Seek & Destroy" blared as we bounced around in the vehicle's guts, tearing through the streets on our way toward payback. I closed my eyes for a moment and let the lyrics settle.

> *We're scanning the scene in the city tonight.*
> *We're looking for you to start up a fight.*

We went in fast. The Bradleys and tanks would soften the buildings before we assaulted through. "Soften" is a euphemism for the hate the Bradleys were going to spray from their 25 mm cannons at a rate of two hundred rounds per minute. Afterward, we would go in and take care of business. The concept was simple: the mech guys wound them, we go in and kill them. The short drive was just long enough to get me fully invested and then some. If you can't get out of it, get into it. It was time to torch the nest.

Our track's gunner opened up as we plowed toward the building. The cannon's violent chug-chug-chug was soothing. It tied in with the other Bradleys as they let loose. The rhythm of the barrage sounded like righteous destruction. An Abrams tank added to the music with a brutal DOOOOVV! Then another in close succession. The track's ramp dropped, and Marc and I led the peel out of the back, buttonhooking toward the building. We fell in behind another squad already assaulting into the burning compound. The softening had set everything ablaze. The flames from burning palm trees scorched the air as we ran toward the entrance. The front of our train entered the building while the rest of us held inside the compound walls. I knelt in the courtyard inferno and scanned anxiously for bad guys. The heat and chaos were constricting—our own collapsing gates of fire. Tony pressed the assault as the train pushed into the building. I followed Marc into the breach as the smoke began to billow around us.

The train had split as half pressed to the second deck and half continued clearance on the ground floor. I moved with Marc into the depths of the two-story structure and the smoke dissipated as we cleared to the back of the house. I came to the last room where the Legend prepared to make entry. I gave him the signal we were ready. The door opened. Two muj immediately sprang in opposite directions.

Hands. Look at their fucking hands. . . . No guns.

I made the split-second decision not to shoot since they were unarmed. Chris and I pounced. I pushed my M4 to the side and launched all 290 pounds of gear, rage, and Frogman at one of the fleeing muj. As my hands connected with his shoulders, jerking him backward, he clumsily attempted to turn and swing at me. I rewarded him with a neck seal and we went down hard to the ground, his teeth cushioning the impact as we connected with the cement floor. Marc rolled to my left and kept his muzzle pointed on the guy's face. The muj attempted another swing and I subdued him with a healthy haymaker. On the other side of the room, the Legend had the other muj on the floor, as well.

I rolled off the limp body as Marc applied the flex-cuffs. I looked over at the Legend.

"All clear, Dauber," he said in a low tone.

He didn't make eye contact with me, but his body language was all business. Marc tightened the cuffs.

"Solid work, Dauber," Marc said.

I gave him a wink. "These guys want to fight, bring it."

I looked down at bloodstains on my gloves. I checked my weapons system, magazine, and optics. I composed myself and made my way back to the main room, where Tony was briefing the next movement. His composure had not changed since we left Falcon.

"The conventionals will come and get these savages. Next building is a two-story structure. Abrams will put a round into the front door. Bradleys provide cover. Luke's chalk makes entry. We kill all combatants on target. Nothing changes. Any questions?"

The simplicity of the plan left no room for questions. No one spoke besides the occasional "Check." I looked around at the other Big Tough Frogmen. I wouldn't want to be anywhere else than next to these bad motherfuckers.

"Stand by for breakout," Tony barked.

We all ran back to our respective tracks and funneled into our original positions in the tracked vehicles.

Slayer was our new soundtrack as the Bradley jolted to life. Still broiling from the courtyard blaze, I burned with rage and adrenaline. Anger had replaced anxiety. We'd crossed the line of departure. The Bradley roared up, guns blazing, to our next target. The driver maneuvered into position and stopped so his gunner could fire its round into the front door. The Abrams's cannon belched out a loud blast, firing a round toward the building. The tink-tink-tink of enemy fire reverberated all over the Bradley's armored skin outside. The snaps and tinks increased as the Bradley gunners returned fire with everything they had. Our driver dropped the ramp. A reflexive voice in my head yelled:

Put the ramp back up! Then a counterreflex answered: I charged forward, pouring out of the track and button-hooking around toward the building.

Smoke and dust from the burning compound swallowed me up. I hustled through it and saw a smoldering car on its side, engulfed in flames. The Abrams had hit the car instead of the entrance. Smoke, flames, and the snaps and cracks from enemy rounds kicked up all around as I bounded toward the building. As I bolted toward the door, I got the eerie feeling that no one was behind me and I was alone. My squad hadn't caught up. I took a knee behind the car and scanned for muj at the target, waiting for my brothers to catch up. I heard the snap-snap-snap of muj guns, and I contemplated my next move. Suddenly, I sensed someone behind me and felt a hand on my shoulder. It was Marc. He and the rest of the squad were there and he let me know. He gave me the signal. It was time to go.

I sprinted toward the front door and kicked it with everything I had. The metal door flew open, and the kick's force propelled me into the hallway and past two rooms. Marc and Biff were on my heels and cleared left while Luke and Nick funneled right and cleared the kitchen. "Clear!" both rooms called as Chucky fell in behind me. I covered down a long hallway at our front. Chucky signaled, and I started my glide.

At the far end of the hall there was a white door with a glass window in it, and a stairwell going up just to the right. I stayed right and cleared the small alcove under the stairs before holding at the bottom of the stairs. Chucky gave me the signal, and we moved. "Frogman to the second deck!" I called over comms, letting everyone outside know not to shoot us when we hit the roof. At the top of the stairs, I saw a small hallway with one door left and one right. I went left and Chucky mirrored right as we cleared each room alone. We pushed ahead to the rooftop. "Frogman to the roof," I passed over comms, in order to make sure I didn't get lit up by the Bradleys. With a signal, I burst onto the roof and found nothing. Chucky and I cleared around the roof and hurried back inside. With all the fire we'd taken, we didn't want to be outside any more than was necessary. We moved so fast, it felt like we cleared the whole house in a blur and we were moving a hundred miles an hour.

We hurried back inside and headed for the stairs. When we reached the top of the staircase, a loud burst of enemy machine-gun fire ripped into the first floor below us. It came in strong and heavy and blew out the glass from the window in the downstairs hallway. The shooter couldn't have been farther than twenty yards from our building. Chucky and I paused reflexively, listening for a beat, looking for threats.

"Man down!" Luke screamed over comms. His voice was desperate and urgent. "We need a fucking corpsman down here now!"

Chucky's eyes were wide with anticipation. I bolted. I took three bounds down the stairs and saw my best friend, slumped at the bottom, staring vacantly at the ceiling. Marc was down, one leg folded awkwardly under him and his gun off to the side. EOD Nick knelt and returned fire out a window, and as I moved to grab Marc, another burst of intense fire came in. I didn't wait. I grabbed Marc by his kit and dragged him around the stairwell's alcove to work on him there. Nick was already laying down some murderous suppressive fire.

Marc was shot through his mouth. His left cheek was covered by purple bruising, and his usually tan face was pale white. I reached around the back of his head and felt the warm blood of an exit wound through my gloves. I flung my med bag off next to me and pulled my medical scissors from my web gear. I started to cut Marc's gear off for a full assessment: airway, breathing, circulation. There was no sign of hope. He'd taken another round in the shoulder.

"We need a fucking CASEVAC, now!" I yelled to Luke.

I knew Marc was dead before I started working on him. There was nothing I could do to bring him back, but I had to try. An intense gunfight was playing out around me, and I wanted nothing more than to loose my rage at the enemy. But I had a job to do. I had to take care of Marc. I had to be a medic and work on my brother.

"CASEVAC's en route!" Luke yelled back. "Will be outside in a minute!"

I finished cutting off Marc's gear so we could move him. I tried hard to do what I could. I couldn't do chest compressions or put a tube in him with so much enemy fire coming in over my head. I had to package him to move.

Moments before, I'd felt like everything moved at hyperspeed. Now everything outside of the immediate space that contained Marc and me slowed down and became a blur of nearly indecipherable images. I was aware of more gunfire. An officer came in with several of his squad. "Marc, we're still with you; don't fucking leave us!" he said. I looked up at him blankly, frustrated and angry. Registration dawned on his face and he shook his head. "He's not dead, right, Dauber?" I didn't answer him. I put my eyes back on Marc.

"Get it together, dude. It's a fucking firefight," I said and pushed him mentally out of my space. He melted into the blur of the scene outside my bubble.

"CASEVAC's outside!" Luke yelled from the other side of the hallway. "Get him up."

I secured my bag and threw it on. Then I struggled to sling Marc's hulking body up in an awkward fireman carry. He was crushingly heavy, and his limp frame hung clumsily as I struggled down the hallway. I made it almost to the front door before I fell. Ned and Scotty from Team EIGHT jumped up to help, and we picked Marc up in a graceless buddy carry. I held one side of Marc's cammies with Ned on the other side and Scotty held both of Marc's legs. We stumbled outside, barely noticing the snaps and pops and rounds impacting all around. As we got close to the Bradley, one of us slipped and Marc went down hard.

"Motherfucker!" I yelled. We all cussed ourselves and the situation, picking Marc back up and rushing him into the back of the empty track.

"Jump in, Dauber," said Ned. We locked eyes for a second and I nodded swiftly.

I turned to Scotty. "I need some help, bro." He nodded and jumped in.

The ramp closed, and we started resuscitative measures on Marc. The driver held nothing back and tore away toward Falcon. For the four-minute ride to the COP, I tried desperately to breathe life back into my friend. By the time we got to Falcon, I had no doubt Marc was dead.

An Army doctor ran up to meet us as the ramp dropped down.

"You gotta take this," I said gravely.

The doc moved in, and I stepped aside. He placed his stethoscope on Marc's heart and listened. He moved it a couple of times. Then he called it.

"He's gone."

It was sometime after 1000. I was numb.

The thing I already knew ripped through me. I walked a few steps out of the Bradley and vomited hard as a wave of emotion consumed me. I fell to my knees and puked some more. I screamed, punching and pounding the ground in front of me. If I'd had a muj within reach, I would have ripped his throat out and beat his head into a pulpy stain on the ground. I've never felt more angry, nor have I since. It was rage born from a sense of powerlessness. There are no do-overs in war, but a warrior can't help but indulge the what-if routine. You always end up mapping the events leading to your buddy's death, trying to locate the point where you could have intervened to prevent it. But it's for nothing. There's nothing you can do to bring him back, and that's a hurt like no other. The doc snapped me back to reality.

"Time to go. Load up, boys. I'm really sorry."

Scotty and I had to make the final lonely ride with Marc to Camp Ramadi. We picked Marc up off the floor of the track and put him on a stretcher. Then Scotty and I climbed back inside the Bradley. I thanked God Scotty was with me. I couldn't imagine having to make that trip alone. The soldiers in the Bradley crew were somber and respectful. It was a safe bet Ramadi had taken some of their friends, too. The ramp retracted, and the Bradley took off. Everything was quiet except for the engine's hum.

I noticed the smell. It's hard to describe the subtle smell of death that early on, but if permanence had a smell, that was it.

Scotty and I fought back tears as we watched over Marc. His eyes were open, staring up into nothingness. I placed my hand over his eyes and closed them. The driver was hauling ass, trying to make the ride as quick as possible, and when we hit a bump, Marc's eyes opened. I closed them again and tried to relax. The driver hit another bump, and Marc's eyes opened again. Then his body suddenly kicked violently. The neural episode scared the shit out of me. I grabbed a T-shirt and covered Marc's face. Then I buried my head in my hands. I couldn't look at his eyes anymore. I looked at Scotty and felt fortunate to have another Teamguy with me. Your brothers stick by your side when you do the dirty work. This time was no exception.

At Camp Ramadi, the gate guards were waiting for us. We drove in and headed straight to the morgue. V was waiting there for us. I got out of the track, and we pulled Marc's body out. It was so heavy—not just the body, but all of it. The physical and mental exhaustion finally swept over me. As we carried him inside, I broke down and started crying, silently at first and then in stifled sobs that racked my body.

"Dauber, there's nothing you can do," he said gently.

I knew that was true, but I was crushed nonetheless. It's the powerlessness. It's the fact that one minute he gave me the signal to let me know he was there; then he was gone. That thing is so hard to swallow. We carried Marc inside and put him down on a table. I looked at him one last time and noticed his mustache, the one he'd grown with the rest of us as a running joke.

"If I ever fucking get capped, you gotta shave this fucking 'stache off," he had told me.

Still choked up with tears, I turned to the Mortuary Affairs soldier and said, "You gotta shave this fucking thing off. He'll kill me if he has to go back with this mustache on."

"We'll take care of it. No problem," he said.

"Come on, Dauber," V said. "I'll take you back to Sharkbase."

Scotty and I climbed into the Hilux with V, and I looked at myself, realizing I was covered in Marc's blood. I was numb.

"We've got another casualty," V announced.

I turned to listen, suddenly intensely uncomfortable with being one of the platoon's only corpsmen and out of the fight. I felt angry at myself.

"Luke caught a ricochet," V said. "Barely broke the skin. He's all right. They called for extract a couple minutes after you left."

We pulled into Sharkbase around 11 a.m. I got out of the truck and walked around to grab my kit, gun, and med bag from the truck bed. V followed and helped me out.

"Just go take a nap, Dauber," he said, putting his hand on my shoulder.

Rest sounded right. Exhaustion had set in fully. I walked to my tent. My hands and feet tingled. I heard my pulse in my temple. I thought of Marc. I couldn't picture his face before the firefight. All I replayed was his forever look.

Spaz was inside. He'd had to sit the op out while his elbow healed. He looked up as I entered and saw the bloody mess.

"Marc's dead," I said solemnly. I stared at Spaz, who had always reveled in my misery just because I was a newguy, and gave him a look that dared him to be a dick about it.

"Jesus fucking Christ, Dauber," he said. He was obviously shocked.

"I'm really sorry, brother. I really am." I heard the mix of sincerity and upset in his voice. I nodded. He got up quickly and headed out of the tent toward the TOC, pausing to squeeze my shoulder on his way.

I dropped my gear, grabbed my towel and soap, and walked out. I walked into the shower with my cammies and boots on and turned the water on high. Blood and dirt washed down as I stripped and tried to scrub away the death. I stood under the hot water for a while, gathering myself. Finally, I turned the water off and grabbed my towel. I dried off and put on a fresh set of cammies. I walked back to my tent, dropped my dirty clothes and gear, and grabbed my camera. I went into Marc's room and took a bunch of pictures. I wanted to record the scene before they packed up all his stuff. Finally, I headed to Charlie Med to check on Luke and the rest of the platoon. Luke's wound was superficial—a little stinger.

Luke approached me. "Dauber," he said. "Would you and Biff like to take Marc back to the States?"

"Yeah, that would be good," I said.

"Good. Ned's gonna go with you guys, too. Take a nap and relax for a couple hours, and you guys will fly out tonight."

"Roger that," I said.

I looked around at the guys. Sheer dejection covered everyone's face.

A couple of hours had passed since I got back to Sharkbase when I lay down in my tent. I closed my eyes and fell asleep almost immediately. My body and mind needed a reset, and I slept hard until about 1700. I woke up and walked outside. I found Chris first, still crying and angry. He wasn't the only one. Everybody loved Marc, and everybody was crushed. All the Big Tough Frogmen were mourning.

Our run of invincibility had ended, and the close calls that foreshadowed August 2 would haunt us long after. The constant questioning and hindsight are the hardest parts. What could have gone differently? What if Marc had been shot in the leg or chest instead? Could I have saved him? I played it all over and over in my head, an infinite mash-up of all the things that could have or should have been. But there is one cruel truth in war: it plays out the way it plays out. And then you have to live with it.

TWENTY-ONE

FINAL SALUTE

You've got friends with you till the end. . . .
Brotherhood's our rule we cannot bend.

—Pennywise, "Bro Hymn"

I GAVE COLLEGE A second try as a twenty-seven-year-old non-traditional student. I was out of the Teams and felt pretty out of place in most of my classes at the University of Connecticut, where I did not blend well with the eighteen- and nineteen-year-old coeds. Attempts to camouflage myself by sitting in the back row and wearing my Oakleys were apparently ineffective, as I was approached during my first semester by a couple of shaggy-looking frat boys. "Dude," they said, "can you buy us beer?"

I laughed, remembering myself at their age. "Sorry, guys," I said and shook my head.

By my third semester, the requests to buy beer were paired with the occasional invite to a frat party. "Can I bring my pregnant wife?" I'd ask. Eventually, the boys left me alone.

Sometimes being a nontrad in undergraduate school felt like being the designated driver on free drink night, except in Professor Garry Clifford's American Foreign Policy lecture.

There, he spoke to me. It was everyone else who was out of place.

"Never in the field of human conflict was so much owed by so many to so few," Clifford effortlessly served up to the class, recounting Churchill's speech in the summer of 1940. "Maybe the world needed to know what was at stake. Those few were willing to sacrifice when others weren't." Clifford's gaze fell upon the class. His words hung in the air, in the space between children who did not yet understand sacrifice.

I smiled to myself.

CAMP RAMADI, AUGUST 2, 2006

"Marc. Lee!" V sounded off the prompt.

"HOOYAH, MARC LEE!" the hundred or so operators echoed in unison. The break in the silence snapped me out of my thoughts. I gripped the handles of the aluminum coffin so hard I felt it dig into my hand. I didn't care. My hands were numb. My mind was numb. My spirit was numb. Marc Lee moved with us, as I ushered him with Biff, EOD Nick, and two others through the ranks on the way to the Black Hawk.

Delta Platoon made the journey through Ramadi from Corregidor. Some of the Tier 1 guys from Sharkbase were there in support. The Marines and Army we worked with were also there. Their presence was felt. We fought and died with them.

Marc Lee was the first SEAL killed in Iraq. There were thousands of American deaths before his and unfortunately there would be more to come, including many more SEALs. The enemy's rounds don't discriminate. It's the harsh reality a soldier comes to realize when he enters a combat zone. We are all brothers. Each life lost over there has its own story, and I've even come to learn many of them. The difference between Marc and the other stories is that I loved Marc.

With one final hoist, we passed Marc into the belly of the bird. Biff, Ned, and I settled in, and I looked again at the scene outside. A bunch of rough men piping Marc ashore on his way to paradise was a fitting send-off. I nodded, full of pride. The rest of Charlie stood in formation until we were airborne. Taking Marc home was heavy, but carrying my brother back was my duty and my honor. I put the muzzle of my M4 down to the floor of the helo, snapped my helmet on, and turned on my NVGs. The August heat was a stark contrast to the rainy arrival I had five months earlier.

Our short helo flight played like a silent film above the desert. The high-pitched roar of the twin-turbine faded into the white noise of cognitive anesthesia. When we landed at TQ I felt numb, like a body still humming after too many hours on a motorcycle.

"It's okay, brother." The Mortuary Affairs soldiers were somber angels, carrying out their duties with the utmost professionalism and constant deference to the gravity of our loss. They understood: first Teamguy killed in Iraq. "We'll take care of him," they said when we delivered Marc to the morgue. We floated listlessly to a temporary berthing area to relax and wait for our flight out.

EOD Nick edited together a Marc Lee remembrance video in the hours before our departure, so Biff and I found a DVD player to watch it on. It was hard to watch. I was still processing the previous hours' events and it seemed too soon to look at pictures of him happy and in another life. The contrast was just too stark compared to the images I had stuck in my mind of him on that floor, staring into nothing. I sifted through the mental slide show, trying to find where it had all gone awry. The abruptness bothered me most. It was cold and merciless, and there was no reasoning with it about how you needed just a little more time. It was like an echo infinitely repeating inside me: *Marc is gone.*

Biff and I didn't talk much. Teamguys aren't the type to do a lot of talking about their feelings. Mental toughness is our default—the reset button. Big Tough Frogmen can handle anything. The death of a brother is no different. I needed to compartmentalize, to channel my thoughts away from powerlessness. Biff had known Marc since BUD/S, and he was dealing with the same feelings. It was something we had to sort out internally.

I sat in quiet reflection on all the good times I'd had with Marc, working and training. I thought about how this man I'd known for less than a year had become like blood. I thought about Maya, his wife, and how he'd talked about her endlessly. They'd made their marriage legal to start getting the benefits, he'd confided to me early in the deployment, but they were planning a big formal ceremony in Italy when the deployment was over.

I thought about how none of that was going to happen now. Maya was never going to celebrate a marriage to Marc in Italy and Marc's mom, Debbie Lee, would never see her son married.

I'd never met Debbie or Maya, and I was anxious. I'd taken the pictures of Marc's room for Maya. His living space on Sharkbase was mostly a shrine to their relationship. I wanted her to see what I saw and to know how deeply Marc loved her, and I worried about how I, someone she didn't know, would convey all this or if I could even do so. I thought again about Heinlein's words about fulfillment. I believed that Marc was too young to die and wished fervently that I could have saved him. But I also knew that I'd been with him when he killed a bad man, and I'd borne witness to how happy he was loving Maya. I hoped that one day, when the dust settled, I would be at peace with Marc's sacrifice.

We crossed the Atlantic in the massive belly of an Air Force C-5, with Marc's flag-draped casket peacefully in line among the six others. There were five from Iraq and two from Afghanistan. Biff and I sat against the bulkhead, staring at the scene in front of us. There was no room for conversation. We stared endlessly. There was time for that.

Dover Air Force Base, in Delaware, is the central receiving and processing point for all remains of U.S. service members. The joint-service Mortuary Affairs detachment at Dover specializes in the solemn dignified transfer of remains from aircraft on the flight line to the port mortuary, where their medical personnel, administrative staff, and embalmers fully document and prepare the fallen for the trip to their final resting places.

We filed down the plane's ramp and lined the path outside while a carry team marched in perfect formation up the ramp to get Marc. A senior officer moved a team of six sailors into place around Marc's casket. With automatic efficiency, they lifted Marc in unison, paused, and marched him down the ramp. We all saluted as they walked past to the vehicle waiting to make the short drive to the port mortuary.

With Marc in the careful hands of Dover's staff, my attention turned to Biggles. We checked into our hotel outside Dover and went to check on our other brother.

At Bethesda Naval Medical Center, Biggles was still in a medically induced coma. Just two days had passed since he suffered a traumatic brain injury and extensive damage to his eyes and face. When I walked into his room for the first time, I didn't know what to expect. I guess I was a little shocked by what I saw. Biggles's eyes were swollen up to the size of purple golf balls on a patchwork of pink, black, and blue skin. It didn't feel right. As we stood around his bed in our civvies, Biggles had no idea we were there. The whole scene made us uneasy. He had tubes protruding from his mouth and one from his head to relieve the pressure. He wasn't the same Biggles I saw on patrol headed down Baseline—now placid with unconsciousness and badly wounded. None of us could say much of anything until I finally muttered, "Be strong, Biggles. We'll be back to see you soon, brother."

During our refuel in Germany, I had called my parents to let them know I was coming home. They were a little surprised to hear I was headed home, but nonetheless they were glad I was coming. My mom and youngest brother made the trip from Connecticut to Bethesda, Maryland. My dad wasn't able to get away and my middle brother had just started the fall semester at UConn.

I'd been on U.S. soil about a day, and I started to notice the feeling that things were different. I love my family and was glad to be around Biggles's friends, but five months in Ramadi isn't easy to just shake off and move right back into everyday America. It isn't combat stress or PTSD. It's just an unshakable feeling that no one back home has any real sense of ownership of the war. Our loved ones knew what we told them and understood as much as we could make them, but the rest of the world seemed somehow clueless about the fact that we were at war or that one of my best friends had just given his life for them. It was a hard conclusion to reach, but I began to understand that most people will never understand the brotherhood.

———————————

"You were in Ramadi?" my mom asked incredulously.

Five months in Ramadi, and I'd never told my family where I was. I kept them in the dark for the sake of operational security and for their own peace of mind. My mother's wide eyes and dropped jaw told me I'd made the right call by not telling them. Ramadi was in the news constantly. Like many Americans with loved ones overseas, she knew the city was the most dangerous place in Iraq.

It feels sort of strange to admit that it had never really struck me that what I was doing would have a profound impact on my family. I guess I was kind of on autopilot and shouldering any of their anxiety was not part of my war. I could see my mom begin to take on that anxiety on a much deeper level and more earnestly. When you come home carrying your Teammate's body and introduce the family to another Teammate who's been seriously wounded, the effect on your family, especially your mom, is profound.

"Well, what are you doing over there, Kevin? Will you have to go back? How did Marc get killed?"

I gave my mother the PG-rated version of everything and reassured her that I would be fine. I had about a month left before I'd deploy back stateside for at least a year, but I just told my mom I probably wasn't going back to Ramadi.

"Don't worry, Mom. I'll be fine."

"I'm proud of you, man," my little brother said.

"Thanks, Mikey. That means a lot."

"Serious, brother. You've come a long way. I remember when Dad, Mom, Sparky, and I came out to your BUD/S graduation. I knew you were going to do good things. I want you to know that."

My mom was talking with Biff on the other side of the table, but the noise of the bar seemed like a million miles away. My youngest brother sat across from me. He was only twenty. I couldn't believe how much he had grown up. His words left a lasting impression on me. I had spent a childhood growing up with Mikey and Mark. However, in the last few years, I had entered a different type of brotherhood. I had been back stateside for less than a day and I felt uncomfortable. Mikey didn't pry.

I smiled. It was good to see my family again.

"You know I speak for all of us—you constantly make us proud."

I clenched my jaw tight and fought back a flood of emotion.

"I love you, man," I responded.

The business-class accommodations from the East Coast to San Diego were an abrupt change from the third-world life I'd been living in Ramadi. We escorted Marc back with Master Chief Bro, who was Team THREE's new master chief. He had put me through SEAL Qualification Training a few years before and had managed to go out on a few ops with us in Ramadi. Bro was a solid operator and the quintessential SEAL master chief.

He flew from TQ to Dover to make the trip back to San Diego with us. Bro had arranged for our dress blues to be sent to Dover so we could make the final leg of the journey back to Coronado. With the autopsy done, it was time to take Marc home.

As we taxied off the runway in San Diego, the captain asked everyone to stay seated while we deplaned to remove Marc's body from the cargo hold and take him on to the final leg of his journey home.

"You're gonna call cadence as we pull him off the plane, Dauber," said Bro.

It caught me a little off guard and I found myself struggling to digest the moment.

"Roger that."

I got off the plane and saw Guy and a handful of newguys from Team FIVE on the flight line, waiting for us. Guy had left Ramadi a month earlier to care for his wife while she battled Hodgkin's lymphoma. One of his duties while he was stateside was to help with casualty assistance duties. It was good to see another familiar face. I needed that.

The scene outside the plane looked, to me, like a shot from Todd Heisler's Pulitzer Prize–winning photo story, "Final Salute." It shows a team of Marines pulling one of their fallen from the belly of a commercial plane in the middle of the night while the passengers watch from the windows inside. Like the Marines in the photo, all of us wore dress blues. And like the civilians in the photo, everyone watched us.

I stood rigidly at attention, calling cadence for the guys carrying Marc toward the waiting hearse. I fought my voice as it started to waver and struggled to hide the emotions brought on by the scene. I tried to ignore all the faces glued to windows, hoping they couldn't hear my choked-up cadence. I wondered if the people had any idea what the scene they were watching really meant, particularly what it meant to me.

The transfer took less than a minute. Guy and his team placed the casket carefully in the back of the hearse and shut the door. Our job was done. I wouldn't see Marc again until the funeral a few days later.

The transition from combat to normalcy began when I landed in San Diego. In the nights before Marc's funeral, I practically lived at Danny's Palm Bar—a big Teamguy hangout in Coronado—with a few of the guys I'd gone to BUD/S with. They were close friends from Team SEVEN. Tanner and BDub were pipe-hitting Frogmen from my tadpole years. They had been to Iraq before, but hadn't had the experiences I had. They were willing to listen. I was ready to talk.

Fortunately, Teamguys know how to read situations and how to pick up on cues. They were acutely aware of what had happened on August 2. Our after-action reports were circulating the West Coast constantly. They already knew what happened and didn't pry. They knew I'd tell them what I wanted to. We talked about our war and the killing in Ramadi. We talked about winning and how there was more work to be done. Mostly, we raised a lot of glasses, many in salute to Marc and Biggles. We drank because Teamguys like to drink, and I hadn't been allowed to for five months. We drank to feel free because there wasn't a lot of freedom in Ramadi and we wanted to get it while the getting was good.

Eventually, I told Tanner and BDub the story of August 2. I didn't need to, but I wanted to. I felt comfortable among my brothers. I realized that there wasn't a possibility of moving on, but there was a need to move forward. I couldn't communicate the same with someone who has never been a part of the brotherhood. They wouldn't understand why we fight, why we drink, or why we don't share that part of ourselves with anyone and everyone. SEALs understand. The more I spoke about the good times and the bad I'd had with Marc and Biggles, the more tired—yet at peace—I felt.

On the day of Marc's funeral, barely a week had passed since I worked on Marc under the stairs in that dingy house. The slow buildup to that day had me emotionally fatigued. I was ready for the "Are you okay?" phase to be over, and Marc's funeral was the last step.

I stood outside the church at Naval Station North Island, watching all the people filter inside. I saw Maya and Debbie and the droves of Marc's friends and family, and I wished that I knew them better. I wanted to tell them about the Marc I knew, the warrior and brother. I wanted to tell Maya everything I knew that she probably didn't, how he'd talked about her constantly in Ramadi, how she was his center. I wanted to tell her and Debbie how I'd wanted so badly to save him, how I knew I couldn't, but tried anyway. As the last of the attendees filtered in, I was about to head inside when a guy from Team TWO materialized in front of me.

"Hey, man, you relieved us in Iraq, in Ramadi. Sorry about your loss, dude, but yo, you guys are killing it out there!"

I wanted to punch him.

"Back the fuck off," I said, pushing past him.

Yes, we had a reputation as one of the most lethal Teams in Iraq. Yes, we'd killed almost two hundred insurgents. Yes, we were like rock stars in the Teams.

No, five minutes before my buddy's funeral starts is not the time to talk to me about that stuff. I had no sympathy for him.

I walked inside the church and tried to clear my head of the Team TWO asshole. I wanted my last few hours with Marc. I needed to spend that time and say a final goodbye. The church was packed— standing room only—so I found a spot on the side and stood by to watch the ceremony by myself. I was one of the few Team THREE guys in attendance. Biff, Ned, Bro, Guy, and Bob were all sitting. I felt tired. Bob, with his bandaged-up knee, caught my attention from his seat near where I stood.

"Dauber, come over here and sit down," he said in a hushed tone. He and his fiancée sat together, and they scooted over to make room for me. I was glad to be sitting with a Teammate. Afterward, the procession moved to Fort Rosecrans National Cemetery, which sits on a hill overlooking San Diego.

I don't know what it is about bagpipes, but they always bring back the special memories I have for my brothers. My wife wanted them at our wedding and I had to say no. It was the bagpipes that got me that day. Not the flag presentation to the next of kin, not the rifle volleys, not the bugler playing Taps. I made it through all of those. The bagpipes at Marc's funeral tempered every BTF molecule I had, and to this day the sound of one puts me right back in that cemetery. Two weeks before, Marc was full of life and we were killing bad guys together. Three weeks before, he had smoked his first insurgent. It was another flood of too many thoughts, and I had to get a handle on them. I just needed to keep it simple: I lost a buddy. It's just one of those things. It's just war. These things happen—even to SEALs.

———————

I will always regret the fact that I never pounded a trident into Marc's casket. They put him in the ground that day after Debbie and Maya held a small, intimate ceremony at the grave site that was reserved for close friends and family. I barely knew Maya or Debbie or any of the Teamguys Marc had gone to BUD/S with who were in attendance. I watched it from a distance, and didn't go over because I didn't want to intrude. I even watched Marc's buddies pound their tridents onto his casket. There are times that I look back at that day and regret not putting a bird on his casket. However, I remind myself that I was fortunate to have truly lived with Marc when we were working in Ramadi.

———————

I paddled my board quickly to get up and over the outside set of waves that was about to clean out the lineup. The frigid Pacific Ocean water sent a chill down to my toes and I turned my head to spit some out. The Imperial Beach ocean water is supposedly some of the most polluted in the country. I didn't bat an eye after having been in the Euphrates. I turned as I crested the wave and gazed back at the lineup. It was a yard sale of boards, asses, and elbows. I chuckled to myself. A Frogman always returns to the water.

The water felt like a baptism, rinsing away all the fatigue I'd been wading through for the last two weeks. Imperial Beach never felt so clean and perfect as the warm Santa Ana winds buffered the chill of the ocean. As the waves swayed me calmly, I felt a deep serenity, and a peace that had been denied me for a long time.

"Okay," I said to myself. "Time to get back after it."

TWENTY-TWO

PAYBACK

"Brave men have fought and died building the proud tradition
and feared reputation that I am bound to uphold. In the
worst of conditions, the legacy of my Teammates steadies my
resolve and silently guides my every deed. I will not fail."

—SEAL Creed

A FEW DAYS BEFORE Hell Week began, a couple of BUD/S instructors pulled me aside. "Lacz," they said. "We have some bad news. Your grandfather passed away. We're really sorry, man. You have the option of going home for the funeral and rolling back to the next class to do Hell Week with them, or staying here with 245. No one would think less of you if you went home for the funeral."

I was very close to my grandfather, and the news was hard to take. Of course I thought about going home and being with my family, about saying goodbye to him one last time. I also thought about the commitment I'd made to get through BUD/S and to become a SEAL. My grandfather had joined the Navy after Pearl Harbor and served in the Pacific. I thought about what he would want me to do and I decided to stay and endure a winter Hell Week. I don't think he would have wanted his death to interrupt my dedication to my class and my training; rather he would have appreciated that when I needed to dig deep and push through the tough evolutions, I thought of him. I think he would have wanted me to see my commitment through, and I believe he would have understood my decision.

CAMP RAMADI, MID-AUGUST 2006

I saw that Biff was lost in his thoughts. We all had something to think about. But there was also only a twenty-minute Black Hawk ride between us and the ground in Ramadi. Twenty minutes to get your head in the game. It seemed like part of Biff's mind was still back stateside. The images of Bethesda, our last stop stateside before we flew out, were sharp in our minds.

Less than twenty-four hours earlier, Biggles had woken up and begun dealing with the reality of traumatic brain injury and life without sight. His face was still swollen and bruised. He personally shed the bandages so we could see the extent of his injuries. Admiral Eric T. Olson, the deputy commander of the U.S. Special Operations Command, was there checking in on his Frogmen. The admiral was well liked within the community and that never changed, no matter how high he climbed. Olson was a big deal, a Frogman officer who had commanded at every level. I was eager to meet the man and personally glad to be there with Biggles and Biff. After the admiral said a brief introduction, Biggles spoke.

"Hey, Admiral," he said loudly, turning his bandaged head in Olson's direction.

I always admired Biggles's boldness. He was never one to mince words or back down. Missing an eye, blind, and laid up in a hospital didn't deter him.

"You ever hear about the SEAL in Ramadi who lost a KYK?"

I passed a wide-eyed look to Biff. He stared at Biggles, incredulous.

"Yes, I did hear about that," Admiral Olson replied.

"Well, he's standing right next to you," Biggles said, laughing sort of maniacally through his damaged jaw.

Biff looked down and shook his head. *Fuck, Biggles.* Olson helped us ease the tension and laughed off Ryan's awkward jab. Biggles's frontal lobe had been severely injured from the sniper round. He admitted candidly that he had little power to control his emotions. Later on that same day, he joked cruelly about how my only real patient as a combat medic—Marc—had died. "You're a terrible corpsman, Dauber," he said with a shitty laugh. I knew he didn't mean it, but the comment hit home. It hurt. Still, that's what I appreciated about the Teams. These guys will shoot it straighter to you than your family will.

Teams and shit.

Years later, long after Ryan had recovered and rebuilt his life, he apologized to me. He remembered the incident and felt terrible about it.

Our flight from the East Coast back to Germany left me feeling like there was something more to be said, but Biff was never a big talker. Marc's death and Ryan's wounds didn't change that. He just swallowed everything and stuffed it down. As newguys, we grumbled often about the decisions that led up to August 2, but those thoughts always led to the same end. And the wrong thoughts can quickly become a liability if you indulge them too much. Operating in the night was our outlet. We talked about wanting payback and how we had a month to get some.

When we touched down at Camp Ramadi, it was game time.

The head shed had understood the impact of August 2 on the platoon and had walked back the Punishers' op tempo while we were gone. The illusion of invincibility was long forgotten. Daytime patrols stopped not because Teamguys were averse to patrolling in the daylight, but because there was true resentment in the ranks toward the reckless nature of the decision-making process.

We got back to our bread and butter. Despite these concessions from our higher-ups, morale among the sled dogs wasn't great. Residual animosity lingered toward the head shed in the aftermath of August 2. Tension in our op briefs was always palpable. Everyone was focused on finishing our deployment without further casualties.

We all knew we had to keep taking the fight to the enemy. The war didn't stop because a couple of Teamguys became casualties. We didn't have the luxury of feeling sorry for ourselves, but our resolve came with a new risk calculus. With less than a month left, you want to take fewer chances. Best not to tempt death when you can see the finish line. We kept our body armor and helmets buttoned up and were a lot more cautious in general. War is a cruel reaper.

I was determined to get some payback for Marc and Biggles before I left Ramadi. I'm not the kind to stay on the canvas when I get knocked down. I'm more the explode-with-a-Polack-haymaker. On every overwatch mission, that's what I was looking for—the haymaker. Scanning with my scope, I was sharper than I had been before August 2. You might say I was trying to will a target into my crosshairs. That's about the gist of it. The quiet surf of Imperial Beach was lightyears away.

_____

Our hide was in a building near the end of Baseline, not far from where Marc was killed and probably nearer to where Marc got his kill behind the rifle. The three-story structure looked out east toward the remainder of the muj-controlled space within Ramadi. The fifth anniversary of 9/11 was less than a week away. I lay prone, looking out a loophole of four missing bricks. My target window was close to the floor of my bedroom hide. I was a good distance back from the hole, but I could see down Baseline and into the Ma'Laab for at least a thousand meters. My target area covered all main arteries into the area. Squirrel was with me, splitting time on the gun, and Tony mirrored our setup across the hall in another room twenty meters away.

The heat hung in the air, as the airflow was minimal. I switched out with Squirrel at 0800 and lased all my reference points out to 1,000 meters. It didn't take long. The building 700 meters down Baseline drew my attention when a muj with an AK walked out of a doorway onto a street. My heart rate jumped as I found him in my scope. With my Nightforce at full-power magnification, the muj appeared relatively small in my scope. I methodically checked my dope card on my buttstock. I dialed my elevation knob from 300 to 700 meters quickly, hoping I wouldn't miss the opportunity. I wasn't about to hold to compensate for the elevation change. At 700 meters, I needed to bring all the marksmanship fundamentals together to deliver a clean shot. Marc and Biggles deserved it. I visualized a center-mass shot as I reacquired my payback target. Still there.

Before Marc's death, my autonomic response to a bad guy in my scope had become less and less pronounced with every kill. All my previous kills were from shorter distances, so tracking this kill at seven hundred meters sent my heart rate up a notch. This was the bad guy I'd been waiting for since I got back from the States—the one for Marc and Biggles. I wasn't about to accept failure.

Muj lit a cigarette and stood smoking outside the building, holding his Kalashnikov in his right hand, its collapsible buttstock folded. An unarmed military-age male squatted on either side of him. They were oblivious to the enemy threat, but my target's AK presented clear hostile intent according to the ROE.

My breathing was fast as I put the crosshairs on the target's chest. I worked to get my body under control and slow my heart rate. Missing was inexcusable. I cleared my mind and focused on breathing. I began to relax every muscle in my body and isolate my finger on the trigger. There is a meditative quality to the process.

Watching my target holding steady helped me relax. The target continued to stand still, smoking his cigarette. He had not a care in the world and was oblivious to me. His calmness slowed my breathing. I calmly settled into my natural respiratory pause. With a quarter lung of air left, I isolated my trigger finger and squeezed slowly. When I hit my pause, the last of the slack slowly came out of the trigger and the bullet leapt from my gun. The flight time was about a half second. I didn't hear the rifle go off. All I felt was the sear reengage as I loosed my pressure on the trigger. The round found its target, dead-on center-mass. The muj crumpled and fell dead. I took a deep breath.

I scanned for other targets as the street came alive with people scurrying around frantically. His pals took off, assholes and elbows. The target's motionless body, lying down for the dirt nap, was the only stillness on the scene. A few hasty minutes later, a black sedan screamed up next to the muj, and a couple of guys threw him in and drove off. I saw no other weapons or valid targets.

"Whatta ya got, Dauba'?" Tony asked from across the hall.

"Got a guy with an AK, seven hundred meters. He's down."

"Rodja' that," Tony said.

I looked over at Squirrel. He never made eye contact with me, but he stared out at the scene with a loose smile on his face.

After August 2, I truly had no sympathy for the enemy. The macabre scene of Ramadi over the previous six months had left me robotic. The images of fellow brothers injured, dead, Marines mangled and torn up, left me with no quarter for the enemy. Anger was a small part of it, but sense of duty overrode all other emotions. Had the patriots in Lexington and Concord been swayed by the sight of a brother falling to British musket rounds, the dream of freedom for the colonies might never have been realized. The warrior drives on. We don't move on. We move forward. Constantly.

As the confusion on the streets began to die down, I let my neck relax and stared down at the dip spit on the ground. The brown puddle speckled with pieces of tobacco was a quiet juxtaposition to the scene on the opposite side of the gun. The sweat began to bead on my forearms as I wiped my brow. The faint aroma of cordite was a welcome change from the smells of the dusty apartment. I reached to my right, plucked the piece of brass off my rucksack, and tucked it neatly into my left breast pocket with the rosary, blood chit, and two hundred dollars cash.

Marc wasn't the first or the last SEAL to die in combat. Wherever there is conflict, a Frogman will be at the forefront of it. Marc was a brother who died upholding the brotherhood, something that only a select few will ever truly understand.

What Marc and August 2 taught me the most was we don't quit. There isn't a test in BUD/S that serves as a prediction for operational capabilities in the midst of adversity. You'll never know until you are put into that situation. You can't train for it. You just have to get outside your comfort zone and hope you're the type who reacts appropriately. I looked back at Squirrel. His gaze had been replaced with a stone-faced glare.

"My turn, Dauber."

"Check," I replied.

War kills and maims with cold indifference, and the best you can hope for is to keep yourself on the right side of the gun.

The withering PKC fire got everyone's attention. Twenty minutes after I successfully practiced some long-range target interdiction, Tony took some machine-gun fire in his room. A burst came through his loophole and peppered the wall a couple of feet above his head.

"What the fahk??" Tony yelled, pushing his gun aside and scrambling to his feet. He looked around the room and zeroed in on

Chucky's Mk 48. He lurched toward the gun, snatched it up, and stuck the barrel out of his loophole, lighting off about a hundred rounds.

"FAHK YOU!" Tony yelled like a madman as he let loose in consecutive angry bursts. "Fahk you, you mothafuckas!" Squirrel and I just sat there looking for the gunner as Tony shot and cussed at the invisible enemy who'd nearly killed him a few seconds earlier. Chucky sat in the corner of the hide and watched him work through his rage. When Tony was done, he stood there sweating and winded as he looked around at all of us watching him.

"Yeah, fahk you guys. What are you looking at?"

Everybody chuckled.

"Ah, what the fuck. Gimme a dip, Dauba.'"

I threw my can of Copenhagen across the hallway into his room, still grinning. Tony packed a dip and got back behind his gun and started scanning.

Man, I love that salty old Frogman. He's got a personality like a mafia henchman. I thought of the Bohdi Sanders quote, "Beware of an old man in a profession where men usually die young." Tony wasn't exactly old, he was probably thirty-seven or thirty-eight. But age in the Teams is really measured in deployments more than years, and by that measure he was ancient. Teams and shit. We sat back waiting for an officer to come get an assessment of the engagement. Ramadi continued to boil in the heat.

TWENTY-THREE

A FINAL OP

"Greater love has no one than this: to lay
down one's life for one's friends."

—John 15:13

For the past decade or so, I've spent Veterans Day at the cemetery. When I was still stationed on Coronado, I'd ride my chopper all the way up to Point Loma and spend the afternoon at Rosecrans, visiting my brothers' graves. As their numbers grew, so did my compulsion to return. I know Memorial Day might be a more fitting day for this tradition, but for some reason I prefer November and the end of a year, the close of a chapter, for my yearly homage.

Since leaving the Teams and San Diego behind, I have made the trip to various cemeteries. Fredericksburg National Cemetery is the final resting place for more than fifteen thousand Union soldiers who died in the Civil War. Just down the street is a Confederate cemetery full of the graves of men who were not allowed to be buried next to their Union countrymen. I visited them both.

Last year I took my wife and children to Barrancas National Cemetery. We walked through the rows and rows of markers, bearing names of veterans who'd died as long ago as the Civil War. The deeper we went into the cemetery, the more wars we saw represented: the Spanish-American War, World War I, World War II, Korea, Vietnam, Iraq, Afghanistan. Every branch of service was there from every conceivable conflict.

Our weapons change, and our wars change, but the warrior spirit unites us all. Every generation of American has answered the call willingly, and I rest easy knowing they'll answer long after I'm gone.

SHARKBASE, SEPTEMBER 2006

I cracked my eyes as the alarm clock sounded its monotone, rhythmic beeping. The AC had cut out sometime in the middle of the night and I awoke in a pool of sweat, the sleeping bag splayed open. Same shit, different day. I swung my feet over the side of the green Army cot, slipped into my flops, and rubbed the lingering sleep from my eyes. I picked up the Copenhagen can from the ground and packed a very BTF-sized chew. Start each day with a success.

I walked out of my eight-by-eight-feet partitioned room and headed to the exit of the tent. I paused. It was quiet then. Bob was in San Diego. Dale was at the TOC and Spaz had already left for the morning. I turned around suddenly, walked past my room, and hung in the doorway of Marc's room. I looked at the emptiness. The only things that remained were the shelves that he had built and the Army cot. I closed my eyes, took a deep breath, and exhaled. I quickly walked out of the tent and didn't look back.

Morale was still low following August 2. The unraveling of our tight-knit dynamic was unmistakable in our daily interactions. Everyone just marked time as we looked forward to the end of our tour. Newguys took care of our regular duties and then slinked back to our rooms to play video games and bitch among ourselves.

Then things got worse.

The Legend had to leave early. His daughter's illness called him back to San Diego, and Chris needed to be with his family. Under different circumstances, he might have opted to stay in the fight, but our war was winding down. It was mid-September, and we were scheduled to leave at the end of the month. Chris had done more than his share of killing in Ramadi. His kill count stood at 101 and comprised roughly half of the platoon's total. Chris had personally changed the dynamic of Ramadi.

The way most of us saw it, we'd all done our share of killing. Task Unit Bruiser had played a huge role in turning the city into a strategic vise. In the Ma'Laab district to the east, our Delta Platoon brothers worked with the Army to put the squeeze on the insurgency while we pressed the offensive from the west. As we approached the end of our tour, there was no doubt we'd moved the chains and put the coalition a lot closer to pacifying the insurgency and winning peace in Anbar.

I sat on the top of Vehicle 1 and looked south to the gates of Sharkbase. The evening stillness was peaceful. I looked over at the Ma Deuce next to me. She was locked and loaded. Somewhere in the distance, an IED blast shook the calmness of the evening.

"Well, Dauber," said the Legend in his usual Texas twang.

"Well, Legend," I replied.

"I got a plane to catch, we ready to roll?"

"That's right," I said. "Cinderella can't miss the ball."

"You'll be home before too long," he replied.

I nodded in agreement, snapped my helmet on, and jumped into the turret. In his civilian clothes, Chris jumped into the shotgun position and looked over his navigation computer. The vehicle checks began from the rear.

The whole platoon made the trip to TQ to see Chris off. As we convoyed across the crater-filled desert plains from Anbar to TQ, the IED threat was barely a thought. Muscle memory, neural numbness, six months of combat—call it whatever. The convoy was uneventful, and we escorted Chris to the terminal. He wore jeans, a black polo, and his crusty Longhorns hat, and he carried his pistol, rifle, and a ruck.

"Hey, brother," Chris said, "you know I hate to leave my boys, but . . . trouble on the home front, ya know?"

"We'll see you back in San Diego in a couple weeks," I said. "You take care of what you need to take care of."

"I will. You keep your head down out there, Dauber."

"Sure. But who am I gonna bum some Copenhagen off of?!"

He smiled and tossed me his can.

I didn't like seeing Chris go. He was my mentor and a damn good Frogman. More than that, he was my good friend and a trusted ally to the newguys. When we griped, Chris listened. He was the type of leader who valued input, even criticism, from subordinates. If he thought our concerns were worth elevating, he always brought them higher. He had been one of the biggest proponents of dialing back the types of patrols we'd lost guys on. Nobody begrudged the Legend for leaving. I think we all felt relief for him because we knew he'd taken Biggles and Marc pretty hard. He deserved a break, but his leaving exacerbated the fractures in the platoon. As we left Chris at TQ, all of us looked forward to our own exit from the sandbox.

———————

With the sun setting behind me, I stood on the dock at the edge of Sharkbase and whipped a raggedy fishing pole toward the Euphrates. A hooked ball of dough plopped into the deep green, and I took a long pull off an unauthorized Jack and Coke. For a minute, I almost felt like I was back home in Connecticut, launching giant plugs for some late-summer stripers. My brother Mark had recently sent me a video of his latest tuna trip. To say I wasn't excited to get back on the water would have been a bald-faced lie.

I had recently acquired a whiskey-filled Listerine bottle in a care package from a buddy back in the States, and a partially drained can of Coke made a convenient and inconspicuous mixer. Moose sat next to me, blowing thick billows of sweet smoke from his hookah, and Scotty, with his own pole and covert cocktail, lounged next to Moose.

After sending Chris off, we all needed something to take the edge off, and Moose had the answers Scotty and I were looking for. The whiskey wasted no time on our alcohol-deprived bodies, and the hookah's sweet tobacco accentuated the deep calm we all felt, shooting the shit on the dock and pretending for a night that we were somewhere that wasn't a war zone. We talked about our friends and retold the best stories from the past five months. Moose told us all about life in Jordan and service in his country's Special Forces. Scotty talked about Wisconsin and his beloved Packers, and I told him why the Packers sucked and that the Patriots were obviously the greatest football franchise of all time. After a while, I got a bite on my line and reeled in a twelve-inch carp. I felt like I was back home. I lit a Cuban cigar and poured myself another Jack and Coke.

"I'm going to miss you guys, Jobber," Moose said.

"Yeah, I enjoyed getting my war on with ya, Moose," I said. "So what's next?"

"Another group of Teamguys to work with. It never changes," he replied.

"Maybe they'll finish this shit show," I echoed back.

Moose smiled and took a big rip off the pipe. He looked off across the Euphrates and said nothing.

We stayed up all night, fishing until the sunrise painted the dawn in subtle hues of pink and orange, and then, in a liquor haze, we packed up and headed to our tents to sleep.

I woke later in the morning on September 29—just a few days until the bulk of the task unit would leave for home. We'd been running turnover ops with our replacements from Team Five and hazing the shit out of the newest guys from SQT who had arrived, to keep ourselves entertained. The turnover patrols were mostly uneventful until we took some machine-gun fire on a recce patrol one night. After the otherwise forgettable patrol, Sal, one of the newguys, asked, "Do I get a Combat Action Ribbon now?"

He received a few blank stares.

"Fucking meatball," Spaz finally replied.

I laughed to myself. *I guess we're not the newguys anymore.* I looked over at Jonny, who was thinking the same thing. It only took six months of war.

The morning of the twenty-ninth was no different from the rest, except the AC was working. I slipped on my flip-flops and headed for the TOC to start another day of packing gear and prepping to leave. As I approached the plywood building, Doc Crispin ran out and hustled toward me.

"Dauber, what's your blood type?"

"O-pos. Why?"

"Delta got contacted on an op," he said, hurrying toward the other guys' tents. "One of their guys is hit pretty bad."

"What? Who is it? What happened?" I asked, following him.

"Muj threw a grenade on the rooftop. Mike Monsoor took the worst of it. They initiated CASEVAC, but it doesn't look good."

I immediately realized that Delta's corpsman was with us at Sharkbase, packing up to go home.

"Who the fuck is the corpsman?"

"I don't know, Dauber. I gotta go."

He disappeared into a tent, and I stood frozen for a second, trying to process everything. I wondered who was working on Mike, and I imagined them trying desperately to stop the bleeding and keep him alive. I knew that whoever it was, he wasn't a corpsman and was likely dealing with a sense of hopelessness comparable to what I'd felt working on Marc, maybe even worse.

News of Mike getting hit spread fast, and everyone waited anxiously for an update on his condition. It took about an hour to find out what happened. All the guys from Mike's platoon who were packing at Sharkbase joined Cadillac Platoon in our mission planning space for a briefing. Jocko told us about the patrol from Delta that had gone out for one last sniper overwatch in the middle of muj country. He told us how the muj launched an assault on the patrol's position after Delta's snipers killed two bad guys. He told us Mike was on the rooftop scanning for targets with his Mk 48 when an insurgent grenade flew over the wall, hit him in the chest, and fell in front of him. He told us how Mike yelled, "Grenade!" before he threw himself on top of it to protect the other Teamguys and Jundis on the roof. He told us Mikey died en route to the aid station. The two Teamguys who had been next to him on the roof survived with superficial wounds.

A couple of days before he was supposed to go home, Mike Monsoor gave his life to save his brothers.

The image was hard to wrap my head around, probably because I just didn't want it to be real.

A few days away.

Just a couple of days.

I remembered my first convoy op and talking to Mikey about how unfair it would be to be killed by an invisible bomb. That was six months earlier, but it seemed like a million years ago. The contrast of that day and the news of Mike's sacrifice struck me as ironic; he ended his tour rushing to meet a deadly explosion rather than avoid it. His heroism didn't surprise me, but it was hard to process.

Just a few more days.

At TQ several hours later, Mike's body lay in the morgue, where all the Teamguys had gathered to say goodbye. From the doorway, I could see a bunch of guys gathered around Mike. I saw his face and some of his wounds from a distance and I turned away. I didn't want that memory of him. The images of Marc on August 2 flashed in my mind. I wanted to keep the image of Mikey the ceaseless gladiator, the funny dude on the convoy, the guy bullshitting in the chow hall. I walked away and found a room nearby with a couple of couches and a TV. Jonny and EOD Nick joined me.

"How the fuck did this happen?" I said to the boys.

Jonny and EOD Nick just shook their heads and said nothing for a minute.

It was bad business not having a corpsman on that op, I thought.

"I can't believe this," I said. "Two days before he's supposed to go home. Why?"

––––––––––––

The next day, we convoyed from Sharkbase to Camp Corregidor for Mikey's memorial service. I stood in the lead vehicle's turret and looked back at the rest of the convoy. We had a much smaller force than when we began earlier in the deployment. A lot of the SEAL reservists had to fill in as turret gunners, drivers, bodies. I put in my headphones and hit play on my iPod. I thought about nothing. The road kept rolling on.

At Corregidor, the Army's 502nd helped put together a big memorial service for Mike. At least two hundred soldiers joined all the Teamguys and support personnel to honor our brother's sacrifice. In the front of the plywood chapel, a large framed photo of Mike in BTF mode stood behind his Mk 48, inverted over a set of Frogman fins. His helmet capped the gun's buttstock, completing the Frogman version of the soldier's cross. A step below the cross was Mike's body armor kit.

Speaker after speaker memorialized Mike, and all of them high-lighted his status as a true warrior to the core—the epitome of a Big Tough Frogman. As they remembered Mike as the great SEAL he was, I looked around and noticed most of his buddies crying.

"Before Mike left, he gave me two gifts," said our team's commanding officer. He identified the two SEALs whose lives Mike saved. "He gave them back to me."

When the remembrances were over, we approached Mike's shrine, two at a time, saluted him, and knelt for one last prayer. For his actions on that rooftop in Ramadi, Mike Monsoor became the first SEAL to be awarded the Medal of Honor in Iraq. He was also awarded a Silver Star for fighting his way to a wounded SEAL and then dragging him to safety while taking intense enemy fire on May 9, 2006.

"Mike Monsoor!" yelled the master chief toward the end of the service.

"Hooyah, Mike Monsoor!" we all replied.

TWENTY-FOUR

LEAVING

"I live, I burn with life, I love, I slay, and am content."

—Conan the Barbarian

'VE ALWAYS LOVED war movies. I grew up watching the Duke in my grandfather's basement, and *The Sands of Iwo Jima* had me hooked. Since then, I've added many films to my collection of must-sees, some of which I watched dozens of times over my deployments to Iraq.

The older I get, however, the more I realize I've never seen a complete war film. Movies have a way of wrapping up a story in two hours and when the credits roll, it's over. In real life, even when your war is over your story isn't. You have to fill in the vacant spaces left by the brothers you've lost. You have to start back at the beginning or move forward toward an end. You will carry pieces of your war with you forever, because it makes you who you are.

A true war story never ends.

TQ, EARLY OCTOBER 2006

A few days after Mike's memorial, I was on a Black Hawk to TQ. I watched the ancient sands of Mesopotamia stretch out for miles in every direction and recalled the helo ride that delivered me across the same expanse six months earlier. A lot had changed, and then again, not much had changed at all.

The same violence of action that propelled me to join the Navy was delivered on the battlefield. I felt nothing for the enemy departed. The old Charlie Platoon motto was "Dead men tell no tales." The enemy dead that littered our six-month push would speak no more. However, I left Ramadi full of the memories of Marc Lee, Biggles, Mike Monsoor, the Marines, soldiers, airmen, and the Frogmen who helped secure that city. I glimpsed out over the night sky as the bird lifted slowly off the soil. I left with memories.

At TQ, we had two days to burn before our flight out. I packed away my M4 and night vision in a conex box and stuffed a fresh dip of Copenhagen. Six months of combat hardening still didn't relieve me of my newguy duties, and I spent some time rigging and loading pallets full of gear before being released to suck up the Air Force life for a while. Ramadi already felt like a long way off. As if I'd been riding on the ocean all day, the sensation of slight *mal de débarquement* surfaced as I adjusted to the formalities of rear-echelon life.

TQ was an ever-changing machine. The constant influx and exodus of operators, Marines, and soldiers presented a sharp contrast to life in Ramadi. The air terminal and chow hall were hubs of activity where the numerous personnel met. I headed to the brightly lit mess facility to refuel the machine. With my tray piled high with meat loaf, macaroni, and desserts, I looked for a quiet table away from the madness. As I sat in the back of the crowded room and shoveled my mountain of food into my mouth, a welcome sight caught my eye. The boys from SEAL Team FOUR made their way into the chow line, with their too-long hair, tattoos, and all fashions that threatened military bearing. Teamguys. I spotted my BUD/S swim buddy, Gilby.

Gilby started in Class 245 with me and was eventually rolled back to 246 with a knee injury around the same time I injured my back. I watched his face light up when he caught my stare. He grabbed some snacks and beelined it to my table with another former classmate, Clark Schwedler, trailing closely. They were on their way into the fight and would soon be deep in the triangle in Habbaniyah and Fallujah.

"Well, look what the cat dragged in," Gilby said, setting his tray down. "How's it going, Mongo?" He called me by my old BUD/S nickname. "Getting your war on?"

"Hey, brother!" I said, standing for a hearty bro hug.

Clark followed: "How the hell are you, brother? It's good to see you. We've been hearing all about the work you guys have been doing. You guys are crushing it." I gave Clark an equal hug.

"Yeah, we got after it, man," I said. "We put a hurtin' on the muj for sure."

"Well, shit, I hope you saved some for us," Clark said.

"You don't have to worry about that. Plenty of getting left to do," I replied.

"Hopefully, the muj didn't make you do any four-mile timed runs!" Gilby joked, recalling my lack of speed.

"Nah, brother. I learned how to shoot a rifle. Moves faster than you and is a lot more capable than your pillow hands!"

Gilby and Clark busted up while the cracks escalated and the food diminished. We caught up for a while and traded some stories. It felt good to see the guys. I hadn't seen them since the days after we got our tridents and they moved to the East Coast. I answered all their questions and passed on as much tactical wisdom as I could muster, and then parted ways.

It was the last time I ever saw Clark. He was killed six months later in a direct-action raid.

The hissing whine of the C-130's hydraulics rustled me awake. The short stop in Germany broke up the monotony only enough for me to take a few more Ambien. As on a long journey, the trip back usually seems shorter. I ached to get back and didn't need my mind ruminating about the long trip. Finally, the bird touched safely down on North Island Air Station in Coronado.

The rumble of the ramp got me moving and the crack of sunlight washed the remaining sleep from my eyes. A lot had changed, and then again, not much had. My family was flying in a week later, so I had no one at the airport to greet me. I was still a newguy and had weapons and pallets to offload when we got back to the Team. I stepped off the bird and soaked in the sunlight. In many ways, the welcome-home scene echoed our send-off, except we were missing Marc, Mike, and Biggles. I looked over at the Jersey barrier off the runway. I thought back to the last pic I took with Marc stateside. I stared at the barrier for a moment. Then I took a deep breath and headed to the buses.

There was work to be done.

I'd been back a couple of days. The musty smells of wetsuits drying and San Diego Bay water permeated my locker. I straightened my ribbons and readjusted my trident. I paused for a moment, thinking back to the day I earned my bird, when Ty Woods had stamped it into my bare chest. I still had that original trident at home in a little box, complete with a smear of dried blood on the back. I thought about the little scar over my heart.

Today, I was headed to another funeral. The buzzing of my cell phone distracted me for a moment.

MEET ME AT BRO'S OFFICE, the text read.

I stared at the screen for a second, then closed the flip phone. I grabbed my Dixie Cup hat and walked down to the quarterdeck. I jumped over the giant "SEAL TEAM THREE" emblem out of superstition and opened the door. I banked a hard left and hustled up the stairs.

"About fucking time," the Legend greeted me as I walked into the office.

"Faster than your old knees go," I replied.

Chris disregarded the comment and passed me his small flask of Tennessee whiskey and can of Copenhagen snuff. I took a long pull and put in a crisp snuff.

"Much appreciated."

"Anytime, Dauber."

"So, what's going on?" I asked.

"This shit." He pointed to the manning chart of Team THREE on the magnetic board. "You're supposed to go to PACOM. Do you really want to deploy to the Philippines?"

After August 2, Master Chief Bro, the incoming master chief for Team THREE, had asked me in Iraq what I wanted to do for my next deployment. I told him I didn't care and gave the choice no other thought. As he stared at me, it became clear that Chris did care and had given it a lot of thought.

"Well, it looks like that's where the Navy needs my skills," I replied sarcastically.

Chris replied with his generous cackle. "Dauber, I'm LPO of Delta Platoon. We're going back to Iraq and I could use a shit-hot corpsman. I have tons of newguys, as you can see. Besides, we could use another bruiser to help with the hazing."

I smiled. "Well, what are you thinking?"

"Easy day. Wind off the Pacific just moved your name over to

Delta," he said as he moved the magnet. "Bro won't care. Besides, there are more muj to shoot in Iraq."

I gave him a sheepish grin. He was right. There was a lot of work left to do in Iraq, and it was work I was born to. I wasn't a man who would lie awake at night haunted by anything I'd seen or done. For me, it was as simple as finding that bad man.

"Consider it done," I said. Chris nodded.

"Let's go bury Mikey."

I tossed him the can and the flask as we headed down to his Suburban.

———

The silence was clean, and a soft onshore breeze blanketed the sunshine-painted slopes of Fort Rosecrans. There wasn't a sound to be heard except the rhythmic thud of fist hitting wood. I had my trident in my hand.

I took a step forward toward the casket. I kept my eyes forward on Guy in front of me. As he saluted and moved off, I walked up. I gazed down on the trident-encased wooden coffin. The amount of gold pinned to it made it look like a shield, sending Mikey Monsoor off one last time. The EOD pin caught my eye. I thought back to when Nick saved our ass. Task Unit Bruiser was successful because of the men. I looked for an open spot for my bird.

I placed my trident on his casket and delivered three sharp hits with my fist. I stepped back, breathed, and saluted. I walked slowly back to the formation.

As I stood at attention, I watched the procession of Frogmen lined up to do the same. They were men, fathers, brothers, friends, killers, and above all else, Teammates. They were there to send a brother off. I couldn't picture myself anywhere else than among this family.

I quickly brushed away a tear that hung on my eyelid. I caught myself. I looked back at the dwindling procession of Teamguys and gritted my teeth. I looked around to my right and left, surrounded by brothers. Pain is temporary. Death is fleeting. The glory of a warrior lasts forever.

The service ended and I walked back among the silence and the headstones. I glanced down at my chest, at my row of ribbons and jump wings. Three tiny holes in the wool of my blouse were all that was left of the bird I'd worn to the funeral. But the scar on my chest remained.

EPILOGUE

THE SUN BEGAN to rise over the water. I knew she hadn't believed me the night before when I told her I'd be there, bright and early, to pick her up and take her surfing. But I had showed up. Reliability is important. I wasn't sure how she would react when I showed up driving the "Murder Van," blacked out with flames on the hood. I was taking chances.

I'd been through much worse and stayed cool as a cucumber. One hundred and twenty pounds of woman shouldn't make me nervous. Yet I sat on a longboard in the Pacific Ocean in Imperial Beach, California, across from one I'd only just met two days before, and I felt an unfamiliar anxiety. I wasn't really uncomfortable, but I guess you could call it a nervous excitement. Her older sister was a friend of mine and had walked her into my garage on Thursday afternoon. I'd been finding excuses to run into her since then. Her name was Lindsey.

We straddled our boards, riding the tide, feeling each other out. I could smell the fear rolling off her. She'd had a hell of a time getting past the surf zone in an ill-fitting wetsuit I hijacked from the Team, try-ing to navigate the first board she'd ever used. The water was rough, but I let her figure it out. She was from Florida: How could she not surf? I wanted to see if she'd give up, and she hadn't. I respected that. Even if all it got us was a chance to sit there in the open water, her face only barely masking her terror.

I took a deep breath and looked into her eyes. They were so blue they were almost clear. She squared her jaw and looked back at me, de-fiantly. She was scared, but not of me. I grinned.

I wanted to touch her, so I grabbed her foot and pulled her board closer. I felt that nervous excitement ramping up again, so we sat there in a contented silence, my hand cradling her foot as it dangled over her board.

It was Saturday. If I let her go, she'd fly back to Florida on Tuesday and my life would go back to normal.

If I let her go.

Around us, the sounds of a sleepy Southern California town grew louder as the sun rose over the water and the rest of our lives.

Seven years later, my wife, Lindsey, wished me luck over a poor con-nection and I ended the phone call. I took a breath, remembered my preparation, and headed into the dingy building. It had been chosen by the set designer for its resemblance to the many compounds the Punishers had taken down in Ramadi. For filming purposes, this com-pound was supposed to be the one where Marc Lee lost his life.

I crouched low, looking at the ground of the dusty floor of the old Moroccan hotel. My helmet was fastened tight, my med bag was on my back, my heater was at my side, and the smell of sweat perme-ated the room. I took a long, deep breath to relax my heart rate. I fo-cused my gaze out into the set as Bradley Cooper's eyes caught mine, snapping me out of my quiet meditation. The last shot of the Moroccan filming session, otherwise known as the "martini shot," was about to commence. I guess the idea is you wrap shooting after the "martini shot" and head out for a well-deserved drink.

I scanned the rest of the room. Eastwood, Cooper, Lorenz, Lazar, Bernstein. I took another deep breath. *Better not whiff on this, Dauber,* I thought to myself. *How the hell did I even get here?*

This is Lindsey's fault, I thought, laughing. She was the one who had fired off the email to the screenwriter Jason Hall in 2012 when she found out *American Sniper* would be a movie. Always protective of us Frogmen, Lindsey focused on this theme: "Please don't mess this up." Despite not knowing me during my Ramadi deployment, Lindsey knew the bond I had shared with the men of Task Unit Bruiser. When Jason wrote back and asked for guidance, she'd nervously approached me, afraid to admit what she'd done without my knowledge.

I gave the Legend a call in September 2012. I caught him up on what Lindsey had done and told him that Hall had wanted to speak with me to get more perspective on Ramadi, sniping, and Chris.

He gave his signature cackle.

"Sure, Dauber. Jason is Hollywood for sure. I don't have a problem at all. Let's make it happen."

Communicating with Jason was almost daily until February 1, 2013, when he finished the first draft of the screenplay. On February 2, I called him to deliver the terrible news of Chris's death.

It all seemed so far away now: traveling to Dallas to be with the Kyle family, inviting Jason and introducing him to my Teammates, carrying Chris's casket as I had Marc's and then Ryan's.

A year later, I found myself in the Malpaso Productions office, face-to-face with Clint Eastwood, rattling off everything I knew about Iraq, Ramadi, Chris Kyle, and my experiences in the Teams. He listened calmly. Little did I know, our conversation was an interview.

Apparently, I did well, because twenty-four hours later I found myself on the range with an old friend and fellow Frogman named

Rick, teaching a novice Philadelphia kid how to shoot like a West Texas gunslinger who had done it all his life. Fortunately, Bradley was a natural and easily sent some brotherly love to head-sized targets at four hundred meters. Midway through the first day he inquired casually, "Ever think about playing yourself in the movie?" I was intrigued.

Lindsey and I filmed the auditions on my iPhone and sent them into the casting director. Two days later, he called and offered me the role in his best Eastwood impression: "Boy's damn good, get him a job."

"No fucking way," I said.

"You bet, Dauber. Great job. We'll get you set up with costume. Plan on coming to L.A. this week and you'll be in Morocco in two weeks."

Cooper looked at the monitor, then back down at me. I could sense his encouragement—*Let it roll, Dauber.* I closed my eyes again and envisioned the dirty two-story structure in Ramadi. The heat, the smoke, the smell, the visceral balance between here and gone. I thought about Marc, Chris, Biggles, Clark, and Mike. Our struggles were being captured on film, and I wrestled with a desire to protect Marc and our last day together and a need to show them what Marc had done for them. I swallowed the beginning stages of a knot and found solace in my breathing.

A tall figure in a camo boonie hat stepped forward. He looked down and asked in a quiet voice, "All set, Kevin?"

I looked up at Clint and smiled.

"You got it, boss."

"Well, all right then. Let's make this picture."

He stepped back behind the camera and Bradley drifted to his right. In quiet reverence, Clint whispered, "Action."

Eight years after I fought elbow to elbow with men I called brothers in Ramadi, I waited anxiously in New York City with one of their widows. In a Warner Bros. screening room in Manhattan, I waited to watch *American Sniper* for the first time. The theater had a feeling like an old friend, but I was anxious. My knee tapped like a machine gun. Maya, Marc Lee's widow, was next to me, as close as Marc had been in the moments before he was killed in Ramadi in 2006.

I took a deep breath.

I stared at the curtains covering the screen. The theater's acoustics reminded me of a wake, and I wrestled with a feeling of apprehension. I thought about my fallen brothers: Chris, Marc, Ryan Job, Clark Schwedler, Darrik Benson, Mike Monsoor. They were all giants among men. We had actually lived the stories that were about to play out on-screen.

The warmth inside the theater was buffered by the chill I had from my walk down Avenue of the Americas in the rain. I am a creature of habit and never fail to prepare for anything. I had walked through this moment in my mind for months, but now it was real. Memories flooded my brain. I stared in silence as I tried to remember my preparation.

Sitting next to Maya, I thought of Marc and the last moments I'd spent with him in the morgue at Camp Ramadi. The image of Marc's last gunfight and the brotherhood we shared played back in my mind. I relived the moments I spent treating Marc after he'd been shot, knowing I couldn't save his life and then trying anyway.

The brotherhood we share as SEALs supersedes life. Marc's gift, like that of Chris and Ryan, carried on long after he was gone. Marc gave me the gift of his family. I came to know Maya, his mother, and his brother more after Marc's death. It's never easy to convey to loved ones the experiences we SEALs share in combat. Whether we choose to describe the details or not, our presence and fixture in the lives of our family members reinforce our commitment to the brotherhood.

You can always tell the way a man loves his wife by how much he talks about her; Marc worshipped Maya. Nearly nine years after those final moments I spent with Marc, I sat alone in the theater with the love of his life.

The opening of the curtain startled me back to the present. I blinked and swallowed the knot in my throat. The screen came alive, beckoning me into the story of our journey as warriors and stewards of the flag. My mind wandered to Ramadi in 2006, and an intense rush of emotions hit me hard, like a Coronado Beach wave in Hell Week. My heart began to slow and my breathing relaxed as the rumble of tracked vehicles filled the theater. The sounds and images of war took me back to the experiences that galvanized and shaped my life.

I remember the brotherhood.

Sometimes Ramadi feels like a lifetime ago. Many of the men I served with are dead now. I don't know if they saw flashes of their lives before they went, but I know that when I go, if mine plays for me, Ramadi will be in it. For all the death we dealt in that city, I never felt more alive than when I ran with the Punishers through its angry streets.

GLOSSARY

Abrams tank: a well-armed, heavily armored battle tank. Its main armament is the M256A1 120 mm smoothbore gun, but it also has a .50-caliber machine gun and two 7.62 mm machine guns.

ANGLICO: Air Naval Gunfire Liaison Companies; their mission: "To provide Marine Air-Ground Task Force (MAGTF) Commanders a liaison capability, with foreign area expertise, to plan, coordinate, and conduct terminal control of fires in support of joint, allied, and coalition forces."

AOR: area of responsibility; a predefined geographic region assigned to a combatant commander where he has the authority to plan and conduct combat operations.

APC: armored personnel carrier; an armored fighting vehicle designed to transport personnel to the battlefield.

AQI: Al Qaeda in Iraq; founded in April 2004 by Sunni extremist Abu al-Zarqawi; used vehicle-borne IEDs, kidnappings and beheadings, and suicide bombers as a means of attacking coalition forces and pressuring Iraqi civilians not to support the coalition effort.

ATPIALS: Advanced Target Pointer/Illuminator/Aiming Laser; small and lightweight aiming system with both visible and infrared aiming lasers and an infrared illuminator.

BDUS: Battle Dress Uniform; standard camouflage uniform worn in combat situations by United States Armed Forces from the early 1980s to the mid-2000s.

BLOOD CHIT: a small sheet of material carried on a service member into combat; depicts a U.S. flag and a statement in several languages that anyone who aids that service member will be rewarded.

BRADLEY FIGHTING VEHICLE: an American fighting vehicle platform designed to transport ground troops while providing suppressive fire; armed with a 25 mm cannon, twin TOW missile launchers, and a 7.62 mm machine gun.

BTF: acronym meaning Big Tough Frogman; used by the men of Charlie Platoon to describe themselves and their actions.

BUD/S: Basic Underwater Demolition/SEAL training; six-month SEAL training course in Coronado, California.

CASEVAC: casualty evacuation; emergency patient evacuation from a combat zone.

CENTCOM: United States Central Command.

CHALK: a small group of soldiers who deploy from a single military platform.

COP: combat outpost; a coalition base for combat operations.

C-17: a large Air Force aircraft commonly used to transport troops and cargo throughout the world.

DA: direct action; a type of combat operation of short duration designed to seize, capture, or destroy a target, or to recover designated personnel or material.

E-DOG: slang for an enlisted member of the armed forces; not a commissioned officer.

E-5: petty officer second class; a rank in the Navy.

EOD: Explosive Ordnance Disposal; EOD technicians are trained in the disposal of improvised explosive devices, as well as chemical, biological, and nuclear weapons.

EOTECH: holographic weapons sight commonly used on M4s.

.50-CAL: M2 Browning machine gun; used extensively as a vehicle weapon and for aircraft armament; air-cooled, belt-fed machine gun that fires a .50-caliber round with long range, accuracy, and immense stopping power; sometimes referred to as a "Ma Deuce."

FLEX-CUFFS: single-use disposable restraints; cheaper and easier to carry than metal handcuffs.

FOB: Forward Operating Base; a secured military installation.

FOD WALK: foreign object damage; patrolling an area to pick up debris; usually reserved for a flight line or a ship.

FROGMAN: a common term for a SEAL; in the Teams, the term originates from the Navy Combat Demolition Units during World War II.

GREEN ZONE: a roughly four-square-mile area in Baghdad that housed the Coalition Provisional Authority. It was heavily fortified and one of the safest military bases in Iraq.

HEAD SHED: slang for the command or control center.

HEADSPACE: space between the barrel and bolt on a .50-cal.

HMMWV: High-Mobility Multipurpose Wheeled Vehicle; commonly referred to as a Humvee; four-wheel-drive light truck; often mounted with a .50-cal in the turret.

HVT: high-value target.

IED: improvised explosive device; a bomb constructed and deployed for use in ways outside of conventional military action; in Ramadi, IEDs were often planted in roads or used by suicide bombers.

IR CHEMLIGHT: infrared chemical light stick; used to mark a location.

IR NETTING: camouflage netting that scatters radar and reduces thermal signature; used to help conceal personnel and equipment.

JDAM: Joint Direct Attack Munition; a guidance kit that converts an unguided, free-falling bomb to an all-weather "smart" bomb.

JTAC: joint terminal attack controller; a qualified service member who directs the action of combat aircraft engaged in close air support from a forward position.

JUMP SCHOOL: United States Army Airborne School; three-week basic paratrooper training for the armed forces, conducted out of Fort Benning, Georgia.

KIA: killed in action.

LEAVENWORTH: Among service members, refers to the United States Disciplinary Barracks, the U.S. military's sole maximum-security penitentiary, in Fort Leavenworth, Kansas.

LPO: Lead Petty Officer.

MA'LAAB: district in southeast Ramadi; in 2006 an area of heavy insurgent activity.

MEALS, READY TO EAT (MREs): a self-contained individual field ration for use in combat or the field; contains an entree, side, dessert or snack, crackers or bread, a spread, a powdered beverage mix, utensils, flameless ration heater, beverage mixing bag, and an accessory pack.

MIL-DOT: rifle scope reticle used by snipers to aid in calculating distance to target.

Muj: term commonly used by American forces for the insurgency; shortened from the Arabic *mujahideen,* or "one engaged in jihad."

NODs: night optical/observation device; a device that allows images to be produced in near-total darkness.

NSW: United States Naval Special Warfare Command; NAVSOC or NSWC; the naval component of United States Special Operations Command.

OIC: officer in charge; a platoon's lead officer.

OPERATION RED WINGS: disrupted surveillance mission in Afghanistan on June 25, 2005, during which four SEALs were ambushed and pinned down; the helicopter QRF was subsequently shot down, killing all eight SEALs and eight Army Special Forces aviators on board; ultimately there were nineteen U.S. service members killed and one survivor.

PACOM: United States Pacific Command; responsible for Indo Asia-Pacific region.

PID: positive identification; required when recovering a hostage.

PKC: variant of the Soviet-designed PK machine gun.

PLO: patrol leader's order; brief given prior to launching an operation.

PT: physical training; often given as a standard of minimum physical fitness for a school or command.

PX: post exchange; military retail store providing service members a tax-free source of American books, clothing, electronics, magazines, snacks, etc.

QRF: quick reaction force; any force that is prepared to react on very short (typically fewer than minutes) notice.

RECCE: reconnaissance; the military observation of an area to obtain information or locate an enemy.

REMF: rear-echelon motherfucker; derisive term used especially by service members in combat to describe soldiers far removed from the front lines.

RPG: rocket-propelled grenade.

SAW: Squad Automatic Weapon; a portable source of automatic firepower; can be fitted with a heavier barrel and bipod to perform as a light machine gun; only requires one person to operate.

SERE SCHOOL: Survival, Evasion, Resistance, Escape school; training designed to prepare service members for all situations prior to and during enemy capture with the intent to escape.

SITREP: situation report; a report on the current situation in a particular area.

SMP: Special Missions Platoon; the most tactically proficient and well-trained Iraqi soldiers; the elite of the Iraqi Army.

SOFT KNOCK: technique used to gain entry into a building and set up a hide.

SQT: SEAL Qualification Training; twenty-six-week course during which students learn the core tactical knowledge needed to join a SEAL platoon; students become SEALs upon graduation.

SQUIRTER: someone, usually the enemy, fleeing the scene of an attack.

SSE: Sensitive Site Exploitation; the act of searching a site for sensitive or valuable materials.

SURC: Small Unit Riverine Craft; a rigid-hulled armed and armored patrol boat; used by the U.S. Marines and U.S. Navy to navigate and maintain control of rivers and inland waterways.

SWCC: Surface Warfare Combatant-Craft; Navy personnel trained to use a variety of well-armed and specialized boats in support of and for the delivery of SEALs and their missions; conduct clandestine reconnaissance and combat gunfire support.

TEAMGUY: a term commonly used by SEALs to describe themselves.

TOC: tactical operations center; a command post for military operations.

TQ: Al Taqaddum Air Base; located in central Iraq approximately 74 kilometers west of Baghdad.

TRIDENT: the Special Warfare insignia worn by designated U.S. Navy SEALs; commonly referred to as a "bird" or "Budweiser."

ACKNOWLEDGMENTS

THIS BOOK WOULD not have been possible without the men and women I served with during my time in the Navy. Thank you to all of my brothers at TU-Bruiser, Charlie and Delta Platoons, and the Naval Special Warfare community. Each one has been an influence on me and I wouldn't be where I am now without them. Also, I would not have arrived home safely had it not been for the SEALs, Rangers, soldiers, airmen, and Marines that I had the honor of working with. Thank you.

First and foremost, I want to thank my wife and coauthor, Lindsey. She has been an inspiration from the day I met her and has continually made me better. This book would not have been possible, nor as impactful, without her. I would like to thank my children—they only screamed part of the time while I was writing this. I hope this book allows them a glimpse into my previous life and serves as inspiration to know that anything is possible.

Thank you to my parents and my brothers Mark and Mike, who

have always believed in me from day one. Thank you to my in-laws and family, who have welcomed me from day one and have supported Lindsey and me unconditionally.

To Mommalee, Maya, and the Lee family: your love and support have been as solid as the day our paths crossed. Wayne, Deby, and Jeff Kyle, you have always known how great a friend Chris was to me. You all are family.

Thank you to Ethan Rocke for spending countless hours working with me. I appreciate the sacrifices you made and I enjoyed our time together. Most of all, I appreciate your friendship. Alec Shane, my agent and fellow Xavier graduate, we did it. To Natasha and the entire Team at Simon & Schuster, thank you for reinforcement and guidance. Don Epstein and Greater Talent Network have elevated my career and I am very grateful. Monique Moss and Integrated PR, thank you for all your help.

Thank you to Lieutenant Guy Budinscak for your help in preparing this manuscript. Your help has been instrumental. To my fellow Frogmen who assisted in the process: Tanner, Bito, Gilby, Biggs, B-Dub, KPM, Maro, and the rest of 246, you know who you are, and your loyalty is steadfast. Thank you, Tony, for being a wicked chum.

Thank you, Scott McEwen, for your friendship and mentorship over the past several years. I have appreciated your advice and watching you do great works in the community.

Dave LeMay, thank you for your friendship, inspiration, and patience during the writing process. My partners at Lifestyle & Performance Medicine powered by Regenesis, John McInnis, Dave LeMay, and Cameron Price: thank you for believing in me. Your trust has never wavered. John Peacock was instrumental in developing my passion for charity and has been a great friend. Joe Branciforte, Chris Monnes, and Alex Strekel have helped me raise money for the Chris Kyle Memorial Benefit and have supported me since high school.

The Wake Forest School of Medicine's Physician Assistant Program offered me admission to their prestigious school and I am forever grateful. To the American Academy of Physician Assistants, I hope my story will inspire other veterans to join our ranks.

Michaela Harr, Andrew Kilgen, Kyle Hendrickson, and Jason Wilson, thank you for your help with this cover. Also, a big thanks to Richard Schoenberg for the usage of his photographs and a decade of friendship and advice.

Adam Young, thank you for promoting me to tell my story when only a few would listen. Thank you to Denny Southern and Scott Braddock for being there at the beginning and having the vision. Thank you to Congressman Richard Hudson (NC-08) for your friendship. Thank you, Dave Janice, for your generosity and friendship.

To the many supporters, both here and abroad, who have journeyed with me this far: thank you. Your encouragement is appreciated.